# Galdrbok

## Practical Heathen Runecraft, Shamanism and Magic

Nathan J. Johnson and Robert J. Wallis

The Wykeham Press of London & Winchester

First published privately in 2000
as 'Galdrbok' in a limited edition
Southampton & Winchester: Whispering Wolves Books

This revised and expanded edition published
Summer Solstice 2005 by The Wykeham Press

© The Wykeham Press of London & Winchester
PO Box 437
Winchester
SO22 5WN


ISBN 0-9549609-0-4

# Galdrbok

# Galdrbok

## Practical Heathen Runecraft, Shamanism and Magic

### Nathan J. Johnson and Robert J. Wallis

Galdrbok ('spell-book') straddles the divide between the academic and the inspirational to provide arguably the most comprehensive and practical 'system' of Northwest European 'Heathen Shamanism' thus far in print. Nine years in preparation and painstakingly constructed by two practicing Heathen shamans, Galdrbok explores the magic of Migration Age Northwest Europe and outlines a complete self-study program of Heathen Runecraft. Galdrbok introduces the essential techniques of Scrying ('to descry'/'foresee'/crystal gaze), and Galdr (magical chants or sung spells), and other powerful techniques involving Runes (whispered secrets and magical letters) for inducing the 'altered states' necessary to enter and explore the nine magical worlds of 'Yggdrasill' – the Heathen World Tree. The book also includes an impressively thorough bibliography for sourcing essential reading on Heathenry, Paganisms and related occult subjects.

Nathan J. Johnson is a teacher and the author of ten books, including Barefoot Zen: The Shaolin Roots of Kung Fu and Karate (Red Wheel/Weiser 2000). Robert J. Wallis PhD lectures in art history, archaeology and religious studies, is the author of three books including Shamans/neo-Shamans: Ecstasy, Alternative Archaeologies and Contemporary Pagans (Routledge 2003), and Co-directs the Sacred Sites, Contested Rights/Rites Project (www.sacredsites.org.uk). Robert & Nathan are founders of the Ulfhednr Heathen group, Hampshire.

# Contents

# Acknowledgements

A number of Ulfhednr (wolf-head) members, past and present, made active contributions when field-testing the material which eventually became the system detailed in Galdrbok: thanks to Andy Comley, Kevin Luce, Simon Macartney and Mike Stobart. We express our thanks to Brian Bates, Graham Harvey and Ronald Hutton for their suggestions and support. Thanks are also due to Russel Bestley, Kevin Luce and Kenneth Lymer for the book design.

Nathan would like to thank: Barbara Eunice Johnson (nee Smith), Doris Smith (nee Davies), and the three unknown men. Also for Ruthy, Tukhura (Tuey), Güdren Fiorgen, Declan, Claire and Father Anthony Gatt.

Robert thanks: first and foremost, Claire Gaudion and my parents Jan Wallis (nee Press) and Simon Wallis. A special thank you to my sister, Katherine Wallis, as promised. A heartfelt 'waes thu hael' to L.L and F.R., denizens of Freyja, and other helpers, as the path unfolds. For their encouragement during the preparation of Galdrbok, I also thank Robert Ansell, Jenny Blain, Andy Letcher and Mogg Morgan.

# Authors' Note

In Galdrbok, for the purpose of accessibility, we have removed non-modern English characters and anglicised all Old Norse, Anglo-Saxon and other Germanic terms. For comments on the original terms, their pronunciation, etymology, and so on, see Gordon (1962) and Simek (1993), and for Old English in particular, Mitchell and Robinson (1992) and Pollington (1996[1993]).

We prefer the Anglo-Saxon name Woden as opposed to the Old Norse Odinn or Old High German Wuotan for the 'classic' Northen shaman god. We do the same for all the gods where such Anglo-Saxon equivalents to the Old Norse exist. Thus, Thor becomes Thunor, Baldr becomes Balder and Tir becomes Tiw. This is purely a matter of personal choice, given our location in the landscape of Wessex, England.

Heathen Wizardry and Witchcraft is rather different from the more common 'pagan' version(s) currently in vogue, since Heathenry is less influenced by 'high ritual magic' and ancient Mediterranean or 'Gallic' practices and deities. The Heathenry in Galdrbok is shamanic in nature, rooted in animistic sacred landscapes, has its own Gods and Goddesses, a distinctive 'lore' and a specific oracle (the runes). Moreover, it is inspired by the village heathenry and cunning craft of Anglo-Saxon England. The very terms 'Wizard' and 'Witch' are, indeed, Old English in origin.

The abbreviations CE (common era) and BCE (before common era) are used over the Christian privileging BC and AD and Crowleyan e.v. (era vulgaris).

Galdrbok was written for both the beginner who is seriously interested in pursuing an initiatory spiritual path, and for the more seasoned occult practitioner. The ideas and practices contained within are of a potentially powerful nature. They should not be considered or attempted by anyone in ill health. The authors and publishers take no responsibility for effects which may result from reading or practising any part of the system, beneficial or otherwise.

## A Suggestion

Readers interested in exploring Galdrbok beyond its text should consider reading Appendix B before proceeding further. This appendix offers a practical approach to the Heathen shamanic initiation system detailed in Galdrbok.

The Ulfhednr group in Hampshire (England) developed, practice and live the Heathen worldview and system detailed in Galdrbok. Readers may contact the authors via the publisher.

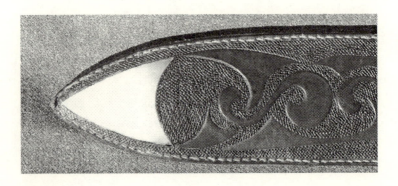

# Treasure Trove

THE GREATEST OF TREASURES, OR SO I AM TOLD
LIES NOT IN FINE SILVER, CUT GEMSTONES OR GOLD
BUT DWELLS IN THE FOLKLORE AND RUNE-CRAFT OF OLD
AND THE CALLING ON GODS, WHO ARE MIGHTY AND BOLD

THUS COUNSELLED ONE 'GREY-CLOAK', WHO WANDERED ALONE
UPON RAIN-LASHED EARTH, O'ER SUN SCORCH-ED STONE
FROM LAND'S-END TO GRIMSBY – SEVENOAKS TO FROME
OFT STAYED-HE WHEN WELL-MET, A GUEST IN SOME HOME

AS HE PASSED-HIGH-O'ER, WINDS HOWLED AND GROUND SHOOK
YET WITH CARE TROD HE GREEN-FIELD AND BABBLING BROOK
HOODED AND CLOAKED, WITH A ONE-EYED LOOK
VENTURED-HE ALE-HOUSE, SOUGHT-OUT 'INGLENOOK'

ELF-KIND, DWARFS, GIANTS – MEN TOO
HONOUR THE GODS, MAY THEY HEARKEN TO YOU
WHILST ONCE 'WE' WERE MANY THOUGH NOW 'WE' ARE FEW
TAKE HEART ALL YE HEATHENS, HERE'S TREASURE – AYE TRUE!

In 'Treasure Trove', 'Grey cloak' is a reference to Woden, the hooded one-eyed master of Galdr/Spells, Magic and Runecraft. Woden is the original Anglo-Saxon inspiration for J.R.R. Tolkien's wizard, Gandalf. Gandalf means 'wand elf'. The 'Grim' in the place-name Grimsby, is one of Woden's travelling names, and Woden the 'traveller' seeks out inglenook fireplaces and the company of men (and other beings) to give and receive stories and news.

# – Preface –
## Roots to Ecstasy - Shamanic Travel on the Northern World Tree

How would you like to travel to another world, another time or place, or forward to possible futures? How would you like to be able to roam freely in otherworldly realms, places of freedom, of mystery and magic, danger even?

Perhaps, in some ways, you already do, for example by reading novels or watching films – as an 'escape'. But these are passive acts and an active 'questing' soul can only ever find temporary relief in such escapes – the unfulfilled heart will always yearn for a more empowering journey; a journey of spiritual transformation with purpose, full participation and personal meaning. In the instant one recognises this one has begun to 'awaken' into the 'otherworld'.

The world of 'spirits', the dead and other beings – the otherworld (or more correctly, 'otherworlds') – is found in mythologies across the world. In the worldview of the 'Heathen' traditions of the North – the topic of this book – the past, present and future are intimately linked and affect one another, as do the 'other' and 'real' worlds: the past is known as Wyrd, the present as Metod, and the future as Skuld, and all are intimately bound by the omnipresent 'Web of Wyrd'. As a concept, and in its various cultural elaborations, the otherworld may be very difficult for the linear and rational Western mind to comprehend or even take seriously. Yet, in Galdrbok, the nine worlds of the Northern otherworld, embodied in the shamanic world tree 'Yggdrasil', are within reach, and the necessary theory and methods for engaging with them, practically, in daily life, are made accessible. Thus, the system outlined in Galdrbok offers the potential for individual (and group) empowerment and transformation, for those prepared to embrace it!

## The 'Why' of Galdrbok

Shamans, medicine men, wise women, indigenous spiritual leaders and others, have in recent years begun to accrue a new 'dignity', gain acceptance and political empowerment, attract sympathy, and are increasingly afforded appropriate status. After centuries of (ongoing) colonialism and oppression, the spiritual practices and world-views of native peoples, their stories and mythologies, are receiving the attention and respect they deserve, are being listened to, recorded and passed on. Native American 'sweat lodges', 'pipe ceremonies' and 'sun dances', for example, can be experienced in England and elsewhere in the modern 'West' (and we assume the majority of our readers are themselves 'Westerners'), but, there are thorny issues of neo-colonialism here; namely the (wholesale) appropriation of non-Western indigenous (sacred) spiritual practices.

Ironically, our own indigenous Heathen practices lie somewhat dormant and neglected. In place of the practical and ritual 'ancestral memories' of indigenous communities, we now have a wealth of documented 'history' – useful and interesting, but often academic, dry, seemingly separate, and widely perceived as of less importance than, for instance, 'technology'. Science, technology, and the precocious sense of 'progress' prevalent in the West have yielded great benefits to many people, yet every 'coin' has its flip side. On the one hand, global inequality and poverty are prevalent, and seemingly occur (particularly) in environments where indigenous peoples endeavour to continue their traditional ways of life despite the impacts of colonialisms. On the other hand, one price we in the West continue to pay for this 'progress' is a loss of connection with our (diverse) Northern (principally Northwest European) 'tribal' cultural inheritances, particularly in respect of indigenous Heathen shamanic practices and the benefits they once provided.

Without looking to our pre-Christian past, modern Westerners seeking 'spirituality' are left to pick amongst the ashes of traditional Christian churches: the Anglican church, for example, has a dwindling number of attendees and a worldview which is increasingly outdated in the modern world. Or such seekers look further afield – abroad to be exact – with such practices as Yoga and Tai Chi, and such religious movements as Bahai and Sufism, now in popular parlance. Meanwhile, the New Age (pronounced, perhaps unfairly, 'newage' by some) perceives an essential (vague) oneness uniting all faiths, removing cultural nuance and diversity.

While indigenous peoples are increasingly reclaiming and feeling pride in their 'traditional' life-ways, we argue that this sense of 'indigeneity' now includes modern Westerners who have a 'feeling' for pre-Christian, Heathen shamanistic/animistic spirituality. Native communities are either recovering or reifying their own spirituality, their own gods and goddesses and their own re-established and earth-centred worldviews. We can and should do – and increasingly are doing – likewise in Northwest Europe.

Galdrbok marks one endeavour to reclaim the Heathenisms of our past and re-empower ourselves spiritually and 'tribally' in the present by providing an up-to-date and workable system of practical shamanism, coupled with a sense of history, or ancestry – something sorely neglected and lacking in our highly eclectic and fast-paced Western society.

Galdrbok is a synthesis of 'old' and 'new'. Modern seekers of 'Magic' are therefore challenged to navigate (within Galdrbok) writings which at times reflect the distant past, yet are firmly rooted in the present. Arcane language (in, for example, the Galdr [pronounced 'galdur'] – sung spells – and the various poems) and symbols (principally the runes) rub shoulders with references to contemporary points of view. This, alongside knowledge gained from exposure to diverse global cultures, positions Galdrbok as being both backward and forward looking; contemporary and ancient.

The impetus behind Galdrbok is to re-constitute a Heathen initiatory path for today, yet stretch the Heathen 'line' back to our fore-fathers and fore-mothers – wherever they came from – and whether we know of them or not. In this respect, the system presented here is in the vogue of contemporary 'Paganisms' in the sense that, while it stems from the present time, addresses contemporary needs, and is written from a modern perspective, it also looks back to an ancestral path and the experiences of many Heathen predecessors over the millennia. Indeed, it can be said that Galdrbok is positioned in three time periods: at the outset, the past and the present – yet Galdrbok, by its very nature, looks forward, by insight, to the future. It is not a matter of re-creating the past or reviving a dead culture, it is not a matter of 're-enactment'. Thus we stand with one foot in the present and one foot in the past, so that we may walk with confidence into the future.

## On 'Authenticity'

'Is Galdrbok authentic?' the reader may ask. A better question might be, 'At what point does a system become authentic?' The answer is, when it works! Nothing is static. Everything grows out of something else. Traditions (as acknowledged by anthropologists) are living entities, giving structure for human experience. As such, traditions, although regulated by their own rules, must grow or evolve when they need to – otherwise they are just so much dead and formal matter.

If 'neo-shamanic' (new shamanism) practices in the West are to be worthy of the title 'shamanism', then these practices must be living vibrant experiences, with practical methods and procedures which are individually and communally empowering. And, practitioners must avoid neo-colonialism – acts of appropriating aspects of indigenous shamanism, especially when many native shamans ask us not to steal their traditions.

Indigenous communities, particularly Native Americans and Aboriginal Australians, increasingly request that

Western spiritual seekers explore their own heritage, not that of an entirely different culture – their culture. This, as a matter of course, is what we aim to do here. As Brian Bates suggests in his 'The Way of Wyrd': '[W]e may equally well enrich our notions of life and being in the world by travelling in time into our own cultural past as by travelling in miles to study distant cultural traditions' (1983: 11). And, as Asterix says to Obelix – after a visit to Egypt, and in respect of Celtic menhirs versus Egyptian obelisks – 'keep it Gaulish, Obelix!' (In our case, keep it Heathen!)

Mindful of these considerations, we term the practitioner of the system presented in this book a 'Heathen shaman' rather than 'shaman', so as not to be disrespectful to other indigenous shamans. And in place of 'neo-shaman', which may imply inauthenticity to some readers, we also use other broadly interchangeable terms such as Mage or Magician, Vitki, Runester, Seidr-worker, Seidrmadr, Wodenic seer, and so on, although these terms most likely expressed quite different magical/shamanic statuses in the past. As stated in the synopsis of the system outlined in this book (see Appendix B), however, the Ulfhednr have no official leaders or positions. We simply use these terms to mean broadly the same thing: to describe practitioners of Galdrbok's system of shamanic initiation who celebrate nature and landscape as animate and enter the worlds of Yggdrasill (the Northern 'otherworld' tree) at will, to communicate and engage with spirit(s), deities and ancestors.

## A Heathen Outlook

Galdrbok presents a 'cultural' system in the sense that it has been formulated today, in the modern West, but this contemporary formulation is inspired by Northwest European imagery and experience. The reason we have chosen this ancient framework is as stated and has nothing to do with cultural snobbery, nationalism or some other right wing view – for we explicitly profess none of these; it is simply feelings, environment and experience, which is, perhaps, the way it has always been in such matters.

The issue of appropriating the past may be a problematic one. But who's past is it, and which past is more authentic than another? Current trends in archaeology itself now argue that there are multiple pasts, rather than a single knowable 'truth'. Also, archaeologists are not the only people who have legitimate access to the past. As Ronald Hutton, Professor of History at the University of Bristol states:

> It is a classic case of a situation in which the experts are feeding the public with information while leaving it free to make such imaginative reconstructions as it wishes...Druids [and other Pagans] are well placed to take advantage of it...indeed, it is almost a duty on their part to do so, for the more people who are involved in the work, and the broader the range of plausible pictures imagined, the healthier the situation (Hutton 1996:23).

In this vein, Galdrbok is one such narrative of the past, re-presented in and very much located in and for the present. We are indeed fortunate that our ancestors left the legacy that they did. Looking out of the window, right now, and noticing the rain-lashed oak trees, trees sacred to Thunor (the Anglo-Saxon name for Thor), set against a grey and ominous sky, it is easy to be reminded why some of us enjoy shamanism with a 'Northern' flavour. With all due respects to the brilliance of the ancient Egyptian priests, the Mayan shamans, and Chinese sages, we can't see the great Sun God Ra (or his Mayan or Chinese equivalent) today, or most days, with the weather being what it is in Britain! Joking aside, there is a serious point here. We acknowledge a vital connection between humans and the landscape with which they engage – if you try, you can feel the land wights (spirits of nature) around you.

While we recognise the effects environment, climate and weather has on 'mood', expression, art, culture and religion, we also strongly believe that 'blood and soil' attitudes, often connected with the runes (or other religions/cultures) are 1) incompatible with serious involvement in Heathen spirituality, and are 2) outdated in a world in which cultural differences are more consciously considered. As we have made plain, there is no room for right-wing politics, Nazism, or homophobia and their ilk in the Runecraft we advocate.

'Galdrbok' roughly translates from the Old Norse as 'Spellbook'. Once, 'Galdr' were likely sung as well as chanted, or simply spoken. Galdr have a 'magical' quality and were (and are) usually crafted poetically. A good 'skald' or 'scop' – (pronounced 'shope', in Anglo-Saxon 'sceapu', derived from 'to shape'), meaning 'crafter of words', poet, or teller of tales (including the proverbial Wizards and Witches) would recite his/her stories, songs and Galdr, having learned them by heart. We encourage the readers of Galdrbok to do the same. This parallels the 'Bardic' tradition of the Celts. Indeed, there is more commonality between the Anglo-Saxons and the Celts than is often imagined.

A considerable amount of modern 'sword and sorcery' imagery stems from various fusions of these two cultural strains. Enduring images of 'magical swords', fortified stockades (hill-forts and, later, castles), court Magicians, wyrms and dragons, wizards, witches, and so on, act as a 'hoard of cultural images'. They flesh-out many an imagined 'magical landscape' in our minds, and literature, from the ancient – such as the Anglo-Saxon Beowulf and wider corpus of Northern Mythology, to the modern – such as Tolkien's 'The Hobbit' and 'Lord of the Rings', and even 'Dungeons and Dragons'. Today, many are interested in the 'arts of enchantment' and spell-casting, but no Wizardry or Witchcraft is complete without an ethical framework.

## A Heathen 'Code of Conduct'

Runecraft, as outlined in this book, rests on a distinctive Northern 'code of conduct'. This does not mean that Heathen values are not shared by other cultures or different peoples, it simply means that it is possible to explain and define what can best be described as the (distinctive) Heathen virtues (as suggested by Tony Linsell in the booklet accompanying the 'Rune Cards', published by Anglo-Saxon Books), namely:

1. The keeping of oaths
2. Loyalty

3. Courage

4. Hospitality

5. Boldness – in thought and action

Linsell further informs us that,

> The person who observed the code and overcame their doubts
> and fears in order to fight against great odds, earned more
> honour and fame than a person with an easier passage through
> life... It was believed that fame enabled an individual to cheat
> death by living on in the hearts and minds of those they left
> behind. Although it was not thought necessary to be a warrior to
> win immortality, facing death in battle was regarded as a more
> testing and revealing experience than growing vegetables...
> Although the values of the Northern tradition are often
> expressed in a masculine way, it does not mean that women did
> not value [these] personal qualities... women often had to reveal,
> and strive for, those qualities [and others] in a different way from
> men (Ibid: 52-53)

We take this ethic further: the path of the Heathen shaman,
like the path of the warrior, is often difficult
and demanding, but it is also extremely rewarding,
and empowering.

The following poem – The Battle – is inspired by the
'Heathen code'. Its content reflects and applauds aspects of
the Heathen code, specifically loyalty, courage and
hospitality, and the conclusion advocates generosity. 'The
Battle' is constructed as nine verses – the number nine is
sacred in the Northern traditions, to Woden in particular,

and, for various esoteric reasons, it will be encountered over and again in Galdrbok. This poem is dedicated to the ancestors who upheld the Heathen code, and to those Heathens prepared to do so today. The first verse is inspired by the first three runes of the Anglo-Saxon Futhorc (twenty-nine Anglo Saxon runes): 'Fehu' – (mobile) wealth, 'Ur' (Aurochs) – strength, and 'Thorn' – conflict and instinctive behaviour. The last verse is inspired by the last three runes in the Futhorc: 'Yr' – weapon, the power to defeat an enemy (or illness), 'Iar' (Beaver) – contentment, and 'Ear' – the grave, death.

The poem echoes all of life's battles, both on and off the battlefield, and is given to counter criticisms levelled at the 'so-called' Northern penchant for war (actually a worldwide phenomenon even on a mundane level). Everything is struggling, all of the time. This is not a pessimistic view. Rather it leads to a clearer understanding of life, and gives rise to an 'enlightened self interest', tempered by the virtues of the Heathen code. We wish to stress that the Northern 'ethos' was and is one of 'pro-active' engagement with life, duty and honour. Besides, who has never felt like life is a battle? (Note that there are nine verses and 36 lines, with 36 being four times nine and both four (the Os rune) and nine being numbers sacred to Woden.)

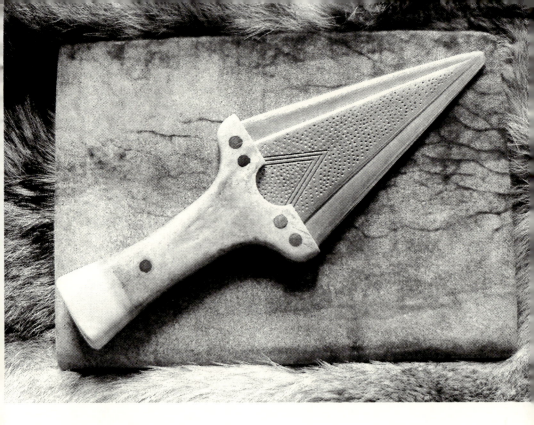

## The Battle

Iron-shod-clatter o'er cobble-stone route
Presaging warriors carting off loot
The glimmer of helm's, dulled-out by fierce blows
The keenest-blades-notched, in-scabbard repose

Mail-shirt a-clinking, axe hafted with oak
Bitter air hanging in grey palls of smoke
Hobbling weary on bones cracked and broken
Murmured farewells to the fallen are spoken

Many do flee them from dread bloody battles
Abandon their posts, filch-out goods and chattels
But caught wending coward's-path, trod-quick-to-home
Heaps punishments grim, on wretches full grown

Turncoats, deserters, cut-purses – and those
Massed ale-breath-vagabonds with kings to depose
Compare-not-to-noble-hearts forged strong and brave
Unsullied by knavery yet with scorn for the grave

As rude bloody-conflict beggars all peace
Champions' base theft, foul-pillage – caprice
'Bout the nature of strife, sore spoken of here
And of ill-gotten gains, I pray to make clear

'Tis no more than battle, ventured each day
In all walks of life and in every way
Thus even the glee-man enters strong in
With cheap jest for weapon, and idiot grin

And if wearest thou, no cold shirt of mail
Carry not sword, nor with axe do prevail
Yet much daily battle must oft' thou conjoin
To carry-off ransom of fair-minted coin

For hearth and home keep not of themselves
For Men, for Dwarves for Giants or Elves
Even Witch and Wizard need them for to eat
And drink them their ale and cook them their meat

Two conquer one, the tongue slays the head
The miser keeps coinage stashed-under-his-bed
Let heart rule the head, if not belly instead
For what use be wealth, to a man who is dead

## On Shamanisms

An underlying theme linking all the chapters of Galdrbok
is the concept of 'shamanism'. Shamanism is a term
constructed by anthropologists to describe certain diverse
healing and ritual practices in many cultures worldwide.
Shamans are people who alter consciousness in order to
engage with 'spirits' (in a 'spirit world') for a diversity of
culturally embedded, community-specific purposes (see
e.g. Wallis 2003), including healing and sorcery. Our
approach thus differs radically from Harnerism (see, for
example, Harner 1980) and other neo-shamanisms.
Harner argues that 'core-shamanism' is based on certain
universal principles which can be disassociated from
cultural contexts. He also argues that shamans are not
sorcerers – they do not use their abilities to cause harm.
We argue, in contrast, that core-shamanism is a Western
ideal version of what is, in all of its examples worldwide,
intrinsically culturally embedded. Furthermore, the
practices of many shamans are 'grey' rather than 'black' or
'white', in the sense that life is a struggle involving both
positive and negative elements – good and evil are too
simplistic a characterisation of the complexity of the
world(s). Embracing the complexity of shamanism, we
emphasise its cultural embeddedness – here in the
Northern or Heathen traditions – and its diversity (as
shamanisms) over an alleged universal, acultural and
apolitical shamanism. Academics and specialists debate
whether   shamanisms   existed   among   Germanic
communities (e.g. Wallis 2003), but it is certainly clear that
certain aspects of Germanic life were shamanic (e.g. Blain
2002) and that our ancestors engaged with Sami (Lapp)
shamans, indicating that cultural exchange indeed
occurred (e.g. Price 2002).

Many people find shamanism appealing because it is perceived to be a 'personal', 'free' and 'eclectic' spiritual path. Indigenous shamanism is certainly highly pragmatic and involves direct human contact with supernatural agencies. But the notion that it is free and eclectic is largely a Western stereotype imposed on shamanism as we have universalised it and removed cultural diversity from it. Indigenous shamans are as much constrained by cultural norms, personal relationship pressures and community politics as we are.

Paradoxically, in any case, it is limitation, or structure, which facilitates transcendence or freedom: it is structure which gives meaning. This is why we present a structured approach to Heathen Runecraft, Shamanism and Magic; what might be described, in short, as a 'Heathen shamanism'. We feel that the common 'newage' notion of 'doing your own thing', and 'making it up as you go along' each time you perform rituals, does not achieve much. Inspirational it may be, but it is also vague and unfocussed. Further, such a modern attitude ignores the vast legacy of indigenous practices left to us by our Northern ancestors. Indeed this legacy has much room for freedom of inspiration – despite its structure – and in many ways relies, shamanistically, on it: there is no room for dogma.

## On 'Shamans' and 'Religion'

Issues of terminology and definition are difficult to avoid in discussions of this sort. Graham Harvey, a scholar of religions, argues that both 'shaman' and 'religion', 'mean a host of things, some of them comparable, some overlapping, but not a few are contradictory. Even more to the point, both words can be defined in many ways'

(Harvey 2003: 4). Indeed, 'many languages have no word that can be directly and unambiguously translated as "religion"' (Harvey 2003:59) and while in the Old North 'shaman' and 'religion' were not 'native' terms, aspects of the sources do compare and overlap with (and sometimes contradict!) these terms. If, as Harvey indicates, religion 'is a native term in some languages, but... in academic discourse it carries particular associations and implications' (Harvey 2003:4-5), then the terms 'religion' and 'shaman' are negotiable.

When negotiating 'shamanic' elements of 'Northern religions', we are clearly dealing with beliefs and practices which are pre-Christian and therefore markedly different from the more hierarchical, institutionalised and somewhat corporate 'religions of the book' we are familiar with in the modern West. On the other hand, early and more localised forms of Christianity (and perhaps Judaism and Islam), for example Gnosticism and Anglo-Saxon village Christianity, were likely more 'shamanic' than current Protestantism and Catholicism. If this appears somewhat contradictory, then it is important to avoid a simplifying definition of religion: 'not only is religion capable of many definitions, many of which are evidently applicable in indigenous contexts, but also the academic Study of Religion now engages with far more complex and interesting understandings of religion precisely because it interacts with indigenous and other life-ways' (Harvey 2003: 59-60).

It is the incorporation of religious practices into daily life, into a 'worldview', which is of interest to the practitioner. Harvey concludes that 'all religion is a matter of action, observance, performance, or practice... In short, shamans and their communities perform religion when they attempt to meet needs for health, food, security and knowledge (Harvey 2003: 59-60). So, for the Heathen shaman, it is important to recognise the empowering (agentic) nature of religion, its 'action, observance, performance, or practice' in daily life (Harvey 2003: 59).

## On Animism

One of the key themes underpinning shamanic worldviews is animism. Animism is another anthropological construct which suffers from many popular and academic misunderstandings. It is often written-off as unsophisticated and/or superstitious, but many indigenous communities might argue that animism actually offers a more sophisticated and holistic way of engaging with the world than the mechanistic, dualistic, biological model of the West (though these may not be mutually exclusive).

According to an animistic worldview, an animating force permeates both 'animate' and 'inanimate' things (thus the dualism of animate/inanimate is simply removed), and people engage in relationships with the 'spirits' of trees, stones and so on. Some stones and other 'inanimate objects', as they are known to Westerners, are considered as much alive as we are, but alive in a different way. Engage with, listen to or feel a rock you are drawn to, and you may perceive its spirit to be very different from your own. It has, after all, been in the process of creation for millions of years.

In the Heathen tradition introduced in Galdrbok, stones, plants and indeed all things are filled with the animating essence termed 'Ond'. Everything is connected by this essence, by threads which comprise the 'Web of Wyrd'. It is the Heathen shaman who 'sees' and traverses this web, a web which is mapped out by the world tree Yggdrasill. Yggdrasill is examined in detail in later chapters; for now, it is relevant to know that Heathen animists in 'the real world' stand in Midgard which is located at the centre of Yggdrasill. In this 'living landscape', we engage with wights (spirits of nature), gods, goddesses, and so on. All of these 'nature beings' – from rocks and streams to trees and hills – are vitally important to Heathen shamans in their engagements with the world(s).

Graham Harvey (2004a, also 2004b) suggests, more academically and precisely, that since animals (and others) can be considered as 'relational communicative agents (persons)', so animism is 'engaging with conscious relational agents (persons)'. More simply put, 'we (humans) live in a world full of "persons", only some of whom are human' – this is 'a radically living world'. As animists, we have an 'adjusted style of communication' (from the mechanistic model) with regard to these 'other-than-human persons'. So, as 'human people' with this adjusted style of communication, we may engage with 'other-than-human-people', be it rock-people or tree-people. But this adjusted style of communication works both ways, since for rock-people there are other-than-rock-people, such as human people and tree people.

If this sounds like an inversion or at least levelling of the Darwinian evolutionary schema, then so be it – which is not to discount evolution itself, only the way in which it has tended to privilege humans as the ascendant species on the planet. It might be argued, for example, that viruses and bacteria are more arguably ascendant due to their numbers, diversity, resilience and success, or that crocodiles are more successful due to the millions of years longer they and their ancestors have been on the planet than modern humans.

Harvey points out that it might be more challenging to engage with some 'inanimate objects' (such as plastic things) as 'animate' than others (say, a tree or a crystal). Consider that among indigenous shamans, though, a 'spirit' of the outboard motor might have offerings made to it in order to ensure a safe fishing trip. Besides, animists need not engage with all things as animate, all of the time. Indigenous animists (and by now we think we can also legitimately call ourselves indigenous Heathen animists!) also do not engage with all things as animate, all of the time. Ond animates all matter, but each of us develops special relationships with specific other-than-human-people, and they with us. In short, we may choose our own 'spirits', but they may also choose us!

With this animistic view comes an element of what Harvey calls 'respect': it is incumbent upon us to lead responsible lives and engage in responsible relationships with all living (all animated) things. In some indigenous traditions, a short 'prayer' of respect and gratitude is offered to hunted quarry, and all parts of the animal (or plants) are used and/or valued. Just as we must do 'violence' to others (killing plants, animals, etc), so they (viruses, predators, etc) do violence to us. In this natural cycle and in these dynamic, respectful relationships, we celebrate life, celebrate the seasons and as a fact of life, also respect death. Indeed, indigenous shamans tend to have an intimate association or connection with death, and some use 'death' or 'dying' to describe their trance experiences. This experience of 'death' can be somewhat frightening at first, but may then become consistently positive and empowering – for individual shamans and their communities.

Generally speaking, attitudes towards death are influenced – if not created – by attitudes towards life. Thus, the value systems, or more properly, the beliefs people subscribe to (or reject) shape their attitudes and responses to death. However, the 'duality' insisted upon in 'rational' 'material' thought can not help but reach a nihilistic conclusion: you live, you die, that's it! But, does a line divide or join 'life' and 'death'? Simply put, from an animistic and shamanic standpoint, the 'cold', 'sharp' line between life and death both joins and divides – the divide becomes permeable, if not dissolved altogether, because all things are understood to be animate and we humans are among other relational beings. Thus an alternative perspective to rational materialism unfolds, one which looks beyond the perceived supremacy of our own species to an animate universe. Today, some people seem to be grasping this intuitively: sketchy ideas on 'universalism' or cosmic 'oneness' are espoused with increasing frequency, yet they often lack the necessary depth, (mostly, ways of making the idea concrete, physical, or life changing, and locally embedded) and consequently, when the moment of 'inspiration' arises (sometimes repeatedly), it is lost.

The answer to the question 'what will happen to me when I die?' which arises in each of us with the first stirrings of self awareness and exposure to the idea of death, is in the West firmly based on rigid and fixed notions of who and what we are (or should be), particularly the idea of the bounded, singular 'individual'. Challenge this concept, and our Modern notions of death can be radically altered. The practice of altered consciousness, which moves the experient beyond 'ego' and therefore 'death' (of the ego), gives rise to new insights (kennings) which at least throw doubt on the reality or accuracy of the question 'what will happen to me when I die?' by challenging the perspective of the enquirer. A widespread perception may be that Hindus, Buddhists, Taoists and others were 'the first' to 'discover' or reveal the so-called teaching of the 'deathless' state, but some shamans in indigenous communities also have this knowledge. The way you perceive (and shape) life is the way you will shape and perceive death; but also (perhaps more importantly) the way you perceive death will shape the way you perceive life!

The 'big subject' to address, in consequence, is individuality. Everyone knows that they can not go shopping or take a holiday when they are dead (excluding the supporters of a de-facto paradise), yet one has only to consider notions such as infinity or eternity, or at least the minuscule position of humanity in a vast universe, to see how simplistic, small-minded and potentially limiting (however beguiling) such notions are. Imagine instead if you were everything, and everything was you – 'you' as a microcosm of the macrocosm, or vice versa. You could start with the (relative) notion that everything is living, all of the time, and that it just keeps changing form. Such may well be the nature of life – movement and change – and you (whatever you perceive yourself to be, and that is the issue) are an inextricable part of it.

Everyone knows that they can not escape death and the separation from family, loved ones, and friends, as well as the loss of power, control and choice which death imposes. And whilst some recognise this and seemingly accept it at face value, practical post mortem (after death) decisions still need to be taken. Many people, depending on custom, consider whether to be burned or buried – when, where and how; but why, if a rational material view is taken that 'you die and that is that'? We, all of us, know we will be dead, and assume that once we are dead we will not feel anything, so why such concern over our mortal remains? The (natural) egocentricity which is part and parcel of being human, as well as respect for 'personhood', individuality and a whole host of other factors, coupled with the requirements of culture or society, largely determine these concerns.

Animism offers a different perspective on these issues. This does not mean death is still not a major event. On a personal basis, or for family members, a friend or relation dying is like a world ending. But in addition, from an animistic point of view, it can be postulated that 'we' are not necessarily what we think we are (individual bounded egos), and our ability to see and to know ourselves and the world(s) in which we live is severely limited by the Western notion of the (rather cognicentric) 'human condition'.

Westerners often have consistently rigid and unyielding value sytems. We argue that an animistic view offers some flexibility and challenges negative views of death based around rational materialism which can lead to a jaded and/or nihilistic and obsessively materialist approach to life. Animism is not superstition, is not 'primitive', is not simplistic – indeed with a diversity of relationships with 'other-than-humans' to be established, animism is clearly a complex and sophisticated worldview (as already made clear). Engaging with other-than-human persons or non-human people – or simply 'spirits' – also includes gods and goddesses, of course, and by chanting Galdr (see Chapter 5) and temporarily altering our personalities and assuming god and goddess forms (essences/complexes – we do not mean 'dressing up' here), our perception becomes greatly enhanced. When the veil of modern Western scepticism is lifted, we are able to 'see' with 'new eyes', and gain new kennings (insights) which powerfully challenge negative views of who and what we are (like).

## Woden and Freyja

In Galdrbok, Runic spirit-questing and self-initiation are based on the examples of two deities we consider to be the 'classic' Northwest European shaman-Magicians, Woden and Freyja. In our suggestion that the god Woden is a shaman-god, we have considerable evidence from the sources. Woden is skilled in magic and sorcery and according to the Icelander Snorri Sturluson (1179-1241), it was he 'who ruled and practiced the art which is the most powerful of all and is called seidr' (Ynglinga saga 7). Other shamanistic themes are easily identified in the mythology of Woden. Snorri tells how Woden can 'shift his appearance... in the shape of a bird or animal' while his body would lie (in trance?) 'as if he were asleep or dead' (see also the Heimskringla). In the Norse myths Woden

rides (the shamanic journey) his eight-legged horse Sleipnir
(a spirit helper) to the worlds (shamanic otherworlds)
comprising the Yggdrasill tree (shamanic world tree)
(Ynglinga saga 7).

According to the Havamal ('Sayings of the High One': see
Larrington 1996), Woden hangs himself in Yggdrasill,
pierces himself with his own spear and after nine nights he
receives the wisdom of the runes – a shamanic initiation.
Yggdrasill means 'Horse (or steed) of Yggr (i.e. Woden)' or
'terrible steed', perhaps a shamanic metaphoric link to
Woden riding Sleipnir. In Grimnismal, Woden seemingly
undergoes 'shamanistic rituals' of 'torture, starvation and
heat' (Larrington 1996:50); he also has the ability to shape-
change at will and he is 'lord of the dead', collecting the
souls of warriors after battle during the 'wild hunt' of the
Valkyries. Furthermore, Woden has shamanic animal
helpers: two ravens – Huginn ('thought', 'mind') and
Muninn ('the thought', 'memory') – who perch on his
shoulders and bring news of happenings in the world tree,
and two wolves – Freki and Geri.

Etymologically, the Icelandic 'Odin' (or Odhinn/Othin) is
cognate with the Old Icelandic adjective and noun
'odr/othr' meaning 'mad, frantic... furious, vehement',
while the noun 'odrm/othrm' (m.) can be 'mind, feeling...
song, poetry (Zoëga 1961 [1910]: 323). As Wotan the name
relates to the modern German 'wut' meaning 'fury',
'intoxication', 'possession', 'rage', 'wrath'. Woden is
derived from the old English 'wod' meaning 'angry',
'obsessed' (see Davidson 1964:147; Fries 1993:208; Bates
1996:169-70), relating to the term 'wodbura', meaning 'the
one who carries the rage' as well as 'poet'.

This evidence (see also Buchholz 1971) points rather convincingly to the role of Woden as a shaman-god. We go further and suggest that Woden was most likely a major patron of Heathen shamans in the migration age. Moreover, it is plausible that Woden's exploits are a record or reflection of the actual experiences of some of his (initiated) devotees. Indeed, a number of authors suggest such shamans may have operated in Anglo-Saxon and Norse communities (for example, Bates 1983; Glosecki 1989).

Yet, Heathen Runic shamanism is by no means a 'male' prerogative. Aspects of the goddess Freyja are also likely to be shamanistic, though few scholars have recognised this (see Wallis 2003: 125-6). As well as the practice of Seidr (pronounced 'sayth', discussed further in Chapter 4), Freyja's character may refer to shamanistic themes when she makes use of a falcon cloak (Thrymskvida 2-5, Skaldskaparmal 56), and, like Odin, raises the dead (in her form as Hild) (Flateyarbok), acts as a trickster deity (in the form of Gefjon) (Ynglinga saga 5, Gylfaginning 1), and endures a trial of fire (in the form of Gullveig/Heidr): 'three times they burned her, three times she was reborn' (Voluspa 21).

Galdrbok promotes equality between the genders we in the West know as 'male' and 'female'. Simplistic classifications which conflate sex and gender and rely on binary oppositions are a modern Western invention. Other cultures have different systems of classification, often involving three, four, or more genders. Interestingly, the Western distinction between male and female is challenged by gender theorists (such as Judith Butler [1990]) who argue that biological sex is as much a Western, mechanistic construction, as gender. The shamanistic path of Freyja may most appeal to women, yet both Woden's and Freyja's path (or both!) is open to anyone – gods willing, of course!

It is imperative that this balance is encouraged because the Northern traditions have for too long been associated with the 'barbarian' Viking stereotype with its beer swilling and horned-helmets (never mind the fact that Vikings never even wore such helmets – Hollywood promoted that mistaken image). Scholars now suggest the evidence from our ancestors points towards a very different view of the Vikings and other Northern peoples of the migration age. Accounts of Heathen Viking raids and pillaging were not only mostly written down by hostile Christian monks and are therefore highly biased narratives, but these raids have also been overemphasised in the literature.

More likely, a typical man of the Old North (be he Anglo-Saxon or Norse, etc) was a farmer concerned with the day-to-day upkeep of his smallholding, not a horned-helmeted sword-wielding murderer! And where are the women in these male orientated accounts? While they are mostly ignored, we suggest they were central to community life, and in some instances with greater status than many men! Not only is Galdrbok aimed at both men and women, then, but we also argue that the quicker the 'horned-helmet' stereotype of the Vikings is ditched, the better.

## Denizens of Yggdrasill

Part of our purpose in this book, is to provide a map and the necessary instructions for effective travel through the otherworldly regions found on the Northwest European world tree. But, does such an 'otherworld' exist? And if so, where is it and how can it be visited?

For practicing shamans, the otherworld does exist and it is not an imaginary or literary creation. Nor is it a grim place (like the Christian 'Hell') where punishments are meted out after death (unless you want it to be!). The 'inner' life knows none of the ('ordinary' world) constructions of time and space, and when we re-activate the ancient myths within ourselves we begin to flesh-out and customise the mythography, making the otherworld navigable and experiential. A crude example might be the common disorientation felt, and the distortion of time commonly experienced, in dreams – dreams themselves are important aspects of one's being and may provide information of a visionary nature to the Heathen shaman.

A diverse range of first-hand spiritual experiences can be had by travelling through the roots, trunk and branches of the world tree. We may encounter the denizens of various 'worlds' such as Dwarfs, Light Elves, and Giants, and of course the Northern deities themselves, such as Woden, Freyja, Thunor and Frigg. We may encounter Ancestors, the Dead, and Dark Elves. We may converse with Magicians, warlocks, prophetesses, witches, wizards, and holy people from long ago and from possible futures. And, in so doing we may gain wisdom, magical accomplishment and much more besides.

In contrast to the various passive 'visualisation' and 'path working' techniques which are popular in Mind Body Spirit books and workshops today, both the active (e.g. shamanic journeying) and passive (e.g. scrying with a crystal ball) practices provided in Galdrbok are structured only up to the point of entering the otherworld as well as offering the signposts of its geography (which is open to personal interpretation and negotiation). At the point of entry, while the mythological background will influence the manner of your experiences, the otherworld experiences themselves are entirely spontaneous. We only provide the basic 'map' – the roots, trunk, and branches. The Northwest European world tree Yggdrasill, an otherworld map, consists of several layers or 'worlds' encompassing different levels of human and other-than-human conscious states. By travelling on Yggdrasill – its roots to ecstasy – and accessing states of consciousness, we can, in the way of many diverse shamans worldwide, fly on spirit-wings. And, travelling beyond the usual boundaries of mind and body, time and space, we can follow in the footsteps of Woden and Freyja, walk 'between the worlds' and enter ecstasy.

# – Introduction –
# Why Runecraft?

## The Runes

RUNES OF WISDOM RUNES OF WOE
RUNES OF HEALING, EVIL TO SLOW

NOT BOOK-LAW, DOGMA, ZEALOUS RULES
RUNES BOLD-WRITTEN ARE MAGICAL TOOLS

HONOURED RUNE-HOARD, HOARY WITH AGE
WISDOM'S TOOL FROM ECSTATIC RAGE

WELL-WON BY WODEN – SPIED FROM THE TREE
GIVEN WITH BLESSINGS TO YOU AND TO ME

## Heathenry Today

The initiatory, shamanic 'Heathen' path offered in this book does not pretend to be the 'true', 'ancient', 'authentic' tradition of the romanticised 'hoary runemaster-shamans of old', nor is it 'channelled' speculation. It is, instead, an authentic spiritual path for contemporary Heathens, based on ancient traditions. As such, it is the product of considerable study and practice, supported by insight and informed conjecture. The conjecture, in terms of interpretation, is necessary to fill gaps left by several hundred years of neglect, during which Heathen practices were persecuted, largely abandoned and in many places eradicated.

The term 'Heathen' is derived from the old Germanic
languages. At the time of conversion to Christianity in
Iceland, it was used by newly converted Christians to refer
– not negatively – to followers of the old Pagan religion. It
later became a term of abuse, but, significantly, it is 'now
being reclaimed by... those who refer to "people of the
heath"... suitably for those who would follow the spirits of
the land' (Blain 2002: 6). Today there are enthusiastic
'revivals', 'reconstructions' or 'reinventions' (depending on
viewpoint) of Heathenry also known variously as 'the
Northern Tradition', Asatru – 'faith in the gods', and forn
sed – 'Old Way' [Blain 2002: 5]), a path which is allied with
other contemporary 'Paganisms'. But this book is not
intended to support or represent any kind of 'Runic
renaissance', per se. There are already books available
which purport to do that. Galdrbok is instead, as stated
in the section entitled 'Preface', an attempt to provide a
contemporary system of Heathen shamanic initiation based
on the legacy of migration age Northwest European
communities in the first millennium CE. In this capacity,
Galdrbok is unlike any other book on the runes
or Heathenry.

The majority of books concerning runes usually present
them as tools for divination only, or as an adjunct to Wicca
(Modern Witchcraft), 'Celtic' Druidry (and other Pagan
paths), or magic. Those that deal with 'magic' tend to
present techniques akin to Kabbala/Qabalah or medieval
and Victorian high ceremonial 'magick', a la Crowley. We
have no problem with that. Indeed, we have been
influenced by such systems ourselves. Heathenry is, after
all, a religion for today (as it was for our Heathen ancestors
in their own time). And in the post-modern climate of

today, it is impossible to explore the Northern sources without thinking about them in relation to the cumulative knowledge we have gleaned from elsewhere. Just as many Heathens today have come to Heathenry after looking into Wicca, women's mysteries, natural magic, and so on, and can not ignore this background (for to do so would assume the past is divorced from the present) so we too have not avoided our own experiences in the occult. All such 'narratives' of the past are equally valid because they 'work'; whether they are authentic or similar to the ancient practices is a different matter, to which we shall return. Unlike these other Pagan paths however, which often seem to regard traversing the tree itself as a subsidiary practice to magic, oracle use and personal growth, we approach the subject from a more 'shamanic' perspective. Indeed, this book concerns itself with the much neglected 'shamanic' aspects of the Northern mysteries, a focus that we believe fires genuine mystical/magical empowerment and spiritual attainment.

One consistently important aspect of shamanisms is the entering of a 'spirit world' for the purpose of engaging with 'spirits'. This moving out of the (physical) body, or 'ecstasy' (from the Greek 'ekstasis', meaning to be outside the body), involves journeying to the subtly mapped territory of the other world. Shamanic 'journeying' (as practiced by the popular core-shamanism invented by Michael Harner), or using the Northern wordhoard 'faring forth', is not the only trance state that many indigenous shamans induce, however, since shamans may also mediate spirits (mediumship) and practice contemplative techniques (meditation). In this book you will find clearly defined trance states known here as Vaniric (mediumistic,

comprising Runic and scrying practises), Disiric
(shamanistic journeying and ancestor communication) and
Aesiric (deity invocation) (See Chapter 4: Trance). We also
present an 'otherworld geography' – the roots, trunk and
branches of Yggdrasill – to provide the reader with a
destination, a route and a vehicle for these trances.

## On Heathen Orthodoxy

Another important point to bear in mind is that ancient
shamans, from whichever culture or time, were/are
practical people. Returning to the point of authenticity in
the context of practicality, a short tale might well be
in order:

We remember sitting with some shamanically-minded
friends on a windy hillside one evening. As sticklers for
'authenticity', we insisted (as far as possible) on wearing
clothing which reflected (our ideas on) the 'days of yore'.
One of us dressed in an Old English leather tabard, boots,
and with woollen 'wraps' (complete with Saxon cloak-pin)
thrown over his shoulders, he cut quite a figure. But how
practical or necessary was it? Perhaps we paid too much
attention to aesthetics and too little to what we were
actually doing? One of our friends was lightly but warmly
dressed in eminently more practical modern mountain
wear. This raised a question: if ancient shamans had had
lightweight waterproof clothing or butane gas lighters for
instance, would they have used them? We think they
probably would have. Have you ever tried starting an
outdoor fire on a wet and windy hillside, dressed in
soaked woollen wraps and armed with a couple of flints
and some kindling?

Aesthetically, we could never understand how a Voodoo priest for instance, could tolerate making 'holy' and ritual objects out of old cola tins, empty squash bottles, old car tyres or whatever was at hand. From our modern and initially rather romantic perspective on 'Runic shamanism', we found it difficult to accept these ignoble materials as suitable. But shamans make them suitable. They imbue them with power and bring them to life. Theirs is a practical vocation, not a hobby, an anthropological study or an excuse to be a consumer of new-age products.

We are aware this narrative raises other issues connected with 'organic' and 'natural' vs. synthetic materials and indeed do not include cola cans in our Heathen shamanic 'kit'. But the important point is that people have always made use of whatever is around them, in the period and place that they live in. For us, like it or not, we have the 21st Century. In our literary, jet and cyber age, we have amassed a vast storehouse of spiritual and esoteric information. Nowadays, silver haired grandparents take lessons in Yoga, Zen Buddhism, Tai Chi, and all manner of other activities. And, everyone seems to know about Feng Shui, the Chinese art of harmonious alignment. There are even techno-shamans who use the World Wide Web as a divinatory device.

Gone are the days when the shrammed and rain-sodden Northern shaman never left his shire, and had nightmares of falling off the edge of the world in a boat. Nowadays we don't believe that the earth is flat...we know it is! But seriously – now the Dalai Lama meets with the Pope, and Prime Ministers and Presidents wear jeans; we are in the postmodern global village.

We therefore argue that practicality in spirituality is paramount. Having failed to learn the lesson several times – having been sticklers for a perceived 'authenticity' – we now recognise that we are not 're-enactors'. Practicality, aligned to a clear-cut purpose is of greater import than perceived 'authenticity', unbroken 'traditions' (Nordic, Celtic, Wiccan or whatever) and artistic aesthetics (dressing up or wishing to be in ancient Egypt, Atlantis, Mu, etc).

Being misguided by inappropriate notions of authenticity based on ideas of 'purity' (i.e., 'pure' Runecraft, 'pure' Celtic shamanism, etc) can waste rather a lot of time. Of course, we cannot discover 'the' 'authentic' 'tradition' or 'dogma' – you see, mercifully, it never existed. Which tradition would be the authentic one, among which of many diverse communities, and at which time in the history of the Northern peoples? Traditions change, they are not static, so we can not find the one true Runic tradition because there never was one, whatever anyone claims about inherited traditions; even inherited traditions, were they to exist, would have undergone change! It is a pity that there are people, often with their heads in right-wing politics, who would like to return us to the fold of an imaginary 'Runic orthodoxy'. The question begging is 'what would this orthodoxy look like?' – given the way in which Heathenry in the North was (and is!) diverse in space and time, the idea of a 'Runic orthodoxy' at all is of course mistaken.

To the seeker of purity, orthodoxy and authenticity, contemporary written discussions concerning the origins of the Runic alphabet(s) are (or can be) infuriating, particularly when authors claim the runes were derived from Mediterranean alphabets, like the Etruscan, Greek or Latin. To the seeker of orthodoxy, this might constitute a 'threat' to Runic sovereignty; it might make the runes – 'our' runes – second rate to the alphabets of others. With National caps firmly on heads, seekers of the single Runic orthodoxy yearn for the very dogma Runecraft has actually managed to avoid. They, unfortunately, find only nationalism instead.

As evidence for the ever-changing nature of tradition(s), we cite Brian Branston who argues, in 'The lost Gods of England':

> The Woden of the Old English never became the warrior king in golden helmet... exclusive patron of princes and jarls such as Snorri depicted in his Edda: he was never preoccupied with the problem of organising his battalions of slain into a doomed army to oppose the Children of Muspell at the Ragnarok. Instead, the Anglo Saxon Woden stalked the rolling downland, one-eyed and wise beyond all knowing in cloak and hood when the weather was fine, stopping at cross-roads to recognise his own dangling from the gallows; but on black and stormy nights he racketed across the sky at the head of his wild hunt (Branston 1957 [1974]: 107).

So, the rune craft practised in, for instance, the south of England in the sixth century, differed radically from that in tenth century Iceland. The Runic glyphs in the various Scandinavian, Germanic and English systems, for example, vary even down to the numbers and orders of the runes. The mythologies also exist in different versions (and some are re-writes of others). Anglo-Saxon Heathens, according to Branston at least, seem not to have acknowledged a Ragnarok (death of the gods), a major theme in

Scandinavian mythology. Valhalla, the 'hall of the slain', within Asgard, the home of the Gods, only appears in Old Norse literature and most of these Norse myths were recorded late in the history of their use (after the tenth century). Where the Icelandic Odin of Snorri's Edda transforms into a snake in order to drink from the mead of poetry, the earlier Poetic Edda has no such tale. And where in the Old Norse sources this Odin had a spear named Gungnir, we have no such record for the Woden of the Anglo-Saxons.

Clearly, this diversity renders a Runic orthodoxy impossible. In desperation, seekers of authenticity may next begin to question the authenticity of the scribes, or even wonder whether the storytellers got the stories right in the first place! What if they had forgotten bits, or, gods forbid, changed them? With an approach like this, one can soon become confused and demoralised. If we were to search for the 'original' Heathen religion (rather than religions – plural) of the North, we would not find it. At the time of its practice, it was disparate, fragmented and diverse. To revive and practice it today, we must take into account all of the sources – of which we are very fortunate to have so many, in contrast to other Pagan paths – and reconstruct a composite, contemporary spiritual practice. Simply put, there is no dogma to cling to, no official version to follow, no authentic 'genuine' tradition. Some readers of this book who were raised in a Judeo-Christian background may subconsciously seek a Runic equivalent, a 'Torah' or a 'Nicene Creed'. You will not find it here, for what we provide is a practical and negotiable system of Heathen shamanic initiation, not a 'Runic bible'.

## About 'Galdr'

Heathenry today is not essentially a revelatory religion, and Heathen shamanism is not dogmatic. It is instead, extremely pragmatic and therefore effective. Galdrbok is not concerned with re-enactment and our reconstructive Heathenry does borrow from other esoteric traditions – we are not runic purists. As such, Galdrbok is not 'channelled' speculation, and offers a practical, systematic approach. As an example of how we are not sticklers for authenticity at the expense of practicality, Galdrbok includes a number of classic techniques of trance induction, one of which, deity invocation (see Chapter 4: Trance), uses Galdr (sung spells) which employ sound vibrations or 'sonics' derived from ancient Sanskrit Mantra – and before that, probably 'Indo-European' language groups (see Chapter 5: Galdr). Intriguing links between Indo-European and Germanic worldviews have also been explored by Alby Stone in his book 'Ymir's Flesh'. Far from being incongruous, we believe such comparisons produce new 'kennings' ('understandings' – see the Cen [torch] rune in the Appendix). As we demonstrate, the 'sonics' in our Galdr may be linguistically related to the runes, the names of deities, and places and events in Northwest European lore and mythology. Moreover, the trance states and sonics presented are of the utmost importance to Galdrbok's system of Heathen shamanic initiation, providing – if used as detailed – safe and systematic methods for producing the necessary altered consciousness required for effective shamanism. Essentially, these techniques work and they work extremely well.

# – Chapter 1 –
## The Otherworld - Recovering the Magic from Childhood

**M**agic – now, there is a loaded word, if ever there was one! There are connotations of 'trickery', the magic circle and sleight of hand. But magic is also a word very well known to children, conjuring up magical realms, special powers, and images of wizards, elves, faeries, dwarfs, trolls, enchanted castles, and of course princes and princesses. But magic in this sense for adults, perhaps sounds rather patronising?

We argue – and this is a theme running throughout Galdrbok – that magic is as much an integral and important though neglected part of the 'Western psyche' as conversations about the weather. As children we easily re-create the magical world of faeries and dragons taught to us in traditional fairytales. These 'make-believe' fantasy worlds sometimes become places into which we retreat when the mood takes us, a habit some of us retain into adulthood.

Those who regularly and spontaneously daydream, however, run the risk of being described as living on 'cloud nine' or in 'cuckoo-land'. Daydreaming is generally seen to detract from what the individual is 'supposed' to be doing (read 'achieving') in the 'real' world and is therefore considered to be unproductive. As we grow into adulthood, we begin to discard the magic worlds we once knew, having been encouraged to do so by parents, teachers and others in 'authority'. Enchanted realms and faeries at the bottom of the garden no longer exist for the grown-up who learns to label these experiences as 'unreal', as daydreams. And yet we seem anxious to pass on this legacy of elves, faeries, trolls, Santa Claus and the tooth fairy to our children! It seems we fear the cultural hole their removal would leave. But what kind of message does this example of double standards give to our children when they are later told that all the beings they were once encouraged to meet are actually 'imaginary'? The ability to consciously dream might be one of the things which makes us human. Unfortunately, this amazing and precious gift is often undervalued.

Dreamers who dream fiscal dreams, corporate dreams and pragmatic dreams for utility mechanical purposes are celebrated as creators, inventors, geniuses and even world leaders. Of course, these people are not dreamers but 'visionaries'! Without doubt, science has brought about many important developments in health care, technology, and so on, and these should not be derided. But perhaps the rampant materialism of the modem world is due in part to the encouragement and preponderance of utility, materialistic dreaming over and at the expense of what we call, for want of a better expression, 'magical dreaming'; that is, concrete proposals over mystical reverie. Perhaps the price we pay is stress, depression and even neurosis.

So poorly is dreaming regarded in some busy quarters that it is considered to be a veritable nuisance, even when it occurs at night, which, as everyone knows, is the proper time to dream of course! Interfering with a good night's sleep as they do, dreams are all right so long as they are nice, so long as we experience, for instance, being richer, slimmer, sexier, and so on.

Excessive linear thinking for utility function (dominated as it is, according to psychologists, by the left hemisphere of the brain) robs the individual of that 'something else' – that magic from childhood we have talked about. On a similar note, C. G. Jung described it as the 'divine and numinous'. For the left hemisphere of the brain, the faces of mythical giants, grey wolves, brooding black ravens, and vast ethereal landscapes hanging invitingly in a timeless sky, become nothing more than rain-filled clouds, as we scurry off to tap the barometer, consigning the otherworld to myth, romance, and fantasy, as we go. Such visions have no place in the worldview of the overworked and stressed people who are increasingly common in today's fast-paced society.

In modern times, however, the opiate of television is not without its impact on imagination, emotions and creativity. It has, to a considerable extent, taken over from the storytelling of old, when audiences were 'spellbound' by the tales of a visiting 'skald' or 'scop' (a poet, similar to the Irish and Welsh 'bard') – even if they'd heard the tales many times before. Film is audio-visual and like most modern labour saving devices, does the (mental) work for us. Yet, a narrated story will always activate inner vision, promote mental exercise and generate pictures built up by the individual, for the individual, thus making the whole experience participatory and interactive. 'Imaginative' participation is vital to mental well-being: just look at children play!

Current psychology has only recently woken up to, and taken seriously, the importance of dreaming and the 'imaginal' (as neo-Jungians call it, e.g. Noel 1997) – something well known for generations by many indigenous communities. Dreaming serves useful and important functions in these societies, contributing to what we in the West term spiritual, psychological and physiological well-being (such terms may not exist or may be more permeable in indigenous cultures). One reason for this is that dreams are seen to connect with a cohesive visionary or experiential 'otherworld' or 'spirit world'. Indeed, for our Northern ancestors as well, dreams were perceived to come from outside the dreamer, not from within the sleeper's psyche or subconscious – hence perhaps the term 'nightmare', to be ridden by a horse (or to wake up in a cold sweat as if one had galloped like a horse).

In addition to paying attention to the dreams which come whilst asleep, indigenous and prehistoric shamans mastered the art of dreaming whilst awake, entering altered conscious states at will (and sometimes not at will!). Thus, they tapped into the power of the vast uncharted regions of the cosmos, mirrored both within and without themselves: as above, so below – to quote a well-known esoteric axiom. The ability to alter consciousness is common to all humans. In altered conscious states, escaping from the strictures of linear thinking, and by transcending or at least facing fear, ego and other conditions, we too can effectively challenge conventional perceptions and, in ecstasy, enter the otherworld – the world of the spirits. While you may not have the faith that 'spirits' exists, many psychologists who study them agree it is mistaken to deny the positively empowering potential of altered conscious states. You can at least begin practising with this in mind.

Notions of altered consciousness immediately bring to mind 'drugs', chemical or organic. We do not take a proscriptive attitude to drug-use, but all of the techniques provided in Galdrbok are 'drug-free'. 'Entheogenic' substances do provide means of access to spirit realms and the use of indigenous entheogens such as Henbane and Fly Agaric by our ancestors is discussed by, for example, Rätsch (1992), Devereux (1997), Leto (2000), Blain (2002) and Price (2002). Altered consciousness may also conjur ideas about the 'enlightened' states produced by Buddhist and other meditation techniques, and in Tibetan Buddhism and Nepalese shamanism, where Buddhism and shamanism meet, altered consciousness and enlightened transcendence may indeed be related – but it is important also to state that we feel such states of being are 'Orlog' related (see Chapter 7: Magic) People are not somehow 'better' than other people due to their 'enlightened' state. Practical Heathenry celebrates what it is to be human and rather than seeking a singular state of 'enlightenment', Galdrbok systematically engages with the variety of altered conscious states available to us. As stated earlier, Heathen Runecraft is not interested in 'religions of the book' which have largely neglected empowering animistic worldviews. Of course, what is right for one person is not right for another.

In indigenous communities, experiences of other worlds are recorded in mytho-poetical terms which weave pictures, invoke feelings and provide inspiration. This is evident in such mythologies as the Norse and Celtic where the skilful use of words in these sources, make the visions and experiences accessible to us, even across the barrier of time. And this transmission is an essential principle, usually accomplished through the use of poetry, song, parable and metaphor.

When discussing 'other', 'spirit', 'known' and 'real' worlds, it is clear that while words are useful, they also have their limitations. The spirit world is not easy to describe since in many ways it works in ways which are beyond the strictures of language. Hence, many shamans express themselves visually, through 'art', as well as or instead of words. Words do not provide experiences in themselves – unless, that is, they can somehow be 'magically' shaped.

This shaping of words is the basis for the magical chants called Galdr (see Chapter 5: Galdr) used to induce altered consciousness. And word and image meet in the sacred 'runes' and the binding of them into sigils – 'bind runes' or in Old Norse 'Galdrastafr' (see Chapter 7: Magic) – magical seeds which are planted in other worlds to bring forth changes in the 'real world'. Directly connected to, and embracing the 'known' ('ordinary') world, experiences in the otherworld were and are not separate from events in the ordinary world because one world influences and affects the other (remember, 'as above, so below'). Indeed the boundary between these worlds may be less defined than is commonly imagined.

At its simplest, this 'imaginal' component of the otherworld is so important to health and spirituality that it has the potential to challenge and relieve the stresses of modern living. Furthermore, and well beyond the psychologist's wordhoard, the otherworld is filled with spirits and the dead, and is a realm in which almost anything is possible.

It seems highly likely that throughout human history people have felt a pull towards other worlds, places of death and dreams. Shamans worldwide have described their otherworlds and provided various poetical, visual and metaphoric 'maps' of them. These descriptions vary in detail from community to community, as does the land, the customs, and the languages, and the same is likely true of shamans in prehistory. But, together with this diversity, this cultural variation, there are distinct threads of consistency.

One of the most common and enduring models of the otherworld, particularly in communities with a resident or visiting shaman, is the world tree, a huge universe-filling, and universe-comprising, 'symbolic' yet living tree. This world tree was (and is still) described and explored, not from the intellectual perspective of science (the new kid on the block), but from direct communion with the reality of creation/nature, un-dissected by the surgeon's scalpel or the microscope. Beyond the compartmentalising rationale of science, the otherworld tree is united in a glorious and organic whole, depicted in symbolic form and described in mytho-poetical language, something which might be described as the 'language of the soul'.

The world tree encompasses and depicts all things; it is simultaneously a mythical, mystical, more-than-symbolic image of the reality that is creation, existence and demise, and reality itself. Yet it is much more than a passive 'symbol' to be looked at; it can be your worldview and can be actively engaged with, by shamanic means. The world tree is within and without, internal and external, both and yet neither! It is immaterial and material. The world tree is the representation of a tree, and a 'real' tree, again, neither and both! There is little point in trying to consider, let alone trying to travel the world tree using conventional rational, scientific thinking, with its natural gravitation towards the 'concrete' and 'material'. Leave the scientific behind. This does not mean losing all rationality, for a healthy measure of scepticism helps to sift the wheat from the chaff; but in our view at least the scientific model will most likely never fully comprehend the otherworld.

Chambers Dictionary defines the word 'materialism' as 'any doctrine which denies the independent existence of spirit and maintains that there is but one substance-matter'. We need pay little attention to this 'dualism' as indeed it is doubtful that our ancestors did. The mind-body split likely did not exist before the French philosopher Descartes. As we noted before, why must we be forced to see spirit as either separate from matter or non-existent? Why can we not consider spirit as dwelling in matter, or even reject the dualisms 'spirit' and 'matter' as too restrictive in the first place? As animists, if we accept that organic matter has life, however limited evolutionary science might consider it to be, so we may say a tree has a life and a 'vital principle', an animating force. That is, the tree has 'tree-ness', the very thing which makes it a tree and not something else, like a dog for instance! The vital essence of being a tree is that which is passed on from the tree via its shoots, seeds, berries, or nuts.

So, the tree has a spirit (the spirit of tree-ness) which existed before the tree and continues to exist after the tree, being both independent from it and connected to it. If a tree inherits 'tree-ness' in this way, then why can't a world inherit the spirit of 'worldness'? In fact it does, in a galactic seed form. So, it is the same for humans. This perception is not new; it has been around since ancient times. Sadly, having fallen out of fashion in our fickle times, it is merely referred to today as 'primitive' animism. The Web of Wyrd which animates all things is the animating force of the Northern traditions. Give us animism over materialism any day!

## Entering Otherworlds: The Runes and the Crystal Ball

So how does one go about entering these otherworlds? Well, the system of Heathen shamanic initiation presented in this book which enables otherworld journeying is summarised in Appendix B. Take some time to briefly look over the basics of the system now, if you have not done so already. Much of it may not yet make sense, but all will be made clear as you read on. You will see that you are currently at the point of stages one and two in the summary, having reached this part of chapter one.

The first priority for putting Galdrbok's system into practice is twofold: you should familiarise yourself with 1) the runes (the Anglo-Saxon rune poem is translated in the Appendix) and with 2) the technique of scrying using a crystal ball. These practices will enable you to enter the otherworld. They mark the groundwork for all other aspects of the system discussed in this book.

We therefore suggest that you now finish this chapter and begin to practice rune casting and scrying before moving on to the following chapters! This is also the time to obtain and begin working with other ritual tools, 'power' items and paraphernalia. You might consider working with a ritual blade of some kind for cutting runes (physically and spiritually), a Gandr (wand, 'shamanic' rattle, and the like), Staff (a larger Gandr, practical for walking of course!), 'shamanic' frame drum, and/or whatever else one may deem necessary for ritual work. This groundwork is prerequisite to undertaking the more advanced practices which are presented in the following chapters (especially in Chapter 6: Ritual).

The rudiments of rune casting and scrying are discussed in detail in the remainder of this chapter. We begin by introducing the oracles themselves – the runes and the crystal ball. We then outline the oracular practices of rune casting and scrying associated with these tools.

## The Runes

Reticent academics attribute no more to the runes than a system of utilitarian writing – an alphabet. Most scholars agree that runes were, however, put to magical uses. But the use of the runes as a divination device – as an oracle – is less acknowledged.

Etymologically, the old English 'run' (pronounced 'roon') means 'mystery, secrecy, hidden knowledge'. To argue against the reticent academics, it is highly significant that each rune comprises a letter, but is also much more than that. Each rune has a word, term or concept associated with it; a specific stanza of the Anglo-Saxon rune poem; and perhaps an ideographic interpretation (such as cattle horns for Fehu and Uruz, and the icicle for Isa). In this way, for the contemporary Runester, the runes have more in common with Egyptian and Mayan Hieroglyphs or the Hebrew letters, than with Greek and Latin scripts, even though the origin of the runes may lie in Southeastern Europe.

The runes are certainly important to the gods. We know that Woden had the original 'vision' of the runes and that his shamanic self-sacrifice enabled this vision (Havamal 138-144, see Larrington 1996: 34-35). But there are many other references to runes in the Eddas. We read in Hymir's Poem (Hymiskvida) that the gods 'shook the twigs and looked at the augury' (Larrington 1996: 78); a source suggesting that the gods marked rune-like staves, if not the runes themselves, on wood for oracular use. Historical accuracy aside for the moment, since we will never know 'for sure', we speculate that it is indeed the runes that we are dealing with in this instance: though they are not specifically mentioned, Woden's explicit connection to the runes is evidence enough.

There are many references to the runes as magical tools. In Skirnismal (Skirnir's journey) Frey's servant Skirnir threatens Gerdr by saying 'Giant I carve on you and three runes' (Larrington 1996: 67), referring to the 'Thurs' or 'Thorn' rune and perhaps the magical magnification of its power by carving it three times. In the Lay of Sigrdrifa (Sigrdrifumal), the Valkyrie Sigfrida teaches Runic wisdom to the hero Sigurd, referring to the 'Victory' rune of Tiw, the 'Ale-runes' and 'naud' (the need rune), 'Helping-runes', 'Speech-runes', and so on, and the ways in which they can be used for magic (Larrington 1996: 167-169). For the contemporary Heathen Runester, such sources offer exciting practical kennings regarding rune-use.

One of the most cited but perhaps least reliable of the historical sources for using the runes as an oracle is Tacitus who, in striking similarity to the description in Hymir's poem, describes Germanic divination in the first century CE thus:

> They retain the highest opinion for omens and the casting of lots. Their method of casting lots is always identical: they cut off a branch of a nut-bearing tree and cut it into strips, which they inscribe with various marks and cast entirely at random onto a white cloth… [The] priest… gazing heavenwards, picks up three strips one at a time and interprets their meaning from the inscribed signs (Germania 10, translated by Mattingly 1948).

There are further descriptions of Runic magic in the Icelandic Sagas, particularly Grettis Saga and Egils Saga. A 'witch', in the first source, carves runes to destroy Grettir and reddens them with her blood. In the second source, Egil similarly carves and bloodies the runes on a horn of ale, which, thanks to this act, shatters because it contains poison. Egil also visits a farm where a girl is sick. He discovers the cause to be runes, carved to make her fall in love with the carver. Egil, in turn, carves further runes to cure her. There is also the practice recorded in Egils Saga of a nidstong (involving the 'derision pole', see Simek 1993: 232) with a horse's skull and runes on top of the pole (Simek 1993: 200). Archaeological contexts, for their part, testify to the magical uses of runes:

> [P]articular words or phrases with an apparently mystical significance – alu, for example – appear often in the Runic record, as do seemingly nonsensical or repetitious strings of characters with no evident practical purpose. Likewise, the carving of individual runes on weapons or in places where they could not readily be seen, such as on the underside of grave-markers, seems to attest to some magical significance (Orchard 1997:134).

In material culture, runes inscribed onto weapons and items of jewellery, for instance, often form coded messages which may be equivalent to magical spells. Examples include the sword-pommel from Faversham with a Tiw or 'victory' rune, the inscribed urns from Loveden Hill and Spong Hill, and the Bramham Moor rune ring. In analysing these, 'few of the Runic inscriptions on early Anglo-Saxon objects have been interpreted' (Arnold 1997:152).

The so-called 'Alu runes' mark a good example of enigmatic runes, found in over twenty inscriptions from the third to eighth centuries (see, for example, Pollington 1995:72-80). One of the current interpretations is that this inscription is connected to the Hethetic 'alwanzahh', 'to charm', Greek 'alúein', 'to be beside oneself', and Old Norse 'ol', 'beer'. This suggests alu had a basic meaning of 'ecstatic magic' (Simek 1993:12-13). The inscription perhaps related, then, to the poetic mead of inspiration Odrorir 'the one that stimulates to ecstasy' (Simek 1993:250) drank by Odin from Mimir's well of inspiration, Mimisbrunnr. Furthermore,

> [O]ne frequently recorded practice was the carving of runes into bits of wood, which was supposed to have a significance in harmful magic... as well as in... death magic. Runes were less used for their magical importance as letters composing individual words, but rather as concepts. Thus the repetition of certain concept runes (such as th = thurs 'giant', n = naud 'plight') were supposed to emphasise the message (Simek 1993: 1999-200).

Again, there are valuable kennings regarding ancient practices to be had by the contemporary Runester, when examining these sources. The available historical and archaeological evidence points strongly towards both a magical, divination and utilitarian written use (if the three can be pragmatically disengaged) for the runes.

According to archaeological finds and historic sources from various parts of Northwest Europe, there are a number of Runic alphabets. They all have similarities, but differ in terms of the number, shape, and sometimes order of runes, as well as the poems associated with them, if any. Some major rune rows include the Younger Futhark of sixteen runes, the 'common Germanic' or Elder Futhark consisting of twenty-four runes, the Anglo-Saxon Futhorc with its twenty-nine runes, and the Northumbrian row comprising thirty-three runes.

Which of these variations to choose for your rune set? Well most contemporary Heathens use the Elder Futhark. However, the most complete and informative of the rune poems to use for interpretative purposes is the Anglo-Saxon Futhorc (see Appendix). Either set, indeed any of those we have mentioned, is suitable for divinatory purposes. We leave it up to you to choose. Bear in mind, though, that some of the Futhorc repeat themes in the Futhark (the Grave with Mann for instance, and Beaver with Joy), and the subtle differences between them are for the Runester to ken. Consider also, that the final four runes of the Northumbrian row do not have stanzas of a rune poem associated with them, making interpretation potentially more difficult.

The cosmogony we present in this book (see Chapter 2: Cosmogony) is tied to the meaning and order of the Futhorc. This 29-rune cosmogony, combined with a 24 rune Futhark, however, is not in any way incompatible, as our discussion will make clear. Our intention is to present a coherent, systematic approach to Runecraft which none the less leaves room for the freedom of inspiration. From experience, we suggest that the cosmogony we offer adds considerable depth to divinatory practices which employ any of the traditional rune sets.

You can either make your rune set yourself (from wood, stone, and so on) or you may buy them, and there are some attractive rune sets available. More basic examples are made from artifical materials and rune cards are also practical. You may prefer to make your own runes, imbued with your own energy, in the knowledge that you have been with these runes since the first branch was cut or first pebble collected. Other people will feel happier purchasing (or trading) a set, perhaps one that is more unusual, fashioned in silver or bronze for example. The most important thing is that the runes you choose are right for you, that you use them frequently, that you grow to love them, and that they become a part of your life. The importance of this will be illustrated below, after discussion of the other major ritual tool of the Wodenic Seer, the Crystal Ball.

## The Crystal Ball

The crystal ball is used for the practice of scrying, also known as 'crystal gazing' or 'crystal divination'. 'Scrying' derives from the term 'to descry' meaning 'to catch sight of', 'to discern', or 'to foresee'. The use of crystal balls for these purposes is commonly associated with the Romany (gypsy) people, but there is a precedent perhaps extending back to the British Neolithic.

Various 'special' portable artefacts including carved stone balls were exchanged between Neolithic communities and have been excavated in 'ritual' contexts, such as the passage tombs of Ireland and Scotland. The carvings on some balls are typical of the 'entoptic phenomena' or geometric shapes seen in vision during trances, and such entoptics – including zigzags, filigrees and luminous dots – are also reproduced in many rock art traditions (e.g. Wallis 2002a). With their similarities to various engravings in Neolithic tombs, it seems likely that carved stone balls were portable panels of engravings, used as gazing tools by shamans to facilitate the onset of trance and to induce and/or record visions. Perhaps, then, Neolithic carved stone balls were part of complex divinatory systems which facilitated oracular communication with ancestor spirits. More on such 'trafficking with the dead' in later chapters!

Neolithic carved stone balls, if they were used in this way, may be seen as a precedent to the much later Anglo-Saxon crystal balls. While there are no records of these Anglo-Saxon stones being used for scrying either, they were certainly 'special' amuletic objects (Welch 1992). Crystal balls are found in inhumation burials in Anglo-Saxon England, where they are always associated with female burials or burials with 'gender anomalies' (Wilson 1992: 96, 113, 138). It is interesting that the context is female, since the mediumistic trance that crystal balls can be used to induce is characteristically 'passive', 'open' and 'sensitive' (for the reception of shamanic wisdom) – characteristics which Westerners, rightly or wrongly, associate with women. On the other hand, the stones found in graves with gender anomalies might conceivably have been used by a

Pagan Anglo-Saxon berdache-like figure (for discussion of the multiple-gendered 'berdache', see e.g. Roscoe 1998).

The crystal ball figures strongly elsewhere in the history of Northern Europe, in addition to these links between quartz stones – and crystal balls – and a possible Northern shamanism. The British Museum has in its collection a crystal ball From the Merovingian period in Gaul and Germany (c. 500-750 BCE), used by Childeric the Great. We also know that a number of alchemists used crystal balls for scrying, from Trithemius of Spanheim who wrote a treatise on angelic magical invocation using a crystal ball, to Henry Cornelius Agrippa at the outset of the Renaissance. More famously, Dr John Dee is alleged to have used a 'shew stone' in order to communicate with spirits. This stone (perhaps), along with some of Dee's other magical equipment can also be seen in the British Museum (in the Enlightenment Gallery). More recently, Francis Barrett's 'The Magus' (privately published in 1801) discussed the use of the crystal ball for scrying. This broad and fragmented history, alongside the nineteenth-twentieth century revival, has contributed towards the crystal ball becoming one of the Magician's tools par excellence, with the most famous example perhaps being Merlin and his legendary use of the crystal ball.

Choosing a suitable crystal ball can be a difficult process – after all, the choice these days is almost bewildering. Suffice to say that any stone sphere which appeals to, and resonates with, the Runester will be fine. Some people prefer clear quartz, milky quartz or rose quartz, others prefer quartz with fissures or smoky quartz, and others still prefer dark rutilated quartz or some other mineral composition. Equally popular is a glass sphere, and even a plastic one might 'work'. As with the runes, the importance here, once you have obtained your sphere, is to use it often.

One of the most characteristic features of the stone is its shape. A spherical shape is most suitable for holding the stone and guiding vision. Indeed, the spiral forms on Neolithic carved balls accentuate this, and many of these stones seem to have been purposefully made as spherical as possible. Often, Neolithic stone balls were ground or polished, which, like the crystal balls used today, diffuses light in a way conducive to scrying practice. So, almost any polished or reflective spherical object can be useful for scrying practice – the 'dark mirror' springs to mind here. Indeed it need not be a handheld item, since many people suggest using a bowl of dark coloured water, or even scrying at a well or in a small pool (Chalice Well in Glastonbury, Somerset, understandably being a favourite!).

We would add, never the less, that quartz appears to be the stone par excellence for the crystal ball. While Neolithic stone balls are often naturally rounded river pebbles of white quartzite, many indigenous shamans worldwide hail quartz as a special stone, as far apart as some Australian aborigines and the Amazonian Jivaro (Harner discusses the relevance of quartz crystals to shamanism in considerable detail in his 'The Way of the Shaman'). In Anglo-Saxon burials, beads made from pebbles of quartz are not uncommon and appear to have been used as amulets (Meaney 1981). There is also the rarer crystal ball in some grave contexts, mentioned above. In Anglo-Saxon folklore, quartz is associated with fire and light, and it had a role in healing the sick (again, see Meaney 1981). Indeed, it may be that Anglo-Saxon crystal balls fastened to a chain were dipped into water, and then the water drunk or used as a salve in order to aid healing. Quartz is certainly highly regarded among today's Western crystal users because of its 'healing' and other qualities.

Furthermore, quartz has various strange and interesting properties which many shamans seem to have appreciated, such as the releasing of a piezoelectric 'charge' when struck; it might also be viewed metaphorically as 'solidified light', with the appearance of ice, or containing bright rainbows (see Harner 1980). We have found with our own stones that it is beneficial to be aware of and to explore these properties. Smoky quartz, for instance, has a grounding effect which is most useful for the Vaniric trance states induced by scrying, while rutilated quartz is said to enhance psychic faculties.

## Ethical Considerations

A short word on the ethics of how runes and crystals are obtained is timely at this juncture. As animists, we believe that such 'inanimate' things as quartz spheres and runes crafted from yew wood are spiritually 'alive'. From a scientific angle, basic physics shows all things have a vibration so that in a sense they are alive! (The importance of vibration in terms of sound is discussed further in Chapter 5: Galdr). Therefore, it is important that the Runic Seer is ethically aware when it comes to obtaining runes and a crystal – they should not be perceived as mere material commodities, nor should they be purchased without discretion.

With respect to making runes, it is highly inappropriate, and indeed would negatively affect the runes you are making, to hack away indiscriminately at living trees in your quest for a rune set. Ideally, use wood which has been cut in a woodland management program, or seasoned wood which has either fallen, or can be found hung against other branches in trees. If you must cut a living branch, be sensitive to the tree spirit: consider its perspective on the matter, and deeply reflect upon your potential choice. At the very least, you should sacrifice something of your own in return – an offering of ale or mead, for instance.

Evolutionary concerns (i.e. humans are 'more evolved' than trees) matter little at such times. If you are prepared to communicate with a tree, then you have not only to consider it alive and in its own way 'conscious', but also on a similar 'level' to the human. These considerations are all part of shifting the rational, Western, ego-driven mind-set into a spiritually aware, animistic consciousness. Such an attitude is definitely a part of challenging and disrupting rampant materialism and sceptical rationalism!

Obtaining crystals is a different matter altogether. There are increasing reports of damage to the earth as greedy prospectors 'blast away' at rocks with dynamite to reach crystal seams. It is an unattractive fact that quartz – treasured and respected by many – is in some places sold by the kilo! For this reason we suggest you approach the matter of acquiring a crystal and working with it, as a very serious undertaking. Choose your stone carefully – and choose with the intention of using the same stone for the rest of your life. One aim of scrying is to build a rapport between yourself and the spirit of the stone – it will become one of your spirit-helpers after all. For this reason also we argue that carrying – the notion of 'ownership' is irrelevant to the relationship developed with a sphere – one crystal ball (and perhaps only one crystal of any sort) per person will more than suffice for the ritual purposes discussed in Galdrbok.

If you do decide to change your crystal, then the rapport you have built up so far – the 'Orlog' (see Chapter 7) or the 'connection' between you and the crystal – can be transferred to the new crystal using a ritual of your own devising. Some short heartfelt words, combined with a joining of the new stone with the old, or in the absence of the old stone, a token holding its 'essence' might suffice. But perhaps you may want to 'start again', completely, and will not want to pass the 'Orlog' from one stone to another.

You can cleanse a crystal by cleaning it in mineral water (though do not hold it in running water, it may crack!) while chanting relevant runes, and the stone could also be buried for a suitable time (e.g. nine days) for the earth to clear the 'Orlog', and free the stone from all negative 'on-lay' – that which may have negatively 'touched' it – but this is not obligatory.

Fortunately, you do not need to amass a huge 'kit' of ritual paraphernalia to practice effective Heathen shamanism. It is up to you to find, make or buy inspirational items. The items in your kit can involve all sorts of materials, from stone and bone to leather and wood. Many indigenous shamans employ such 'natural' and 'organic' materials, though you may choose not to. It is not unusual to find an indigenous shaman using a cola can and cola bottle caps combined to make a rattle, for example, as we marked in our introduction. Bear in mind also that in indigenous communities lifestyle does not have much room for 'animal rights'. Some scholars have said 'there is no room for vegetarianism in shamanism', and while this may be true for much indigenous shamanism (with the shamanic horse sacrifice in Siberia for instance), you should follow your own Wyrd, be it involving Veganism or being a devoted carnivore!

In all of these matters of personal choice, be it regarding runes, crystal sphere, and other 'tools' for your practices, you might take heed of a rune cast if necessary in order to make an appropriate, informed decision. When you find a road-killed bird, for instance, you might like to use the runes to advise you about the advice Wyrd has regarding the use of its body or 'Lich' (see Chapter 7), before removing the feathers, skull, etc. If the answer be yes or no, you may decide to ad lib, or even compose, a small ritual to honour the dead animal; a hand gesture, a simple 'waes thu hael' (in Anglo-Saxon, 'be whole') or 'fare-well' done with genuine feeling might suffice (see also MacLellan 1994). Remember that taking on the responsibility of what the oracle advises is a major part of aligning with Wyrd. Often, what you 'want' and what Wyrd advises are very different things.

Having chosen your rune set and crystal ball, what is their importance? We have already hinted at this, but also, why do we advocate them over other oracles? Indeed, what is an oracle? The next section discusses oracles more generally and the importance of the runes and stone sphere to this system of Heathenry. We then outline how to cast the runes and scry with a crystal ball.

## The Importance of Oracles

Simply put, oracles provide a means of communicating with the otherworld and the Wyrd Sisters, deities, ancestors and other 'spirits' can thus be engaged with. Oracles can be for personal use or used on behalf of another/others. Examples of oracles, which most people have heard of, include such 'lots' as the tarot, I Ching, and for our purposes, runes. Human beings can also be oracular 'tools' in themselves, in the form of seers, mediums and those who become possessed. These people communicate with deities, ancestors or other spirits, or have such spirits/persons speak through them. In ancient Heathenry, such persons were known by many names including Volva (wand – or staff-bearer), Spakona/Spamadr (Seeress/Seer) or Seidkona/Seidmadr (worker of Seidr, that is a seer or shaman) and they are not uncommon in the literature (see, for example, the sagas of Kormak, Erik the Red, Vatansdaela, Grettis, Volsunga, Eyrbyggja, Gull-Thoris, Viga-Glum, Heidarviga, Harald – and the list goes on). The increasingly popular practice of 'oracular Seidr' among contemporary Heathens (e.g. Lindquist 1997; Blain 2002) takes this form (discussed further in Chapter 4).

The basic reason for using an oracle is to decide an issue by taking the problem outside of one's self (your decision-making mind) into the hands of otherworld agents, principally the Wyrd Sisters, who steer personal 'Orlog' (again, this term is explained in Chapter 7): 'Wyrd is too vast, too complex, for us to comprehend, for we are ourselves part of Wyrd and cannot stand back to observe it as if it were a separate force… So we carve runes into wood or bone and cast them' (Bates 1983:78). Using an oracle bypasses the usual thinking process, with its personal opinions, allowing users to detach themselves from the immediacy of their own problem(s). We advise that the purpose should not be to discover illicit information, or to gain 'power' over others since this kind of ('black') magic generates its own problems. By asking the runes for advice, your interpretation of their meaning does of course involve its own element of decision-making – 'what does this rune mean (in relation to these other runes)?'. But the influence of the 'rational mind' is reduced when the rune-cast and its interpretation happen in altered consciousness, and when this 'rational mind' must contend with non-rational data – an ideographic rune with more than one meaning to be elucidated.

As well as being useful for decision-making, oracles are practical tools for mediating between parties with differing views. One example, although not strictly speaking an oracle as such, is that of the captains of opposing sporting teams 'trusting to luck' and abiding by the toss of a coin. Although, such 'good sportsmanship' contributes to 'fair play', the 'luck of the draw' sometimes affects the outcome of a particular event.

Once you learn to remove prejudice or doubt during oracle use, and engage strongly with the advice of the oracle, you will begin to feel Wyrd at work. Often it seems uncanny and quite amazing, and one begins to feel a deep sense of reverence for, and gratitude to, the ancestors for developing such a magnificent oracle. Clearly, oracles were once socially important in matters of reconciliation. Indeed, 'flipping a coin' over who gets to use the river first, is better that unnecessary bloodshed, loss of life, damage to resources and the inevitable centuries of feuding.

At their simplest, there are two basic types of oracle, the character and use of which we next discuss:

1. Intuitive Oracles: Scrying with a Crystal
2. Operative Oracles: The Runes

## Intuitive Oracles: Scrying with a Crystal

Intuitive oracles include frenzied dance, clairvoyance and clairaudience, serene reflection, some meditation techniques – and scrying. Dreams are also important in the ancient Heathen sources (see, for example, Kelchner 1935), as are auguries – patterns in nature such as the flight of birds. It is therefore pertinent for Heathen shamans to monitor their dreams and find kennings in the patterned ways of the natural world. These 'intuitive' methods are simple in terms of equipment (i.e. only your five – or six! – senses are required), but they can also demand considerable effort and the results can be difficult to verify. Hence, the ancient seer – the Delphi oracle, for instance – was often required to be 'pure' or with 'conscience'.

Conscience, as it pertains to ethics, is a relative term and there is not room here for a philosophical debate on what constitutes 'right' ethical frameworks. Most of us struggle with our conscience everyday when making decisions. Does one choose to be selfish, as is it sometimes seems is necessary, or does one choose to be altruistic which may be much harder? There are implications for how we engage with one another as humans and engage with non-humans. Much literature marketed as 'New Age' is blinkered by an emphasis on 'personal growth', with many books and workshops focussing on 'me, me, me' at the expense of 'we', 'them' and 'us'; and, when not attending to personal growth, practitioners egoistically claim to be 'healing the world'. We argue one's own spiritual path is important as a matter of course, and that respect for the planet we live on is integral to a Heathen worldview, but each individual path weaves around and intersects other paths – the paths of our local fellow humans, spirits and other beings. Any spiritual path must therefore deal with issues of 'community'. There is rarely a stand alone mage.

Conscience in the sense being discussed refers to respect with regard to other humans and non-humans. It also refers to community responsibility and the importance of making right choices in our daily lives as we engage with others. Over time, the practices offered in Galdrbok may bring shamanic wisdom for individuals and, no less, wisdom for communities. Woden relates a simple example in the 'sayings of the high one' (Havamal):

> About his intelligence no man should be boastful,
> rather cautious of mind;
> when a wise and silent man comes to a homestead
> seldom does shame befall the wary;
> for no more trustworthy a friend can any man get
> than a store of common sense
> (Larrington 1996: 15)

'Listening to your heart' can guide your conscience towards right judgement and such decision-making may involve a 'store of common sense'. But cast runes, or invoke Tiw if need be, to help make in informed choice (see Tiw's Galdr in Chapter 5: Galdr). Conscience relates to the various parts which go to make up the Wodenic shaman's being (see Chapter 7), since as these are harmonised, positive 'Orlog' or 'conscience' is produced. We leave arguments over exactly what the ethical sense of right and wrong is to philosophers and politicians.

Genuine oracle use should not be confused with 'fortune telling'. Yet, the crystal ball is an oracle which has been improperly associated with this for many years. The practice of scrying involves gazing single-pointedly at an image (in this case, the crystal itself – but see discussion of Galdrastafr in Chapter 7: Magic) until only the crystal sphere occupies consciousness. This is an effective technique of sense inhibition which allows consciousness to regroup the senses. The result is heightened perceptual awareness – the 'sensitivity' and 'openness' required for the 'sixth sense' to engage. The purpose of using the technique of crystal gazing, then, is to throw the seer into a light trance state where the habitual babble of thoughts and the linear thinking process can be bypassed. This leaves the seer open to intuition and insight. Your eyes remain open, but by staring at the crystal they are denied any stimulus and can therefore send back only minimal 'real world' information. Scrying thus facilitates a temporary retardation of the function of the optic nerve, in order to obtain 'second sight'.

In the early stages of scrying practice, sit comfortably in a dimly lit (preferably with candlelight and perhaps some incense) room with the crystal in front of you (in your hands or on a stand), and spend as long as possible simply gazing at it. This 'gazing' should be done in a relaxed way, blinking when necessary and taking short breaks, rather than staring at the stone and straining the eyes. The difficulty with scrying is that it is so simple that there is very little more to say, and thus it can be difficult for some people to get to grips with. As an extra pointer, we strongly recommend using a sphere over other shaped crystals because the round shape focuses vision in the desired direction.

Most usefully, regarding practice, we can say that the visual point at which the oracle begins to 'work' is somewhere around halfway between your eyeball and the stone. This distance is comparable with 3D holographic pictures in which you can only see a jumble of geometric images until you 'look' in the right way, and suddenly an image pops out! The required 'sight' when scrying begins as a kind of 'misting over' of the crystal (and your wider vision) – hence the well-known descriptions of apparently clear crystal balls becoming 'cloudy'. Also, your peripheral vision around the sphere is altered, until the clouded crystal dominates. The haze or clouding over which appears in the crystal might be usefully described and contextualised in Heathen terms as Nifelhel, the cloudy part of Helheim (see Chapter 3: Cosmology). An effective means of getting 'into the stone' is to apply other visualisation techniques, such as taking an image, for instance a rune, into the meditation – chant it, hum it, sing it, stare at it, and look repeatedly back and forth from the rune image to the crystal until you can 'hold' the rune in the stone.

As we discuss in later chapters, scrying is a method for moving beyond the space-time continuum and into the region beyond death – outside the circles of space and time, as the Typhonian Magickian Kenneth Grant (Grant 1980), might put it. Indeed the modern Western concept of linear time may have been unfamiliar to ancient Heathens, as it was in many pre-industrial cultures: to our ancestors, there was a perception of 'that which was' and 'that which is coming', which presences time more immediately than the Western model of 'past' and 'future' (Gundarsson 1990: 7-8). 'Seeing through' the clouds of Nifelhel, then, takes us into the realm of the dead; that is, beyond ego consciousness. In every scrying experience then, we face, experience, and engage with death, albeit in a less intense way than is experienced in Disiric and Aesiric trances (discussed in Chapter 4: Trance).

Having sat scrying in the manner described above for around half-an-hour (though scrying can last from minutes to hours), every day over a week or so, you will get results. In most cases, you will know what these results are, and feel them, after a handful of sessions. If not, persist! Scrying is not an easy practice for everyone who tries to learn it, so it may well take some perseverance. You will then know what it means to have a relationship with a stone! We have likened this relationship to awakening the 'amorous function', and you may well feel you have in some way 'fallen in love' with the spirit in the stone. Remember that the properties of the crystal, its vibrations, are affecting you, in pleasant and productive ways. Once you are more experienced with gazing, you will find it **easier** every time, and you will be able to practice in almost **any** environment (including bright sunshine). To keep up your levels of perseverance, scry in different locations. The variety of your living room, a Yew forest, and a Neolithic long barrow, for instance, will help to keep your practice regular and inspiring.

These early scrying sessions will open up possibilities for other scrying experiences. For some practitioners, 'visions' are seen most clearly with the eyes fully open and there are anecdotal accounts of luminescent sightings within the crystal. This is similar to the 'day-dream' in which you are 'awake', with eyes open, yet feel that you are dreaming and not really awake – a state where images may 'pop' into your head and can be quite startling or unsettling. For other people, inducing visions with the eyes open is more difficult. Once the 'clouding over' sight is achieved in the earlier sessions, it may be productive to close your eyes and 'see' that way. This may induce yet deeper trance states (see Chapter 4: Trance). Indeed, lapsing in and out of 'outer' and 'inner' sight can be a useful practice in itself, facilitating an element of 'walking between the worlds'. Such a practice is useful in the early stages of scrying practice since it is far easier to meditate with eyes closed than open. Gently shifting between inner and outer sight, then, will get you familiarised with both worlds.

A final technique which might help you develop your scrying experiences is what we have termed 'Walking in Wyrd'. This involves starting out in a seated posture and inducing the light trance brought about through gazing at your stone, then standing up and walking around the

landscape while continuing to scry with the stone. There is
a definite balancing act between looking at the crystal and
ensuring you don't trip over a branch or rock! But this is a
useful method for testing your scrying abilities, since your
'wider' vision (including the immediate, animated
landscape within view around the stone) should be as
much affected by the practice as that directed at the stone.
When walking in Wyrd this wider vision helps you to find
your way in the 'ordinary' world. It also helps you find
your way in, and familiarise yourself with, the otherworld
territory of Midgard (discussed further in Chapter 3:
Cosmology). Various land wights and other spirits may be
seen when walking in Wyrd, thus this practice facilitates a
're-enchanting' of the land, and purposeful engagement
with living landscapes.

## Operative Oracles: The Runes

The second division of oracles, operative oracles, depends
more upon equipment, numbers, images, lots, marked
stones, sticks, dice, cards, and so on, from which a message
can be directly 'read' – and the classic example in the
Heathen traditions, is the runes. Your runes can be kept in
a bag (easily made from leather or a piece of material, with
a thong to close it), lot-box (see the Perthro rune in Chapter
2: Cosmogony, and Appendix A) or some similar container.
This container also acts as a device for casting the runes.
You can reach into the bag and 'pull a rune blind', or if you
do not trust your hands, shake the bag until one or the
appropriate number falls out, perhaps onto a special cloth
you have made. Some Runic practitioners shake their runes
thoroughly beforehand to ensure they are well prepared,
and attune themselves by focusing on the question to be

asked. They may also ask the Wyrd Sisters or Woden (or some other deity/spirit agency relevant to the question at hand) for guidance.

A most simple (but by no means ineffective) way of getting familiar with the runes is to cast a rune in this way, or to mentally choose a rune you feel an affinity with. Go on to recite, learn by heart and scry on the appropriate stanza of the Anglo-Saxon rune poem (see Appendix A). Meditate for a while on the rune and its significance. If the meaning eludes you, be patient and bear in mind that it may take a long time to fully internalise each rune's meaning. The Anglo-Saxon rune poem is a practical way of getting to grips with the meaning of each rune, which is why we suggest you learn it by heart. By practising often and learning the rune poem, you will make excellent headway.

In respect of interpreting runes after 'casting', bear in mind that Wyrd does not always want to answer your call. A reading in such circumstances may be rather enigmatic, or you may simply not be in the right state to interpret the meaning. Rune casting is not always an easy operation! And the runes may well sometimes tell you to go away/forget it! If so, reconsider exactly what it is you are asking and why you are asking it, and perhaps try again later. Consider that the more direct your query is, the more likely your answer will be clear but yes/no questions are best avoided in oracle work. Full details on the meaning(s) of each rune can be found in Appendix A (see also Chapter 2: Cosmogony).

A useful elaboration on this practice of casting and then scrying on the rune is to 'sign' the rune and then 'send' it.

To sign, mark the symbol of the rune in the 'air' with a blade/sword/dagger, wand (Gandr), staff or rattle, if you have one, or else use a finger. You could even use a suitable twig laying nearby. Visualise the rune in bright burning red as you 'sign' it. To then 'send' the rune, blast, fling, point or cast the signed image through the 'air' and into 'Ginnungagap' (see Chapters 2 & 3) with the Gandr. While doing this you could vibrate the sound of the rune (a form of Galdr). Signing and sending runes facilitates the energising of the rune with-in you and with-out you. In all, these elements of practice count towards a rather powerful use of the runic oracle combined with magic.

Another elaboration on rune casting and scrying, if you would like to use the runes but not cast, is to use runes associated with a deity to harmonise with that deity. So, having invoked the deity using the mundane poetry and sacred Galdr (discussed in Chapter 5), decide upon the runes associated with that deity which you will use in the working (for example, the runes As and Gebo for Woden). Vibrate, sign and send these runes. In addition to sounding basic rune sounds (for example, Ansuz, Ansuz, Ansuz), it is also advantageous to vibrate the 'seed sounds' for each rune as suggested by Thorsson in his 'Futhark: A Handbook of Rune Magic' (1984; see also Gundarsson 1990). For Ansuz, Thorsson suggests the following seed sounds: ansuz ansuz ansuz, aaaaaaaaa, aaaaaassssss, aaaaaaa, aaaaaaaaaaa (repeat) (Thorsson 1984: 27). The sonics for each rune are reproduced in Appendix A at the end of this book. These seed sounds are comparable with the seed sounds on the lotus petals in Mantric Yoga (and Thorsson has clearly been influenced by this spiritual system in his interpretations of

Runecraft). They focus the consonant sound of each rune around the 'sacred' vowels.

This kind of simple ritual is very powerful. The runes express forces or agencies in nature: 'As' is the wind, for instance, and 'Eh' a horse, though the runes are of course much more than one thing and have more than a single meaning! Indeed, the deities are themselves forces of nature rather than abstract principles, just as they also embody aspects of our selves. Such terms as 'symbol', 'metaphor' and 'archetype' are woefully inadequate though, and somewhat restrictive. The links between 'As', the wind (or breath) and Woden are not incidental since Woden is the wind, just as Thunor is thunder and lightning. So, doing the sort of ritual we have outlined above offers a practical kind of sympathetic magic which brings you into harmony with, and allows you to reciprocate with, the environment around you. On a windy March (in the 'March winds') Wednesday in England, the above ritual done with some gusto to contact Woden, would work well!

The runes mark a more clearly defined method of oracle use than intuitive oracles, but they are also open to abuse (such as some forms of fortune telling, mentioned above). However, full acceptance of an oracle is to throw oneself quite literally into the hands of... something. But what is this something? Let us look at the true implications of following the guidance of an oracle. All wilful acts carry 'Orlog' (known in other traditions as karma) so that we must live through (and accept) the results of our actions and behaviour. But we are only responsible for our own actions (though of course we can and should feel responsible for the actions of fellow humans in general), and that is the key to it. In using and following an oracle (intellectual and emotional objections aside for a moment) we are following 'divine law' and have abdicated choice. Notice though, that we do not say this relinquishes responsibility and free will: using and living by an oracle actually requires immense responsibility and entails developing what Crowley termed the 'true will'. Thus, oracle use for the Heathen shaman involves according your life with Wyrd (this refers to the Perthro stage in the cosmogony).

Living one's life by the use of an oracle prevents the collection of negative 'Orlog' and is the easiest and shortest route to living a sacred life, or a life of 'luck'. It is therefore important, as mentioned above, that the oracle is not asked direct negatives, such as questions surrounding 'to kill' or 'steal', etc. Even with well-framed questions, you will notice how quickly the ego jumps at threats to its sovereignty, with a whole load of 'what ifs?' regarding 'correct' reading of the runes. One must learn to accept a reading. If you are unsure about this, do not consult! Cerainly, practice aids familiarity with your oracle and thus acceptance becomes easier over time.

Thus far we have described the basic elements of oracle use, and supplied some useful methods for starting out in Runecraft. Hopefully, this will help you to get to grips with the material and learn some basic techniques. These important techniques described so far then, are:

1. Casting runes and interpreting their significane
2. Learning by memory the rune poem

3. Signing, sending and vocalising the runes
4. Learning the technique of scrying

These techniques are the groundwork for all of the rituals which follow in the later chapters of Galdrbok. As much as you may want to skip to the next step, we advise that you do not do so. Patience and perseverance are required. Never forget, though, that your efforts will pay off. Not only will you be recovering the 'magic of childhood', but you will also be developing all aspects of your being which are malleable – your 'Hugr', 'Hamr', 'Hamingja' and 'Orlog' (see Chapter 7). For the dedicated, the rewards are immense – in many ways beyond description!

# – Chapter 2 –
# Cosmogony - Origins

One consistent characteristic of indigenous shamanisms is proficiency in cosmogonical and cosmological lore. These terms are somewhat tongue-tying. The primary branch of lore we are concerned with in this chapter is the study and cross-referencing of the various elements which go to make up a given cosmogony. Cosmogony is a term which delineates how we, as humans, fathom and understand the origin of universe (world, macrocosm, multiverse – or whatever other terms we use to define it) and all things in it. In conventional scientific terms this would be the 'big bang', or in Christian terms the 'creation'. Cosmogony is the precursor to a cosmology – how all things in the multiverse are arranged – the subject of the next chapter.

In many respects, the cosmogony (along with the cosmology) is the 'playground' of the shaman. Integrating the cosmogony with the cosmology and travelling in, with – through – both, is to travel in and beyond time itself; not the (seemingly) rational, linear time, as we have it in the modern West, but in the ever-changing 'moment' of constant change and constant movement. The notions of travelling 'forward to the past', or 'back to the future' might give some idea of what it feels like to 'internalise' and live out/re-experience the cosmogony, which is after all a living, breathing continuous event and should never be regarded as simply a 'primitive' history of how the universe (or multiverse) was made.

A skilled shaman in trance may drift effortlessly in star-seeded galaxies, encounter terrifying vortices of immeasurable size and depth, and find a galaxy in a microbe. Quasars, pulsing quarks, spiral vortexes, flashing grids and lines, regular and irregular patterns may all be experienced in trance, and these reflect the 'mind' becoming like the cosmos, as the shaman 'changes' into a vehicle for and a representation of the revelation of the spirit(s) animating all things. Accordingly, there is a sense of 'freedom'. The worlds of the Yggdrasill tree really can be visited and entities (spirits, etc) really can be engaged with. Desire is the critical ingredient, and a good grounding in cosmogony provides a 'map' for the desire to 'explore'.

Cosmogony is an intrinsic part of all human communities. It formed a major part of ancient Heathen mythology and the descriptions left to us by our ancestors are valuable for constructing a cosmogony for contemporary Heathens. The study and incorporation of cosmogony (and cosmology) into a 'personal vision' is vital for the serious Wodenic Seer who must learn (shamanically speaking) to sit at the top of the world tree and watch it come into existence, breathe, thrive, and expire, many times over.

The Northern mythological sources pertaining to cosmogony are somewhat difficult for modern Westerners to understand, with their speaking of the meeting of fire and ice, multiple giants and gods, a vast chasm and a sacred cow. If we are to make use of this cosmogony as

Heathens today, it is important for it to become relevant in our daily as well as spiritual lives – it must have pragmatic uses. As stated earlier, in offering the cosmogony we present here, we have shamelessly shored up the breeches in Asgard's walls with imported bricks where required – again, judge the masonry for yourself. This cosmogony is one possible interpretation of many and we hope you will find it theoretically consistent and methodologically practical. After studying the Eddas, Sagas and other sources in some detail, we have elucidated the following kennings with regard to Northern cosmogony.

First of all, we present a 'cosmogony lay', a simple poetic introduction to the cosmogony set out in Galdrbok – including the 'birth' of Ymir from Ginnungagap, the birth of gods and people – alongside a corresponding rune in the Futhorc rune row. In itself, this lay can be used in ritual to re-member how the cosmology came into being. Following this, we present a more detailed, esoteric account of the cosmogony: we have elucidated an apparently logical and profound sequence in the rune row. Other authors have explored the cosmogony of one or more rune rows, but our conclusions are very different. Most significantly, all parts of the cosmogony we present are intimately linked through a mass of kennings, or correspondences, to the rest of the system presented in Galdrbok. This will become increasingly clear as you read on and, over and again, we refer back to aspects of the cosmogony. Runic correspondences between the Anglo-Saxon rune row and cosmogony mark just one of the kennings. Where other accounts of Northern cosmogony appear only to have a use in and of themselves, not as part of the rest of a given system, the cosmogony and associated initiatory system presented here are complete and holistic with regard to all parts making up the whole – roots, truck and branches.

In proposing this Heathen cosmogony, we do not claim that our associations between runes and mythological themes were, necessarily, the way they had it in Anglo-Saxon England or anywhere else in ancient Heathen Northern Europe. Galdrbok is a practical and powerful system for Heathens today, inspired by the storehouse of knowledge left to us by our ancestors. Simply put, it works! And by saying that it works, we mean more than simply working for individuals, for a tradition must work also for a community. We leave issues of 'legitimacy' and 'authenticity' to those who pursue a single 'truth'!

It is important to state that the Runic (and other) associations in Galdrbok are not fixed or dogmatic. Fehu, the first rune, for instance, is not restricted to or limited by its placement at the opening of the cosmogony. The way the runes are placed, however, seems to us to be extremely profound, even if our ancestors may never have perceived them in this way. Indeed, as we have been at pains to argue, that is of no great relevance! The point is that linking the runes in this way makes the ancient cosmogony relevant for us in the present. The runes do of course go much further than cosmogonical correspondences alone. But practitioners will find that relating the runes to the cosmogony brings a new and fuller perspective to oracle use.

We suggest you approach this chapter by avoiding rationalising the information presented to you as much as possible. Try to 'feel' the conceptual framework of creation suggested. Try to avoid getting bogged down with grasping it intellectually. Do not struggle with it; let it wash over you. Return to it later, if you prefer, rather than trying to digest the entire thing in one sitting. For source literature on the subject of Northern cosmogony, you may like to read the following: Crossley-Holland, Larrington, Simek, and Snorri (see Further Reading). But it is more important to put the cosmogony into practice – into your worldview – than simply read about it. Indeed, now that you are well rehearsed in rune and scrying practices, the next stage is to 'internalise' the cosmogony, to make it part of your personal vision, and to accomplish this before moving on to the later chapters.

A simple technique which helps to put the cosmogony into practice is to work with one aspect of it at a time over one month (that is, do one rune / part of the cosmogony, per day, over the best part of one month). Start by working with one rune, its cosmogonical associations, stanza of the rune poem and stave shape. Take these elements into scrying practice and find kennings and connections between them. As the days pass by, feel the whole cosmogony coming together in a coherent whole. By the end of one month in total, you will be substantially familiar with the cosmogony. It is from this basis, knowing where you came from (cosmogony), that it is possible to know where you are (cosmology); but of course cosmology is for the next chapter!

# Cosmogony Lay

I, BORN OF GIANTS, REMEMBER VERY EARLY…

BEFORE ANYTHING GREW, SWAM, FLEW, CRAWLED OR WALKED IN MIDDLE EARTH, THERE WAS NO-THING – GINNUNGAGAP [0]: VAST, EMPTY, FECUND, ALIVE. BUT, EVEN THEN, THE WYRD SISTERS THREE WERE AGED: URD, METOD AND SKULD HAVE ALWAYS SPUN-OUT THE THREADS OF WYRD WHICH STEER THE LIVES OF ALL THINGS.

WITHIN GINNUNGAGAP, A TIME AND PLACE BEYOND MEASURE, THE POLAR REALMS OF NIFELHEIM, WITH ITS FREEZING ICE, AND MUSPELHEIM, WITH ITS BURNING FIRE, MET. A MISTY RIME FORMED AND THE PRIMAL ANCESTOR, YMIR, A MIGHTY HERMAPHRODITE GIANT, WAS BORN [1. FEHU]. SUSTAINED WAS S/HE BY THE FOUR TEATS OF AUDHUMLA [2. UR], THE COSMIC COW, WHO NEXT EMERGED FROM THE RIME. AUDHUMLA LICKED AT THE ICE OF NIFELHEIM AND THERE EMERGED A GIANT NAMED BURI [3. THORN], ANCESTOR OF THE GODS.

YMIR SLEPT, AND IN DREAMS, PERSPIRED. THERE EMERGED FROM THE RIPE LEFT ARMPIT A GIANT [4. OS], AND FROM THE RIGHT, A SECOND GIANT [5. RAD]. THE FIRST IN THE LINEAGE OF THE JOTUNR WERE MADE. BUT YMIR'S PROGENY WAS NOT YET ENDED, FOR ONE LEG MATED WITH THE OTHER AND A SIX-HEADED GIANT WAS BORN [6. CEN].

NOW BURI AND BESTLA TOOK THEIR TURN TO JOYFULLY FORNICATE, AND BESTLA GAVE BIRTH TO THE FIRST OF THE GODS: WODEN [7. GYFU] 'THE BREATH', VILI [8. WYNN] 'THE SPIRIT', AND VE [9. HAGEL] 'THE VITAL SPARK'.

THESE GODS, THREE, BROUGHT DESTRUCTION AND IN THAT DESTRUCTION, TRANSFORMATION. THERE WAS A NEED [10. NYD] WITHIN THE CHASM OF GINNUNGAGAP, FOR (A) WORLD(S) IN WHICH TO LIVE. WODEN, VILI AND VE PLOTTED TO KILL YMIR, AND DISMEMBERED THE PRIMAL GIANT THEN, USED THE BODY PARTS TO MAKE THE WORLD(S): FROM THE SKULL AND BRAINS THEY MADE THE SKY AND CLOUDS UNDER WHICH WE LIVE; AND FROM THE FLESH, THEY MADE THE EARTH UPON WHICH WE WALK, SLITHER, SWIM AND FLY. YMIR'S BLOOD AND SWEAT BECAME THE STREAMS, RIVERS, LAKES AND SEAS, AND THE BONES ARE THE MOUNTAINS. THE TEETH ARE STONES AND SCREE, AND FROM THE HAIR THEY MADE THE TREES, WHILE EYELASHES SEPARATE INANNGHARDHS (BEINGS ON THE INSIDE) FROM UTANNGARDHS (BEINGS ON THE OUTSIDE, OF MIDGARD).

SURROUNDING THE INANNGHARDHS, EMBRACING THEM, IS THE GIANT AND MIGHTY YEW YGGDRASILL, MOST WONDERFUL OF TREES, GROWN FROM YMIR'S FLESH. YGGDRASILL HAS SEVEN WORLDS: IN MIDGARD LIVE HUMANS AND OTHER BEINGS OF THE EARTH, INCLUDING THE FIRST HUMANS, ASK [11. ISA] AND EMBLA [12. JERA], ALONGSIDE ANIMALS, BIRDS, FUNGI AND PLANTS. BELOW MIDGARD IS JOTUNHEIM, HOME OF THE JOTUNR (GIANTS), WHOSE ELEMENTAL POWERS BATTER MIDGARD. LOWER STILL IS DOKKALFHEIM, HOME TO THE SHADY AND MISCHIEVOUS MOUND OR DARK ELVES. WHERE THE SEETHING CAULDRON, HVERGELMIR, LIES IS HELHEIM. HERE THE GODDESS HEL AND THE ANCESTORS RESIDE. ABOVE MIDGARD IS SVARTALFHEIM, WHERE IN CAVERNS DEEP THE DWARFS SMITH MARVELLOUS THINGS FROM PRECIOUS METALS AND STONES. IN THE BRANCHES OF YGGDRASILL IS LJOSALFHEIM, WHERE THE LIGHT ELVES RESIDE IN THEIR BRIGHT REALM. AMONGST THE HIGHEST BRANCHES OF YGGDRASILL IS ASGARD, HOME OF THE GREAT GODS.

THUS SET OUT, COMPLETE, THE YGGDRASILL YEW [13. YEW] IS EVERYTHING. IT IS A WINDSWEPT TREE OF WISDOM. FOR NINE LONG NIGHTS, WODEN HUNG ON YGGDRASILL, PIERCED BY HIS OWN SPEAR, SACRIFICED TO WODEN, SELF TO SELF. IN WILD ECSTASY, HE HAD A MIGHTY VISION, SEIZED THE RUNES, SCREAMING, AND THEN FELL DOWN FROM THERE. NINE MIGHTY SPELLS HE LEARNT FROM BURI, WODEN'S (GRAND)FATHER. WODEN DRANK MEAD FROM ODRORIR, RECOVERED, QUICKENED AND GREW WISE, FELT WELL-LEARNED OF THE MYSTERIES OF SEIDR-MAGIC FROM THE WITCH-GODDESS FREYJA.

IN THE FOOTSTEPS OF THE SHAMAN-GODS WODEN AND FREYJA WE FOLLOW: OFFERING SELF TO SELF IN SACRIFICE, FLYING OUT FROM MIDGARD, TRAVELLING THE WORLD TREE IN SEARCH OF WISDOM. HEATHEN SHAMANS HEED THE RUNES [14. PEORTH], SEEK STRENGTH AND RESILIENCE [15. ELKSEDGE], SUCCESS [16. SIGEL], RIGHT JUDGEMENT [17. TIW], AND MAGIC [18. BEORC]. IN TREE-TRAVEL, RIDING SLEIPNIR [19. EH], WE DIE [20. MANN] TO THIS WORLD, SUBMERGE (WITH SOME TREPIDATION) [21. LAGU] INTO THE OTHERWORLDS, AND THUS WE SEIZE THE MYSTERIES OF THE SPIRAL [22. ING], GAIN WISDOM AND INSIGHT [23. DAEG], AND THEN, OURSELVES, FALL BACK HOME [24. ODAL] FROM THERE, AS WODEN DID...

THUS INITIATED, WE JOURNEY ONWARDS FOR GREATER SPIRITUAL STRENGTH [25. AK] AND DIRECTION [26. ASK], THAT WE MAY FACE SHADES AND, ARMED [27. YR], CHALLENGE DEATH, ACHIEVE HAPPINESS AND CONTENTMENT [28. IAR] IN THIS LIFE, AND SO DIE A GOOD DEATH [29. EAR]... RAGNAROK COMES TO US ALL!

DO YOU UNDERSTAND YET, OR WHAT, MORE?

I, BORN OF GIANTS, REMEMBER VERY EARLY... BEFORE ANYTHING GREW, SWAM, CRAWLED, FLEW OR WALKED IN MIDDLE EARTH, THERE WAS NO-THING – GINNUNGAGAP [0]: VAST, EMPTY, FECUND, ALIVE.

## A Northern Cosmogony

Galdrbok's cosmogony is composed of three phases based around the three Norns (or 'Nornir'): Wyrd, Metod and Skuld. These names equate with the Old Norse nouns Urd, Verhandi and Skuld, but note that the more correct spelling of Skuld in Anglo-Saxon is Sculd, and that Metod might also be known in Anglo-Saxon as Weorthend (Branston 1957:71). These 'Wyrd Sisters' as they are known, are in some aspects comparable with the three fates of Greek mythology, in the sense of 'past, present and future'. However, the Wyrd Sisters are not the same as the Greek fates, for a better translation of their respective temporal meanings would be 'life unfolding', 'life becoming', and 'life ending' (a 'debt' – death as the cost of life). Branston (1957:71) suggests Metod (also 'metud' and 'meotod'), for example, is derived from the verb 'to mete'; hence Metod is 'the measurer'. As a whole, the concept of 'Wyrd' is in some ways comparable with the Chinese Tao. In the cosmogony there is a corresponding Wyrd phase, a Metod phase, and a Skuld phase. One of the most evocative and poetic descriptions of the Norns as the composite Nornir, 'Wyrd', which neatly encapsulates their character and meaning, is offered by Tony Linsell:

> The Web of Wyrd passes through all space
> and time, affects all things, determines the
> life of all beings. Past, present and future
> are all enmeshed in its threads. Everything
> is connected by Wyrd and even the Gods
> are subject to its power (Linsell 1994[1992])

It is important to bear in mind, as Brian Bates makes clear, that despite its omnipresence, Wyrd is open to negotiation – thereby also disrupting the concepts of 'fate' and 'free will':

> There is no need for your free will. Although the Wyrd Sisters spin the web of wyrd and weave the loom of life, they do not thereby determine it, for they are agents of wyrd and are therefore just as much a part of the pattern as we... The pattern of life is not woven ahead of time, like the cloth to be worn later as a tunic. Rather, life is woven at the very instant you live it... The task of the sorcerer is to become fully aware and sensitive to all nuances of his life design as it unfolds (Bates 1983: 113).

Our lives as individuals are not entirely determined by 'fate' – the Heathen traditions are more complicated than that. The first task is to elucidate Wyrd's pattern, the second task is to 'smith' it. First, by using and living according to the runic oracle, the Heathen Runester is attempting to 'tune in' to Wyrd. The pattern of the runes in a rune cast reflects the pattern of the 'web' of Wyrd as related to the Runester. Each Runester can then adapt life accordingly and thereby be 'in sync' with Wyrd. The second task is to smith this pattern. Importantly, the pattern laid out for each of us is only a pattern, however, a template, related to your 'Orlog' (fate). As such, the template is malleable and subject to your 'Hugr' (will) (see Chapter 7: Section - The Heathen Shaman's Being). Shaping life according to the Way of Wyrd and the path of initiation outlined in this book is the aim of the Heathen shaman.

As you read on, you will note that we make considerable use of number in this cosmogony (and elsewhere in this book). These kennings, between number, rune and stage in the cosmogony, are part of a simple numerological scheme we have set out in Galdrbok. This numerology cross-references with many aspects of the system, from the numerological sequence of the cosmogony (this chapter) to the number of worlds on Yggdrasill (Chapter 3: Cosmology), and the number of words in each Galdr (Chapter 5: Galdr). This numerology is akin to a simple form of Gematria, the Qabalistic mathematical technique of exploring the spiritual symbolism of numbers (and the numerical significance of words, though that branch is not explored in this book). Each number is understood to be symbolic, to contain certain significances, much like a rune (the Anglo-Saxon 'run' in this sense meaning 'mystery'). Each number is also significant when considered in relation to other numbers. For example, the number 12 is symbolic in its own right, but it is also significant for such reasons as being composed of the numbers 1 and 2, for the fact that 1 + 2 = 3, and because 12 is a multiple of 2, 3, 4 and 6. As the following Wyrd phase demonstrates, number is demonstrably an important aspect of the runes as they are used in this book. By following a simple numerological 'game', it is possible to tease out mathematical significances of the runes, with multi-faceted implications for our understanding of runes and cosmogony in our daily lives. Our use of number, then, is not to limit the possibilities of cosmogony, or reduce cosmogony to numerical data, but to enhance oracle use and for this cosmogony to have practical applications.

## Wyrð Phase

The Wyrd Phase begins with the coming into being of the Norns themselves. Since the Norns are omnipresent in heathen mythology, and since even the Gods are subject to the power of Wyrd, then it makes sense that the cosmogony starts out with the Wyrd Sisters themselves. This does not mean Wyrd is a 'creator' as in the creation myths of the 'religions of the book', or that this 'beginning' is the only beginning. Indeed there are no creators of this sort in this Heathen cosmogony because the Germanic deities are unlike the singular 'god' of other religions, and because 'time' is not perceived of in such a linear way, with a beginning and an end. As you will see, time spirals, it may turn in on itself and the cosmogony itself comes into being and terminates many times over. In effect, the Norns, standing outside the circles of time, are themselves the spinners and weavers of time, and are thus without number.

Name: Wyrd: 'Life Unfolding' (the past)
Name: Metod: 'Life Becoming' (the present)
Name: Skuld: 'Life Owing', a 'debt' (the future)

In the 'beginning' there was No Thing, the abyss, a void, a fecund, womb-like space, known in Nordic terms as Ginnungagap. Within the fertile (animate/conscious/sentient matter) Ginnungagap, a mist forms from the combination of the polarities of Fire and Ice. Thus the 'worlds' (as they are commonly known) of Muspelheim and Nifelheim, are not like the worlds of the cosmology, such as Dwarf world and the Elf worlds. They are understood in this system as elemental spheres existing within the gap, rather than 'worlds' in themselves. Following the Norns, within the gap, a misty 'rime' forms from the meeting of fire and ice. From the ice emerges the first primordial being, the giant Ymir (Aurgelmir):

**Number: 1**
From no-thing, a position or point is formed, indivisible, incapable of multiplication or division by itself.
**Rune**: *Fehu* (Germanic), *Feoh* (Anglo-Saxon) – Wealth, Mobile wealth, Fertility, Potential.
**Heathen Cosmogony**: Ymir (Aurgelmir) is born, who in the beginning was alone, one, simply being, the primal giant ancestor.

**Number: 2**
A second point emerges, joining the first by a line. The process of duplication, the emergence of the will and purpose of the original point to duplicate itself.
**Rune**: *Ur* (Anglo-Saxon), *Uruz* (Germanic) – Aurochs, Cattle.
**Heathen Cosmogony**: Ymir becomes hermaphrodite, the more than one: Tuisto-Ymir (cf. Sanskrit Yama), that is, 'two'. Next to emerge from the dripping ice is Audhumla, the cosmic and sacred cow. Ymir is fed by milk from the four teats of Audhumla.

A crucial point to make here is that since there is no accepted entrance point in the mythological sources for one being over another, it is difficult, if not impossible (and indeed unnecessary) to argue for who 'comes first' in terms of Ymir and Audhumla. We could easily end up with a 'chicken and egg' scenario if we pushed this idea too far intellectually (also known as a Wodenic paradox!). The order of the runes provides an indication of one acceptable direction – Audhumla is second because of the Ur (Aurochs/Sacred Cattle) rune – but this need not be a fixed and unchanging scenario.

The same 'chicken and egg' situation could emerge when locating the Giantess Bestla (and indeed her father Bolthorn) in the following sequence of the cosmogony. More important, and consistent with this cosmogony, are the 'major' players (including Ymir, Audhumla and Woden). Indeed, Stone (1997) argues 'Bolthor' and 'Bestla' are simply the progeny of Ymir (and Borr / Borri is one and the same as Buri). Simply put then, it is the main players that we have focussed upon in order to provide a coherent and workable cosmogony which can be re-membered.

When considering the entrance of male and female beings into the cosmogony, also, a 'chicken and egg' problem could emerge. The risk is of raising the issue 'which sex/gender came first?' and it is unnecessary to privilege one over the other. Further, it is important to avoid modern Western conflations of sex-gender and binary oppositions, as marked earlier. Thus, we suggest that in all instances, such as with the humans Ask and Embla (see Isa and Jera runes, below) the first being should be regarded as ambisexual/hermaphrodite and reproducing asexually, the second sexual so that with the two beings together sexual reproduction is possible – thereby overcoming sex-gender issues. Important themes running throughout the cosmogony, with both practical and esoteric implications, are those of fertility and sexuality.

## Number: 3

A third point emerges, thereby facilitating three dimensions and therefore measurement. This is a surface, a triangle. It represents discrimination, giving rise to awareness: the self, its will, and its awareness.

**Rune**: *Thorn* (Anglo-Saxon), *Thurisaz* (Germanic) – Thurs/Giant.

**Heathen Cosmogony**: Next to emerge from the ice (licked out by Audhumla) is Buri, the ancestor of the gods. He is a giant as represented by the Thurs rune. Note that Bur/Borr is etymologically similar to Buri.

## Number: 4

A fourth point must arise, defined by three co-ordinates, which formulates matter, a three-dimensional solid – the manifestation of solidity. Potential has become actual: from an original nothing something has emerged. The forming of order from chaos.

**Rune**: *Os* (Anglo-Saxon), *Ansuz* (Germanic) – Mouth, a god (Woden).

**Heathen Cosmogony**: Meanwhile, Ymir sleeps, and in his sleep, he sweats. From this process emerges autogamy / masturbation / theogonic heat: from under his left armpit emerges a giant (woman or man). If this number/rune resonates with the concept of order from chaos, then chaos is represented by the thorn rune, and order by the As rune with its connotations of voice and communication which require structure, grammar and other language rules. In addition, it is recorded that Woden has giant ancestry.

## Number: 5

Time and motion: change and events become possible in the space – time continuum.

**Rune**: *Rad* (Anglo-Saxon), *Raidho* (Germanic) – Riding, Movement.

**Heathen Cosmogony**: Also formed under Ymir's armpit is a giant (man or woman). The potential now exists, for the first time since Ymir's autogamy, for the 'physical' (Os) riding/movement (Rad) of sexual intercourse and reproduction.

## Number: 6

Now comprised of the 1-5 above, the point (see 1, above) is self-conscious and able to define itself. In time and motion the self can define itself, can become self-conscious. Self-awareness and experience. The kenning rune fits neatly with this mystical numerological conception of self and personality.

**Rune**: *Cen* (Anglo-Saxon), *Kenaz* (Germanic) – Understanding, Kenning.

**Heathen Cosmogony**: One of Ymir's legs produces a six-headed giant with the other leg. Following the numerological sequence of manifestation thus far, consider that the giant is comprised of 1-5 above, becoming in itself '6' – self-aware – as represented by its six-heads. Logically, the sixth rune resonates well with this six-headed giant.

## Number: 7

At this point, the will has the potential to know itself further through other vehicles of expression. The point's/self's idea of bliss/ecstasy

**Rune**: *Gyfu* (Anglo-Saxon), *Gebo* (Germanic) – Gift, Sacrifice, Sex Magic.

**Heathen Cosmogony**: Ymir has completed his procreation. Now Buri begins his (the further vehicles of expression). He mates with Bestla, giving birth to Woden ('breath', in Old Norse 'Ond'). Gebo is the rune of sacrifice (Woden as a shaman-sacrifice). In terms of Woden's sacrifice and shamanic ecstasy to attain that sacrifice, this is indicative of the point's ideas of bliss (i.e. ecstasy).

Considering this rune in the cosmogony marks the birth of Woden, it is uncanny that in his volume '777', Aleister Crowley attributes the Raven (and all the corvids/carrion eaters) to the Qabalistic sphere of Netzach, which is sphere seven – equating with our seventh rune – on the Hebraic tree of life (termed Otz Chiim). In complement to these creatures of death (carrion eaters), Crowley also associates the Lynx with this sphere, the creature of Venus – which is also intimately linked with Freyja (see Chapter 5 for discussion of deity totems and shamanic shape-shifting, termed Hamfarir in Old Norse). Thus we have a classic example of resonances between spiritual systems (Heathenry and Qabalah), and suitable, intimate link between Love and Death. And of course, Woden and Freyja are themselves intimately linked, for example taking half the slain each and sharing the shamanic practice of Seidr. Seidr seems to have a sexual component (Price 2002), hence the associations of the Gyfu rune with sex, orgasm and sex magic.

At this juncture we might best state again that these associations between runes, cosmogony and esoteric lore are not intended to be fixed and nor should they be seen as dogmatising the system, perhaps stipulating, for example, that Woden and Freyja must be associated with, and only associated with, the seventh stage of the cosmogony. This is by no means the case. These points are simply kennings which facilitate a coherent cosmogony, as well as further insights into the links between cosmogony and cosmology,

and consistency across these aspects of the system of
Heathenry set out in Galdrbok.

## Number: 8

The point's idea of knowledge. With will, the 'point'
(individual) can now become fully incarnate with an
element of free will (negotiated by Wyrd).
**Rune**: *Wynn* (Anglo-Saxon), *Wunjo* (Germanic) – Joy.
**Heathen Cosmogony**: The coupling of Buri and Bestla next
results in the birth of Vili, characterised by 'spirit' or 'soul'.
It is interesting that this corresponds with the Qabalistic
sphere of thoughts and that in Old Norse 'Odr' means
'will' (and/or poetry, and therefore inspiration). Since this
is the point at the centre of individuality or ego, it is not
surprising that Joy is the associated rune, for it is this
emotion and feeling which the ego constantly craves. Note
that Joy is also related to ecstasy and that Vili is a
brother/aspect of the shaman god Woden who appeared in
the previous stage of the cosmogony.

## Number: 9

The realm of dreams, and the point's idea of being.
Chaos/disruption occurs in the order of numbers.
**Rune**: *Hagl/Hagel* (Anglo-Saxon), *Hagalaz* (Germanic) –
Hail, Snow.
**Heathen Cosmogony**: The third and final result of the
coupling of Buri and Bestla is the birth of Ve. Ve represents
the blood or heat of life, and is thus associated with the
body. In Old Icelandic 'Ve' means 'shrine'. One form of the
shrine is the human body itself (see Chapter 6: Ritual) – a
vessel to be celebrated and enjoyed. Furthermore, the
creation of Ve predicts and anticipates, in the number 10,

the final stage in creation. That is, the creation of the body, the shrine, the tree Yggdrasill, and its worlds (recall the maxim 'man is a miniature macrocosm').

This is the creation of the first three gods (Woden, Vili, and Ve), ending with Ve and his associations with Hagel, the number/rune of yet further change and transformation. In Hagalaz, the number nine also hints at the creation and full manifestation of the nine worlds of the cosmology. And, this creation must insist on further change, or at least severe disruption as hinted at by the Hagalaz rune, a rune of change and disruption. Accordingly, at this point in the cosmogony, Ymir is dismembered by Woden, Vili, and Ve – certainly a case of disruption! As a result, Woden, Vili and Ve create the nine worlds of the Yggdrasill world tree (see runes Nyd – Yew). In this sense, Ymir 'needs' to die (see the next rune in the cosmogony, Nyd) and must be the ultimate sacrifice in order for the world(s) to exist. The Hagalaz rune is a rune of chaos (i.e. Hail), since Woden, Vili and Ve mete out a certain degree of disruption! Hagalaz is also a rune of dreams: by way of comparison, the Aboriginal Australian 'Dreamings' also bring aspects of the world into being.

**Number: 10**
The point's idea of itself fulfilled in its complement, as determined by 7, 8 and 9. This is the need for a body/shrine within which to incarnate/exist, and as a vehicle with which to regain zero. This is not yet the point of the manifestation of the body itself, but the 'need' for one.
**Rune**: *Nyd* (Anglo-Saxon), *Naudhiz* (Germanic) – Need.
**Heathen Cosmogony**: Anything beyond 9, a sacred

number of the North, and in accordance with the system of numerology, is a reiteration and replication of the 1-9, cosmogonically. It is also the number of returning to zero (1 = 0). Indeed, one end is a new beginning. As Aleister Crowley states in 777, we need 'the Kingdom': 'earth appears for the first time in Malkuth'. Stage 10 represents the point's idea of itself fulfilled in its complement, as determined by 7, 8 and 9, known to Heathens as Woden, Vili and Ve.

The Nyd rune itself resonates with the need for the creation of the worlds – the Cosmology – and the need for Woden, Vili, and Ve (the first gods) to dismember Ymir and create the worlds. Consider also that the perennial battle in Norse cosmology is that between the gods and the giants. This battle could be said to begin at this point in the cosmogony: the gods kill a giant, sparking off war. Following Ymir's dismemberment, Woden, Vili and Ve use Ymir's body parts to form the nine worlds of Yggdrasill. With the number 10 – with the first gods, and with the first death of a giant – we see the construction of the world(s), though the construction is not yet complete (see rune 13, Yew). Ymir's body parts are used by Woden, Vili and Ve to form the following aspects of the world(s):

1. Blood/Sweat: seas and lakes
2. Flesh: earth
3. Bones: mountains
4. Teeth: stones and scree
5. Skull: sky (supported by four dwarfs – Nordri, Austri, Sudri and Vestri – who represent the four directions and four elements)
6. Hair: trees

7. Eyebrows/Eyelashes: to fence-off Midgard
8. Brains: clouds

Our 'mapping' of Ymir's body is a synthesis of accounts in the Prose and Poetic Eddas. We suggest there are eight main components of Ymir's body which are utilised in the bringing forth of Yggdrasill and the nine worlds. It seems highly significant, then, that Woden's horse Sleipnir has eight legs (referring to Ymir's body parts) and, furthermore, that Yggdrasill – meaning 'Yggr's steed', or 'Terrible Steed' – is a representation of Sleipnir. If we were to extend these eight aspects and take blood-sweat, and eyebrows-eyelashes to be separate aspects, our Ymir-map would then be comprised of ten components. Ten, significantly again, is the number of material manifestation, of this stage in the cosmogony, and of the construction of the world(s). (The cosmological 'map' of Yggdrasill with its nine worlds is discussed in detail in the following chapter).

The cosmogony does not end with stage 10, nor is the creation of all beings completed with the presence of Ymir, Audhumla, the Giants, and the Gods. The order of the Elder Futhark indicates the cosmogony extends further, incorporating 'humanity' into the system. Humans are (thank the gods for us!) a necessary and integral part of the cosmology, residing as we do in Midgard. So:

**Number: 11**
**Rune**: *Isa* (Anglo-Saxon/Germanic) – Ice.
**Heathen Cosmogony**: Woden, Vili and Ve next create Ask, the first human. Like Ymir, the first person is ambisexual. Crowley's '777' states that 11 is 'the general number of

Magick, or energy tending to change', that is, magical expansion. Indeed, the creation of our own species might be viewed as a magical event. Note that the number 11 consists of two Isa runes, resembling a pair, a couple, and a human marriage. This is the potential which will become actual in the number 12, with the creation of Embla. The creation of Ask anticipates the creation of Embla, since humanity can not procreate without 'two'.

You will have noticed by now, in reading this cosmogony, that each number flows into the next, that each part of the cosmogony embraces the next, and that a number/part of the cosmogony can not do without the parts which stand either side of it. This is one aspect of the holism and completeness which defines cosmogony per se, and which, we propose, underpins the entire, coherent and consistent Heathen cosmogony presented in Galdrbok.

**Number: 12**
**Rune**: *Ger* (Anglo-Saxon), *Jera* (Germanic) – Fruitful year, love and sexuality.
**Heathen Cosmogony**: The next being to emerge in the cosmogony is Embla, the first human capable of sexual reproduction. Note that one sex or another is not ascribed here to Ask or Embla, but merely the actuality of sexual reproduction, for reasons outlined above. Again, themes of sex and fertility are consistent in the cosmogony, with implications for esoteric extrapolation. We have here, then, the 'split' of the one (the 1 of 11 which gives rise to the 1 of 12, and the one human cell) into two (male and female, the 2 of 12, two cells of a new human life). This is represented symbolically by the split nature of the Jera rune as it is represented in the Elder Futhark. Note that Ask and Embla

are thought to have been made from two trees – perhaps Ash and Elm – and that it is a third tree which arises next in the cosmogony. The Yew tree Yggdrasill is itself 'born' at stage thirteen, heralding the completion of cosmogony (creation of the worlds) and setting out of cosmology (ordering or arrangement of the worlds) (see Chapter 3: Cosmology).

**Number: 13**
**Rune**: *Eoh* (Anglo-Saxon), *Eihwaz* (Germanic) – Yew.
**Heathen Esoteric Kennings**: 13 is the number of the Yggdrasill yew tree, which is now fully created thanks to the death and dismemberment of Ymir, and creation of humans to be placed 'on' it (who are themselves made from trees). Note that 13 is 1 + 3 = 4: referring back to the fourth rune, Os, denoting creation/manifestation, and this is of course the creation/manifestation of the Yew, the world tree Yggdrasill. Incidentally, the Os and Yew runes are connected by Woden: Os being a Wodenic rune, Yew being the tree upon which he endured shamanic initiation in order to receive the runes. It is with the number 13 and the Yew rune that not only Yggdrasill comes into being, but also the potential for Woden to receive the runes – ultimately a gift to us. To have a rune-set made of Yew runes links well to the cosmogony!

It is important to consider the logical unfolding of manifestation in the runes 10-13. While the potential for manifestation, for completeness, was outlined in the number 10, at that point this was simply 'potential', or as the tenth rune denotes, a 'need'. Following the coming into being of humans (Ask and Embla), with runes 11 and 12, the construction of Yggdrasill by Woden, Vili and Ve from

Ymir's dismembered body is completed at rune 13, Yew. Thus, the cosmogony (the creation) and cosmology (the order of the worlds) is now complete.

Stages 1-13 embody the first 'Wyrd' third of the cosmogony, the coming into being of the world(s) and all the beings in the worlds – the advent of cosmology. It is not too difficult to appreciate that cosmogony and cosmology are ongoing – with each new life, for instance, and with each death. But it is also worthwhile to consider the Wyrd phase as having already happened for most of us, since we already exist in the middle earth when we first come to Runecraft. Following in the name of the Norn associated with this section, it is 'life unfolding' or more crudely 'the past'.

Following the Wyrd phase is the middle, central, Metod phase. And it is here, having acknowledged how the world(s) came into being and having come to understand our place in the worlds (runes 1-13) that we can now explore these worlds. The runes of the Metod phase are shamanic tools – it is here that practice begins, since the thirteenth rune is the springboard for the second phase of the cosmogony and outlining of Heathen Runic practice. Woden's shamanic initiation on the tree is the impetus for our own shamanic journey.

## Metoð Phase

Since the Elder Futhark row continues beyond the Yew rune, so our interpretations of the remaining runes cannot end at the point of the Yew rune simply because that might be convenient (the same is true when we reach the final Odal rune in the Futhark, when in the Anglo-Saxon Futhorc the rune row and rune poem continue). That is, the cosmogony, the bringing into being of the worlds may now be complete, but the cut-off point can not be arbitrary. So, what of the rest of the Elder Futhark, and beyond that, the Anglo-Saxon Futhorc's five extra runes? (We do not discuss the extra Northumbrian runes since there is no rune poem associated with them – certainly a cosmogonical examination of them might be in order in future work). In short, the runes have more to narrate, specifically regarding shamanic initiation. The cosmogony from 14-29 has a triune aspect, narrating 1) shamanic experience (as undertaken by Woden and Freyja, for example), 2) the 'life concerns' of human beings and the shamanic tools we may use to follow in the footsteps of Woden and Freyja, and 3) the sustaining of the Wyrd phase of the cosmogony.

1. The Metod phase narrates the specifics of shamanic experience, namely the entering of trance and receiving of shamanic wisdom. In Northern traditions, Woden and Freyja undertake these experiences. This is the esoteric/mythological basis for the Heathen system of shamanic initiation detailed in Galdrbok. Woden and Freyja's shamanic experiences, in turn, provide a template for our own spiritual journey – a journey which inevitably leads to death (rune 29, the Grave) and beyond (2 + 9 = 11, the number of magical expansion; see the Isa rune

discussed earlier). As the Wyrd phase marked out 'life unfolding' – a cosmogony, so this middle phase then, is the phase of the present, of 'life becoming', of the Wyrd Sister known as Metod. In moving towards rune 29 we may appear to in fact be moving away from the source (0), and this is certainly one aspect of the sequence, from life to death. But it is also clear that this is a returning towards to the source, since, as the process moves full circle and we move ever closer to 29, so the 29 will become 0 – the rune row ends, only to begin once more, with rune 1, Fehu.

2. In addition to this 'spiritual' component, the second aspect of the Metod phase involves a narrative of the 'material' preoccupations of humans. Thus, the ultimate end for us all – a truism of life – is physical death, as represented by the final rune in the Anglo-Saxon Futhorc, the Grave. In this sense, while each rune relates a positive spiritual initiation (each rune as a stage towards shamanic wisdom), it also has a challenging material aspect which attempts to sway us from the path. It is certainly easier to sit passively and watch the television than it is to make an active shamanic journey! Determination and conviction are required to 'stay on the path'. The fully prepared initiate who reaches 29 might fully embrace death and as such 'die a good death', while the unprepared and uninitiated may likely fear death and be consumed by it.

By this we do not equate 'dying a good death' with the warrior hero and Valhalla (Hall of the Slain) of Northern mythology. Rather, death has two meanings here. First, this is the death or 'little death' experienced in every trance ritual when the Heathen shaman moves outside the circles of space and time, and therefore outside death. Second, as animistic Heathens, leading lives with a sense of responsibility towards all of nature (as 'animate') we recognise the fact that as we all live, we all must die. We celebrate the seasons in our annual rituals – the 'wheel of the year' (see Chapter 6: Ritual) – and just as we celebrate the return of life in the Spring and Summer, so we must also, as a fact of life, respect the death we see all around us as Summer turns to Autumn and Autumn to Winter (of course death happens throughout the year, but the dark half of the year is represented mythologically as the dead or sleeping spirits of nature). When it comes to our own death, after many 'little deaths', the territory of rune 29 Grave is no longer such a 'foreign country'. The aim is not to know what is beyond death, for that can only ever come down to belief; the aim is to be able, through shamanic and other significant life experiences, to seize the moment of death and stake our claim that just as we have lived a good life, so we will die a good death. In Galdrbok, a pertinent ritual for preparing for death through ritual is 'Hanging on the Tree' (see Chapter 6: Ritual). A fascinating account of ritual death is also described/suggested by Humphries and Vayne [2004]).

3. Finally, this Metod aspect of the cosmogony narrates the protection and sustenance of the previous Wyrd part of the cosmogony, for as we sustain ourselves and should also sustain our Earth Mother(s), so the Wyrd stage is sustained by the Metod stage. As the personification of the present time, of 'life becoming', one role of Metod is as the 'sustainer', with Wyrd the 'creator' and Skuld the 'destroyer'. So, the first aspect of the cosmogony (1-13)

represents the creation, Wyrd, while the second represents sustenance, Metod, and the third, destruction (death and/or ecstasy), Skuld.

According to the Metod phase, having established the creation of humans in the Wyrd stage, we next learn of our shamanic purpose, and the format or tools available for Heathens to achieve that purpose: to 'wander wilfully' (journey shamanically) the worlds of Yggdrasill in search of knowledge, healing and empowerment. To this end, Woden, as the shamanic god par excellence, is an exemplary teacher. He hangs on the tree (rune 13, Yew) in a shamanic initiation of self-sacrifice. During this initiation, Woden receives the runes, and it is these runes which are a major tool enabling the path of the Heathen shaman during the Metod phase. Indeed, the logical sequence of the runes allows us to see the path behind us and ahead of us, as well as where we stand in the moment.

The Metod phase (as with both the Wyrd and Skuld phases) can not exist in and of itself. What has been sustained must be destroyed. Thus, the creation (Wyrd phase) contains within it the sustenance (Audhumla) which anticipates the Metod phase. And the sustenance contains within it the death/destruction of the Skuld phase, which esoterically can be understood as a 'shamanic death' in the form the Mann rune which, according to the rune poem, points explicitly towards death (later manifested in the Grave rune of the Skuld phase). And, of course, death/destruction inevitably leads to rebirth. As a final kenning, related to all three phases of the cosmogony, it is worth noting that the Wyrd phase represents human birth and early life, the Metod phase represents mid-life and the sustaining of life, as well as a shamanic re-birth, while the Wyrd phase is concerned with later life and death. And of course, all three can be experienced in one Heathen shamanic ritual.

**Number: 14**
**Rune**: *Peorth* (Anglo-Saxon), *Perthro* (Germanic) – The lot box, container of the runes, a gaming piece.
**Heathen Esoteric Kennings**: Woden received the runes in a shamanic death trance and brought the oracle back for the benefit of humans. This is one of the most crucial aspects of the entire cosmogony, for the runes are a gateway to the wisdom of Wyrd, to shamanic initiation and insight, and to Woden himself. We can use the runes to communicate not only with Woden and other deities, but also with the source of all: the Norns, determining as they do, the life of all beings. By embracing the Runic oracle, we can attune to Wyrd, and with increasing skills in interpretation we may align ourselves more closely with and also negotiate Wyrd's map for our lives. Since 1 + 4 = 5, so the lot box provides us with the movement (see rune 5, Rad, in the cosmogony above), the means to move onwards up the tree, the means to shamanic wisdom.

Rune 13, Yew, provides the potential for undertaking shamanic initiation and exploring shamanic ecstasies and wisdom, a component part of which is use of the Runic oracle and crystal ball. The following Perthro stage, denoting the altered consciousness attained in oracle use, marks the point at which aspirants may perceive what we have termed 'Thunor's lightning bolt'. This is the process, by means of scrying, of attaining a vision of the tree – in a lightning flash – in order to fleetingly (a link here to the

Bifrost/Bilrost bridge, the 'fleeting rainbow') glimpse the 'Aesiric trances' represented by Asgard and Disiric trances represented by Hel (see Chapter 4: Trance). This step is an initial traversing of the tree through a 'vision' of it in the crystal. The worlds themselves are explored later when the initiate undertakes shamanic travel proper (see Eh rune, number 19).

In contrast to these esoteric insights, Perthro for the uninitiated symbolises merely the 'entertainment' and games (gaming pieces) spoken of in the rune poem. When interpreted esoterically, these games are of course 'rune games', and the exploration of them – shamanically – is far beyond the simplistic interpretation of life as a mere 'game of chance'.

**Number: 15**
**Rune**: *Eolh* (Anglo-Saxon), *Elhaz* (Germanic) – Elksedge.
**Heathen Esoteric Kennings**: The Anglo-Saxon rune poem states that Elksedge 'grimly wounds and burns with blood any man who grasps it'. It is both painful to touch, and resilient and hardy. In this vein, Woden's traumatic, painful and unsettling shamanic initiation gains him a rebirth, and in consequence, greater hardiness and empowerment. Bearing the pain of initiation brings strength and resilience. For the Heathen seer, the responsibility of shamanic initiation is not to be undertaken casually. But such an initiation may bring spiritual reward and strength, and the strength to continue on the challenging spiritual quest.

Since 1 + 5 = 6, so this rune is the reification of the individuality represented by the sixth rune, Ken. Thus, for individuals concerned only with material wealth, the strength of Elksedge reinforces the false priorities of individuality – bounded beings driven by material gain and ego. Elksedge gives them the strength and resilience to refuse the spiritual path, to be firmly fixed in their bodies and the world of externals. For Runic initiates on the other hand, the esoteric kenning of Elksedge is the transcendence of individuality in shamanic ecstasies.

Furthermore, embracing the oracle and listening to its wisdom also brings the resilience and empowerment associated with Elksedge. For example, this empowerment is the certainty that life is not simply a haphazard amalgam of random events over which we have no control. Instead of the nightmare which is hyper-relativist post-modern individualism, one's life is known to be steered by the Wyrd Sisters, a life full of power and purpose. The Elksedge rune also symbolises protection, with the glyph itself representing a hand raised in warding. Elksedge is therefore a protector of the previous Wyrd phase of the cosmogony. In the altered conscious states induced at this stage in practice (associated with oracle work), Runesters tend to be more psychically sensitive. So, with appropriate invocations, the Elksedge rune protects Runesters from any otherworldly entities which may inadvertently or intentionally harm them.

**Number: 16**
**Rune**: *Sigel* (Anglo-Saxon), *Sowilo* (Germanic) – Sun.
**Heathen Esoteric Kennings**: From the strength and resilience of Elksedge follows the 'light' of the sun, the realisation that we have 'successfully' completed the first stage in Galdrbok's system by exploring oracle use and trance. This is also the start of 'getting life right', that is,

adhering to Wyrd (by starting to use and by following the
Runic oracle and scrying). Simply put, the initiate is at the
beginning of the Heathen path, and has made the first
'right' step on it. As a rune of 'success', Sowilo also
promises that by adhering to a Runic life, spiritual rewards
will follow.

This part of the cosmogony also corresponds with the first
part of the Havamal, 'the sayings of the High One' (see
Larrington 1996). The Havamal can be seen to be divided
into three sections of teachings, all of which are given by
Woden, the High One. In the first part, Woden is initiated
(hangs on the tree, which we associate with the Yew rune).
In the second, which is here pertinent to the Metod phase,
Woden (retrospectively, that is, post-initiation) relates
ethical teachings: crudely put, the second set of teachings
describes how to be a 'good person'. And in the third,
Woden relates his magical abilities.

The ethical teachings of the High One accord in some ways
with what Buddhists describe as 'the eightfold path' of
right speech, right thought, etc, and with the 'eight limbs'
of Yoga). Such embracing of ethical teachings in light of
oracular insight 'opens the way' to the 'intelligence of the
heart' – as Schwaller De Lubicz (1981 [1979]) claims was
developed by Ancient Egyptian initiates. The ethical
teachings of Woden thus pertain to the development of an
ethical conscience. It is interesting that 16 is 6 + 1 = 7,
corresponding with the rune Gebo. Gebo denotes Woden's
self-sacrifice on the one hand, and 'giving' on the other –
giving in the sense of physical 'gifts' or 'presents', but also
giving in the sense of altruism and the conscience which

develops with the 'opening of the way' described by De Lubicz. Indeed, the rune of the sun fits neatly with the character of Light Elf Home and its associations (see Chapter 2: Cosmology). From this logically follows:

**Number: 17**
**Rune**: *Tiw* (Anglo-Saxon, also Tig), *Tyr* (Old Norse), *Tiwaz* (Germanic) – the god Tiw.
**Heathen Esoteric Kennings**: In the new spiritual life hence gained, the initiate may gain shamanic wisdom, as guided by experienced oracle use and by engaging with deities and other spirits. This confers the ability to make informed decisions based on the intelligence of the heart, gleaned from the familiarity of Runic practice and thus the ability to meter out justice. Tiw is significant in this regard, in his form of the 'judge' who meters out justice. There are kennings here with Aleister Crowley's notion of the 'True Will' and his maxim 'love is the law, love under will'. 17 is 1 + 7 = 8, a reification of the eighth rune Wunjo – joy, thus reflecting the ecstasy of Crowley's 'love under will' and De Lubicz's 'intelligence of the heart'. An inkling of these altered states of being may be experienced when the heart Hvel (chakra) is open during some scrying rituals and during the onset of shamanic ecstasy.

**Number: 18**
**Rune**: *Beorc* (Anglo-Saxon), *Berkano* (Germanic) – Birch.
**Heathen Esoteric Kennings**: Berkano is the rune of fertility, regeneration, magic and healing by magic. 8 + 1 = 9, thus referencing the nine worlds, and a number of Woden. Woden is indeed heavily associated with the Birch rune (see Linsell 1994[1992]; Aswynn 1994). In the Anglo-Saxon

Nine Herbs Charm', for instance, Woden strikes an adder
into nine parts with nine 'glory' (likely birch) twigs, most
likely marked with runes:

> A wyrm came crawling, he tore a man apart
>
> then Woden took-up nine glory-twigs and struck
>
> the adder so that it flew apart into nine parts
>
> (adapted from Pollington 2000: 215)

This charm is enigmatic and difficult to interpret, but there
are interesting kennings to be drawn. At the very least there
may be a reference to dragon-slaying. In addition, the
connection between Woden, the wyrm/adder and the
number nine is important: in the cosmogony, Woden's
intrinsic involvement in the manifestation of the triune
aspect of Woden-Vili-Ve is completed at rune 9. The
number nine is recurrent in various sources associated with
Woden. In Havamal 140 Woden states: 'Nine mighty spells
I learnt from the famous son of Bolthor, father of Bestla'
(Larrington 1996: 34). The famous son of Bolthor is Buri,
Woden's father and the ancestor of the gods. Perhaps one of
these nine spells enables the striking of the adder into nine
parts. Or perhaps Woden learnt this spell as a result of the
shamanic wisdom gained during his self-sacrifice on
Yggdrasill. Woden is often linked with snakes: one example
is when he shape-shifts into a snake in Snorri's telling of the
myth of the mead of poetry (Skaldskaparmal 1, see Faulkes'
1998 [1987] translation of Snorri).

The 'twigs of glory' in the Nine Herbs Charm may refer to
the beautiful silver branches of the Birch tree, which can be
white and dazzling – hence 'glorious' – when the sun (or a
full-moon) shines on them. Birch is described in the Anglo-

Saxon rune poem as 'glorious in its branches' (Linsell 1994 [1992]), which links to the 'glory-twigs', but 'glory' might also refer to the wondrous runes carved on them – of course, Woden's link with the runes is well-known. All in all, this part of the Nine Herbs charm might be enigmatic, but Woden is a major feature in it as, perhaps, is the Birch tree, with both Woden and the Birch being linked to magic.

According to a number of authors it is not only Woden who is associated with the birch tree and with magic: the birch is also linked with a goddess. Some authors claim this is Nerthus (e.g. Gundarsson 1990), an earth mother goddess. Freyja Aswynn (1990) proposes she is the little-known Berchta and Jan Fries also mentions a lady named 'Berchte' (2002[1993]). Both Aswynn and Fries point to the shape of the rune as representing breasts or the breasts and belly of a pregnant woman. If the birch rune and birch tree are magic and goddess-related, then this tree may be linked, most plausibly, with Freyja, a shamanistic deity. Interestingly, the birch tree has a symbiotic relationship with the Fly Agaric (Amanita muscaria) toadstool, used by Siberian shamans to aid altered consciousness and otherworld journeying. And, the birch is sacred to the Sami (Lapp) shamans of Northern Europe, whose ancestors had a close relationship with some Norse communities during the migration age (Price 2002). A hardy tree which grows on the edges of woods and in arctic climes, the birch is a tree of fertility and regeneration, resonating with themes of rebirth, revitalisation, healing – and thus elements of shamanistic practices.

At the material level, for the uninitiated, this rune denotes the inspiration of poetry or intellectual thought. For the

Heathen Mage, moreover, the birch rune is also associated with the powerful ecstasy, inspiration and healing of shamanic trance, and thus with the ecstatic deities Woden and Freyja. In the third part of the Havamal, following his shamanic experience and ethical teachings, Woden speaks of certain spells or charms which he has learnt, as we noted earlier. Concomitantly, this stage of the cosmogony relates to magical abilities. In her book 'Leaves of Yggdrasill' (1994) Freyja Aswynn offers an excellent magical practice utilising the runes alongside Woden's Havamal charms (see also suggestions by Osborn and Longland [1987] and Gundarsson [1990]). So, as our skills in scrying, rune-casting and meditation develop, so other abilities begin to manifest – magical strengths which have arisen as a consequence of dedicated practice and visions of the otherworld. In yogic traditions, 'supernatural' faculties are named 'siddhis' and while they may arise spontaneously for a practitioner, like the magical abilities in Galdrbok's system of initiation their onset usually requires the initiate to be experienced.

At this juncture in our discussion of cosmogony, it is worth commenting on the sequence of six runes which follow Birch – Horse to Odal – which correspond specifically to trance experience and which also conclude the Metod phase of the rune row. The first three – Horse, Mann and Water – resonate with the procedure of entering an altered state of consciousness, and hence, otherworlds. Hitherto, the Wodenic Seer has only descried the worlds of Yggdrasill, but at this point the initiate undertakes shamanic travel proper. Broadly speaking, the horse is the means of travel, Mann is symbolic of the shamanic death required for such an experience to occur (see the associations between this rune and death in the stanza of the rune poem), and water is the experience of submerging into the altered state. The subsequent Ing and Day runes relate the sorts of experiences one may have while journeying the tree, such as visions of esoteric meanings of the turning seasons and the cycles of the universe (Ing), and experiences of ecstasy, transcendence or the 'mystical moment' (Day). Finally, the Odal rune is the rune of the Native or Home Land, representative of the journey home, the return from trance to waking consciousness. It is interesting to note that in total there are six runes discussed here which relate to shamanic journeying, thus referring back to the sixth rune, Ken, the rune of kenning, or in this context, shamanic wisdom. By entering the otherworld, by shamanically travelling the Northern world tree, great kennings may be achieved. These kennings are next discussed in further detail within the context of these last six runes of the Metod phase.

**Number: 19**
**Rune**: *Eh* (Anglo-Saxon), *Ehwaz/Ehwo* (Germanic) – Horse.
**Heathen Esoteric Kennings**: Horse is the rune of exploration, travel and partnerships. Woden, as a guide through the tree and through life, offers valuable shamanic teachings, particularly his 'vision' of the runes. This vision was 'received' from the spirit world and provides a mythical template for our own visionary practices. To receive his vision, Woden undertook what we term a shamanic journey. Concomitantly, the title of the shamanic world tree, Yggdrasill, itself means 'terrible stead' (as noted earlier), perhaps referring to the steed of Woden, his eight-legged animal spirit-helper Sleipnir. In practical terms for Heathen shamans, the horse provides a means of travelling

the tree, in shamanic journeys. So the horse itself can provide the vehicle for travel (if this works for you), or the horse may represent a metaphor for shamanic journeying per se, and whatever other means of travelling the tree works for you (from flying or falling to transforming into a wolf and running).

Note that 19 is 9 + 1 = 10, taking us back to the initial 'need' for creation (minus humanity which appears at runes 11 and 12), the penultimate stage of the Wyrd phase. In the Metod phase it is also the 'need' to travel the tree, via the horse, at this stage of the Heathen spiritual quest. On another level, this part of the cosmogony signifies the importance of partnerships and love. This has two aspects: first, in the sense of earthly, romantic love; second, the love between deities which might be described as 'cosmic love', a state of being outside the self-centred, romantic, material stereotype. Sex magic workings in which deities are embodied are therefore associated with this stage of esoteric learning.

**Number: 20**
**Rune**: *Mann* (Anglo-Saxon), *Mannaz* (Germanic) – Humankind.
**Heathen Esoteric Kennings**: The Mann rune is 10 + 10, taking us back to rune 10 once more, the point at which the imperative for humanity's creation was laid down. As well as denoting the natural human need to seek sex, love and companionship, this rune denotes the friendship group. The Mann rune refers to responsibility for and respect towards the humans and other beings with which we engage. It reminds us that (the spiritual) life is far harder for the 'lone sage' and that shamans are always therefore

very much a part of their community. As essential agents in their communities, indigenous shamans are also inevitably involved in social disputes. So Heathen Runesters should also use their abilities to address, reconcile and overcome community disputes and conventions such as those surrounding issues of class, age, gender, sexual orientation, and standing. This is one role of the Wodenic shaman – a negotiator, diplomat and culture-broker.

The stanza of the rune poem for Mann reminds us that the ultimate destiny of life is death:

> Man in his glee is dear to his kin
> though each must betray his fellows
> when the drihten decrees
> the pitiful flesh condemned to the earth
> (See Appendix A)

The Mann rune thus anticipates the 29th rune, Grave. The death referred to is both material (physical death of the body) and spiritual (the 'little death' experienced in altered consciousness). The San (Bushmen) of Southern Africa, for instance, have shamans who wilfully induce shamanic death – dying to the waking world to enter spirit – on many occasions. Every ritual, every rune cast and every scrying session is for the Heathen Runester a death, a form of transcendence and ecstasy – however small – since it involves leaving Midgard and either descrying (viewing) or entering (shamanic journeying) the tree. Rather than being morbid encounters, these deaths are extremely liberating experiences. It is with death as a well-rehearsed part of being alive that the Wodenic shaman meets physical death – with ecstasy – in order to die a good death. Death will not only inevitably come to us all at the end of our lives, but also to the cosmogony at the end of creation, with Ragnarok. This rune anticipates the ending of the sustaining part of the Metod phase, and the beginning of the destruction part of the cosmogony, the Skuld phase, which begins at rune 25 (Oak).

According to Snorri, Woden may die in order to enter the otherworld: he can 'shift his appearance... in the shape of a bird or animal' while his body would lie still 'as if he were asleep or dead' (Ynglinga saga 7). In his shamanistic-like practice, Woden leaves his body behind and rides Sleipnir in order to travel the worlds of the world tree. In going beyond the internal-external and body/no-physical-body divide, Woden and Sleipnir become one. Sleipnir is both the tree Yggdrasill itself and the means of travelling it. Interestingly, experiments record that in altered consciousness 'synaesthesia' is experienced, the melding and mixing of senses. In synaesthesia, tastes become sounds and colours can be smelled. For Woden and the Heathen shaman, this shape-shifting involves moving outside the space-time continuum, beyond Cartesian dualism. A key to shamanic wisdom then, is the regular altering of consciousness.

**Number: 21**
**Rune**: *Lagu* (Anglo-Saxon), *Laguz* (Germanic) – Water.
**Heathen Esoteric Kennings**: With shamanic travel now embarked upon, marked by the horse (Eh rune), and with spirit moved beyond the body in a death (Mann rune), the Lagu rune marks the point at which the otherworld is actually encountered or, put another way, entered or

submerged into. Many indigenous shamans describe the otherworld and the entering of it as akin to being in or under water (e.g. Lewis-Williams & Dowson 1989: 86-89). These shamans feel themselves submerge underwater when entering trance (the spirit world), and may even use the description of 'drowning'. The Bushman shaman Old K"xau, for instance, described his shamanic initiatory experience in the following way:

> Kauha [God] came and took me... He took me to the river. The two halves of the river lay to either side of us... Kauha made the waters climb, and I lay my body in the direction they were flowing... That's how I lay. Then I entered the stream and began to move forward... Kauha said to me 'This man will carry you and put n/um [supernatural potency] into you'. The man took hold of my feet. He made me sit up straight. But I was underwater! I was gasping for breath! I called out 'Don't kill me! Why are you killing me?' My protector answered 'If you cry out like that, I'm going to make you drink. Today, I'm certainly going to make you drink water'... I fought the water for a long, long time... Then, my friend, my protector spoke to me, saying that I would be able to cure (quoted in Halifax 1979: 55-56)

Since water is used to represent the entering of the otherworld in this indigenous example, so in Northern traditions we might describe entering the otherworld as an entering of Ginnungagap (encountering or crossing the Qabalist's Abyss to enter the 'supernal triad' – note the connection that $2 + 1 = 3$ resonating with the sephiroth beyond the Abyss), the primal waters of gestation. In so doing, this en-trance entails the crossing of the boundaries between the 'ordinary' world and the world of 'spirits'.

Engaging with this world may gain the Heathen Runester wisdom, and enable the magical ability of second sight which Thorsson (1984) associates with this rune. In another sense, the Lagu rune denotes trepidation before the journey. The Old English rune poem for Lagu states:

> Water to folks seems never-ending
> to him who must venture on an unsteady ship
> while high waves terrify
> and the 'sea-stallion' heeds not the 'bridle'
> (See Appendix A)

This is the point in the spiritual path where the journey ahead seems to be long, hard and in some flashes of scepticism, ultimately mortal. In Northern mythology, Woden often quests for knowledge of his own death. Shamanic journeying on the part of the Heathen shaman may also bring such knowledge of the nature of mortality – far from negative, this information can be liberating.

**Number: 22**

**Rune**: *Ing* (Anglo-Saxon), *Ingwaz* (Germanic) – Growth, Fertility.

**Heathen Esoteric Kennings**: While the Lagu rune may denote the difficulties of the initiatory path ahead, the road is not eternally hard, nor is it eternal, as expressed by the optimistic fecundity of the Ing rune. The Ing rune is a counterpart to Jera. The vision embodied in this rune is the ever-turning wheel of the seasons, the potential for growth and fertility, and the potential for succeeding in the spiritual quest. Excellent related and further kennings on the Ing rune are found in Osborn and Longland's 'Rune Games', pages 105-128. Interestingly, the number of this rune is 22, which is 2 + 2 = 4. Four is the number of physical manifestation, relating the Ing rune to nature and the four seasons. There are many esoteric kennings to be had when meditating in/on the ever-turning seasons.

**Number: 23**
**Rune**: *Daeg* (Anglo-Saxon), *Dagaz* (Germanic) – Day.
**Heathen Esoteric Kennings**: The Anglo-Saxon rune poem for Daeg states:

> Day is the drihten's herald, dear to men
> great metod's light, a joy and a hope
> to rich and poor – for all to use
> (See Appendix A)

Daeg is associated with Metod, and it thus resonates well with the Metod phase of our cosmogony. Linsell associates Daeg with 'reason', 'wisdom' and 'understanding'. In a mundane sense, Daeg is literally the brightness of the sun, which, after a nightmare perhaps, brings the clarity and reason associated with the 'clear light of day'. When in an optimistic mood, each new Day can bring with it the reason, wisdom and understanding that the spiritual path engaged with is, despite the challenges and hardships, ultimately life-fulfilling and 'right'. Ing and Daeg are juxtaposed in the sequence of the Futhark/Futhorc, hinting at their similarity, in both shape and meaning, in signifying eternal return and enduring cycles. But where Ing has an emphasis on the wheel/return of the seasons, Daeg signifies Thorsson's (1984) 'Wodenic Paradox': the interface at which night and day meet, the melding of two polarities into one, beyond binary oppositions. Essentially, where Ing is the vision of the cyclical workings of the universe, Day is the 'mystical moment' (Thorsson 1984: 67) wherein the Vitki moves shamanically outside the circles of space and time, only to return to the 'real' world, in accordance with the kenning of the Wodenic paradox. Daeg is 2 + 3 = 5, five referencing the movement which facilitates such shamanic processes (see rune 5, Rad).

**Number: 24**

**Rune**: *Athel* or *Ethel* (Anglo-Saxon), *Odal* (Germanic) – Home/Land.

**Heathen Esoteric Kennings**: In terms of trance experience, Odal is the rune of return, the return 'home' from shamanic journeying to waking consciousness. The initiate returns to the ordinary world with shamanic wisdom. With the number 24, 2 + 4 = 6, so there is a reference to six again (see rune 6, Ken) and to human individuality and consciousness. But at this point in the Futhark/Futhorc, the initiate is now much closer to destruction (sequentially much closer to the start of the Skuld phase and thereafter the Grave rune). So, the reference to six is the opposite of that initially presented by the Ken rune, now indicating the dissolution of rather than the forming of individuality and consciousness.

Note that we have followed the traditional sequence of the Futhark (Daeg followed by Odal) rather than that of the Futhorc (Odal followed by Daeg). It is, we think, futile to attempt to disentangle which is the 'right' way round. Most simply perhaps, where the Futhark arrangement 'worked' for the Old Germans, the Futhorc arrangement 'worked' for the Anglo-Saxons. For the purposes of this system, the more widely known Futhark arrangement has been used. The Furthorc arrangement also works, however: simply swap the runes round and you will find the interpretations still 'fit' – and with further kennings to be had. Choose whichever way works best for you!

## Skulð Phase

In reaching Odal, rune number 24 and the end of the elder
Futhark, the Metod phase comes to a close. Simply put, the
Wyrd phase has brought the world(s) (and human and
other beings) into existence, while the Metod phase has
sustained this creation and narrated the process of
shamanic initiation and shamanic journeying of the worlds
on the part of Heathen Seidr-workers. In the Skuld phase,
the Anglo-Saxon rune poem relates a further five runes
which are significant in this system of cosmogenesis and
initiation. The five final runes take us through the final
throes of what began at birth, with Fehu (1) the rune of
wealth, to death, the grave rune (29).

We would like to note some pertinent numerological
kennings at this juncture. The final number of the Wyrd
stage is 13. This is the number of the yew tree and (given
that 1+3=4) is equal to the number four, the number of
manifestation. The number of runes in the Metod
stage/phase (Perthro to Odal) is 11, referring to Crowley's
number of magical expansion and thus to the initiation and
shamanic experiences of the Heathen Runester in the
Metod phase, as well as the 'expansion' of the initiate
beyond the Metod phase into the final 'Skuld' stage of the
initiation. This Skuld phase is where intense shamanic
ecstasy (in addition to the journeying of the Metod phase)
may be experienced. Moreover, the final rune of the Wyrd
phase (13), plus the number of runes in the Metod stage
(11), adds up to 24. The number 24 is the rune of Odal
which marks the end of the Metod phase and the beginning
of the Skuld phase. It is also the total number of runes in the
Elder Futhark and marks the end of the Elder Futhark, as
well as marking the entering of the additional sequence of

five Anglo-Saxon Futhorc runes. Finally, when the 11 runes
of the Metod phase are added to the last 5 runes which
comprise the Skuld stage (five being the number of motion
and the ability to travel shamanically outside the
Newtonian motion of 'a real world'), we arrive at the
number 29, the final rune which is the Grave (death).
Indeed, 29 is 2 + 9 = 11, according to which we arrive back
at Crowley's number of magical expansion.

**Number: 25**
**Rune**: *Ac* – Oak.
**Heathen Esoteric Kennings**: Oak is the rune of 'trust' and
'honour' (see the relevant stanza of the Anglo-Saxon rune
poem), as well as strength, dedication and loyalty. By virtue
of dedication and loyalty to the spiritual journey thus far,
the initiate gains yet greater spiritual strength, beyond the
'resilience' initially experienced at Elksedge. Oak therefore
represents the dedication and strength required – and
obtainable from the Oak rune – to enable progression on
'the path' in ecstatic, shamanic work. Incidentally, Elksedge
is rune 15 so that the Oak rune, number 25, marks a cycle of
ten runes.

**Number: 26**
**Rune**: *Ask* – Ash.
**Heathen Esoteric Kennings**: As well as bringing strength,
dedication to the spiritual journey may bring further
direction. This direction is expressed in the straightness
and height of the ash tree – the Irminsul Pillar. In the
following chapter (Chapter 3: Cosmology), we discuss the
Irminsul Pillar and its relation to the Ash tree, the central
pillar of the world tree, and the juxtaposition of this tree
with the Yggdrasill Yew. Like the Elksedge and Oak, the

Ash is also a barrier rune/tree, 'standing firm it endures living men as foes'. The ash provides further security and protection. By the Skuld stage of the initiation system, the 'defences' of the Heathen shaman are very strong. This is extremely important, since the further up the tree one gets, the further the potential 'fall', and the more difficult following the path may be. The issue here is having sufficient magical ability, skill, and spiritual strength, to make the rest of the journey. We have pointed out that shamanic work is not a 'bed of roses' – and indeed, even if it were, roses have thorns! It is a difficult path. In the logical unfolding of the runes, there is the ultimate challenge yet to face, death itself, so one must be strong and one must have a method of attack...

**Number: 27**
**Rune**: *Yr* – Weapon.
**Heathen Esoteric Kennings**: The weapon of the Yr rune is both the Bow of the warrior (looking back also to the Yew rune and the Yew longbow), of physical warfare; and furthermore, a spiritual weapon (again, see the appropriate stanza of rune poem). This weapon therefore works on three levels: 1) the weapon of war which results in death, 2) the spiritual weapon which kills 'shades' (hang-ups, fears, etc and other forms of negative Orlog), and 3) another form of spiritual weapon, one of compassion, love, and altruism. On a physical level, there are times when war might be legitimate in order to challenge a situation in which yet more death would result (a case of killing in order to promote 'the greater good'). On a spiritual level, the weapon is deployed to meet and challenge death, be it one's own death, or perhaps to meet a mortal illness when healing a very sick patient. Typically, some indigenous

shamans will tackle 'evil' spirits in the otherworld through the use of weapons wielded in 'the ordinary world'.

In juxtaposition with the previous Ash rune, it is pertinent to note that Woden's spear, named Gungnir, was perhaps made from Ash. Gungnir is therefore the ideal representation of the spiritual weapon which can be used to destroy negative Orlog. Notice also that Thunor's hammer Mjollnir represents a pair of scales similar to the scales of justice when held (or worn as a pendant) with handle upwards. The spiritual weapon referred to, at this stage in the cosmogony, may also be Thunor's hammer in its role of bringing balance and justice (balancing the will of the giants and of the gods). Such balance may ultimately lead to happiness and contentment – the rune of the Beaver.

**Number: 28**
**Rune**: *Iar* – Beaver.
**Heathen Esoteric Kennings**: Beaver is the rune of happiness and contentment, and it is the rune and stage in the initiatory journey which represents these qualities. In the mundane world, this is the happiness and contentment which financial wealth brings; we all need such earthly comforts and the snugness of the home, but money does not necessarily produce lasting happiness. On another level, this is the happiness and contentment brought about by companions, fellowship and family. On a different level, the beaver rune denotes the happiness and contentment brought about as a result of spiritual dedication. Moreover, the initiate may in some rituals experience shamanic ecstasy, which in being outside the circles of space and time is beyond death. And death is the final rune…

**Number: 29**
**Rune**: *Ear* – The Grave, Death.
**Heathen Esoteric Kennings**: Death comes to us all. At the end of this Skuld phase is the destruction, the death, embodied by Skuld herself. Uninitiated, material-hungry humans may only fear death – when 'riches fade, joys pass away' and 'friendships end' (Linsell 1994 [1992]). Most people, in avoiding a 'spiritual' life, 'religious' path, or whatever we are going to call it, rarely face or challenge their fear of death (which is of course quite reasonable considering how difficult and terrifying the thought of death is for the ego). We do not deride material needs and wants – as Runesters we simply feel that there is more to life than this, as many indigenous shamans might attest.

As we have mentioned, indigenous shamans often describe spirit world experiences as a 'death'. This is by no means a metaphor. Shamans believe that they literally die when they enter the spirit world. This is a crucial point in Galdrbok's system of initiation. In his self-sacrifice, Woden dies, but – in similarity to indigenous shamans – returns to the living/'real'/'ordinary' world with shamanic knowledge. The Heathen shaman also endeavours to arrive at such wisdom by similar means. To die and return with knowledge is in some ways not so difficult as one might imagine. We suggest that rune casting and crystal gazing are excellent techniques for entering trance (see Chapter 1: The Otherworld), and that this entering of trance, however 'light', goes some way towards experiencing death – for in trance time and space are displaced. Entering the otherworld may usefully be perceived as a death.

Heathen shamans may, in moments of shamanic transcendence, experience a state of ecstasy. Such ecstasy may perhaps be perceived as an experience of death and a state which may be beyond death. Gaining familiarity with the realm of the otherworld is a major goal for the Vitki, since such familiarity facilitates the ability to 'die a good death'. But although it is positioned at the end of the Anglo-Saxon rune poem, the grave is by no means 'the end'. The Grave rune takes us back full circle to the beginning, to the birth rune, Fehu. Also, it does not seem insignificant that the grave rune is number 29, and that 2 + 9 = 11, the number of magical expansion in Crowley's Thelemic system, thereby resonating with expanding 'ordinary' consciousness into the altered consciousness of death. The grave is also, at the same time as being the last stage of the cosmogony and the shamanic questing of the Runic Heathen, the point at which the spiritual journey may also be said to begin – for an excellent starting point for the initiate embarking on ritual practice is to engage with the dead, with ancestors, by 'sitting out' on burial mounds.

The Yew rune also represents a death and a beginning. It is at the Yew stage that, like Woden, the Heathen shaman-aspirant recognises the need for self-sacrifice, a death, in order to follow the spiritual path which draws him/her. The vision of the tree, the spiritual path ahead is, at the Yew rune gateway on the path, seized using the shamanic tools of the runes and the crystal sphere. With the Horse rune, Heathen Runesters go on to travel the Yggdrasill tree of life and death, a process involving a death (Mann rune) and submergence (Water rune) into the otherworld. Just as indigenous shamans the world over must enter the spirit world many times, each one of them a death and rebirth, so the Seidrmadr must encounter Yggdrasill many times through the tools and rituals set out in Galdrbok (see later chapters!). In fact, the more journeys you undertake, the better, so that your familiarity with the realm of spirit means that the final death may be successfully engaged with.

In the 29th stanza of Crowley's 'Book of the Law' the goddess states: 'For I am divided for love's sake, for the chance of Union' (Crowley 1990 [1976]: 22). This is a well-known and profound statement for many Thelemites (adherents of Crowley's system), for its cosmological significance. Of relevance to the Grave rune is that one aspect of separation/division the goddess speaks of (for there are many kennings to be had in these few words of the 'Book of the Law' alone) is the separation of humans from the gods, and she also speaks of the 'union' (or Yoga) which is experienced when reuniting with that original source. In Galdrbok's cosmogony, union may also be achieved in the number 29, in the regaining of 0 (what we might term 'Nornic consciousness') by following the Runic path of 1 to 29 – and achieving a shamanic ecstasy.

## Further Significances

Our discussion demonstrates how the runes themselves resonate with the act of creation/cosmogony. At the simplest level, this cosmogony ends at 10 (as in the Qabalistic tree of life), with the creation of the world(s) from Ymir's body. The cosmogony can also be said to extend from this point as humanity is introduced (runes 11 and 12), with the thirteenth rune, the rune of Yggdrasill representing the manifestation of the tree on which the worlds might be said to subsist/depend. The rune row and the unfolding of its esoteric meanings continue through the remaining Elder Futhark, since Perthro (rune 14) represents the 'fate' or lot box (or rune bag) through which people can embrace and accord with Wyrd. As a result of according with Wyrd, strength and resilience (Elksedge), good health and success (Sigel) are maintained, 'right' choices in life may be made (Tiw), and magical insights may be attained (Beorc). The Horse (Eh) is a major vehicle for shamanic travel on the tree, which requires a shamanic death (Mann) and submergence into trance (Lagu). In trance, various elements of shamanic wisdom might be won (Ing, Daeg), and the Heathen shaman finally returns to Middle Earth (Odal). The grave is the final point of shamanic ecstasy, a transcendence which can be rehearsed and produced in every shamanic ritual – which is in itself a ritual death. The final moment of ecstasy is of course the end of life; hence sex and death are related (see discussion of the cosmogonical aspects of the Gyfu rune, above).

The succession of runes, their logical unfolding, resonates with the sequence of the cosmogony. It is a profound kenning that every rune cast is a re-enactment of creation. Consider how Woden received the runes while hanging on Yggdrasill, and how some Runesters' rune sets are, accordingly, made of Yew wood. Since Yggdrasill was made from Ymir, so the runes are also actually parts of his bones/flesh/body – you hold in your hand the disarticulated parts of Ymir! Accordingly, ideal materials for runes include yew (or other sacred woods such as ash, oak, apple, thorn) and bone (perhaps best to avoid human bones though!) or antler. In each rune cast the lots are thrown in a replication of Ymir's dismemberment. In turn, the replacing of the runes in the lot box symbolises the remembering of the disarticulated parts of Ymir. This is a simple but profound way of cosmogony mimesis which can be practised on a daily basis (see also the ritual of cosmogony mimesis in Chapter 6: Ritual).

The cosmogony may also be re-membered by embodying the runes one's self. One technique involves runic postures known as Stadrgaldr, best described by Thorsson (1984) and Fries (2002[1993]). In this practice, one stands in postures which mimic the shapes of runes. Standing upright with arms pointing straight and downwards in an 'f' shape, for example, is the Stadrgaldr for the Os/As/Ansuz rune. Inscriptions of people in Runic postures on the two fifth century CE golden Gallehus Horns found in Germany (in 1639 and 1734) – replicas can be seen in the Enlightenment Gallery of the British Museum – perhaps mark the ancient Germanic precedent for this practice. The runes can also be embodied by chanting – or vibrating – the rune sounds, as a type of Galdr. Repeating 'ansuz, ansuz, ansuz' would effectively vibrate the Os/As/Ansuz rune. As well as sounding each rune name, the seed vowel sounds can be incorporated, as described by Thorsson (1984). So for the Os/As/Ansuz rune again, this might involve vibrating 'ass, iss, oss, ess, uss' over and over. Finally, runes can be signed and sent in order to effect magic – you might simply carve the shape of the rune in the air with a finger, for instance (see Chapter 7: Magic). Thus, every rune cast, every Stadrgaldr, every Galdr, every signing and sending, resonates with the cosmogony. Each element of Heathen ritual practice outlined and developed in Galdrbok ties in with the other elements, and ultimately ties into the cosmogony. Such systematic coherency is, for us at least, inspiring and empowering, because a complete 'world view' (or vision of the world[s]) is established.

Taking all these considerations into account, we argue that the order of the runes is of and in itself, magical. It does not concern us that this interpretation is simply that – an interpretation. But it is fascinating that the order of the runes handed down to us by our ancestors contains multiple kennings – and we do not think this order is simply coincidental, arbitrary or meaningless. More importantly, attending to the order of the Futhark/Futhorc is empowering for Heathens today. Why else begin at wealth (birth) and end at the grave (death)? What we argue is not a dogma; we do not want a runic orthodoxy. Rather than arguing for fixed and singular meanings, we have pointed to many layers and meanings within both the runes and the cosmogony. You might consider now (if you have been following Galdrbok to the letter!) what sorts of kennings have you gleaned from the runes and the cosmogony so far, and how these kennings have empowered your life.

## Conclusion

Having provided in this chapter a poetic introduction to the cosmogony, and a detailed esoteric extrapolation of it, we end with a summary of the esoteric kennings we have set out. No doubt there are other kennings to be had, and as they continue to unfold for us, so we encourage you to elucidate your own. We also offer a poetic accompaniment to this lore – 'From Raggedness to Majesty'.

Having discussed a cosmogony, in the next chapter we explore Heathen cosmology – that is, the worlds on

Yggdrasill: the Haven, Middle Earth, Helheim, Dark Elves, Giants, Dwarfs, Light Elves, Vanaheim, Nifelheim and Muspelheim. It is these worlds that were brought into manifestation as a result of the cosmogony. And it is Heathen shamans who, with rune-oracle kennings and accomplished scrying skills, journey to these worlds to engage with the beings therein – and return to Middle Earth with shamanic wisdom and power.

## Cosmogony Summary

### Wyrð Phase: Genesis of Ymir, Auðhumla, Gods and Other Beings:

1. Fehu: Creative and fertile potential. Ymir.
2. Uruz: Auðhumla, the sacred cow.
3. Thurs: Buri emerges.
4. As: Ymir produces the first giant.
5. Rad: Movement. Sexual (rather than asexual) potential. Ymir produces second giant (thus sexual reproduction is possible).
6. Cen: Ymir produces a six-headed son.
7. Gebo: Buri's reproduction begins (sexual, with Bestla, rather than asexual). Note that sex is only possible since 5, the number and Rad rune of movement. Woden (Breath) is born, the god of sacrifice (Gebo/Gyfu /Gift/Sacrifice). A rune of sex magic.
8. Wunjo: Vili is born. Soul / Will / Thoughts. A rune of love magic.
9. Hagalaz: Ve is born. Blood, the heat of life. The potential for the worlds to come into existence, and for the emergence of the tree. The Hagalaz rune represents change and the need for transformation. Ve thus predicts the need for a shrine / a world(s) to live in.
10. Nyd: With the birth of the triple gods (Woden-Vili-Ve) now complete, the killing and dismemberment of Ymir is needed to create the world(s). Creation can be said to continue beyond 10, as human life begins:
11. Isa: the gods Woden, Vili and Ve create Ask, the first human, and:
12. Jera: Embla, the second human (again, with two beings of the same species, sexual reproduction is now possible). Thus,

13. Yew: the final form of the universe is represented by the yew tree, the place where all the beings dwell in their respective worlds. It is also our starting point in shamanic work. This involves following Woden's precedent and offering your own self-sacrifice on the Yggdrasill yew tree.

**Metod Phase: Shamanic/Human Experience:**
14. Perthro: The lot box and wisdom of the runes, received by Woden during his shamanic initiation, hanging on the Yew tree. Perthro marks the beginning of the path towards shamanic wisdom.
15. Elksedge: Strength and resilience is gained from the pain of initiation, and dedication to runic practice. Elksedge also refers to the protection of the previous Wyrd phase of the cosmogony and the sustaining of this Metod phase.
16. Sowilo: Following the runes, negotiating one's life in accordance with Wyrd means living life right. Responsibility towards and respect for humans and other beings is required, as told by Woden in the Havamal. 'Success' in life (that is, following the spiritual journey) follows.
17. Tiwaz: runic and scrying practice brings conscience and the ability to make right judgement (for example, by using the runes and invoking Tiw, the judge).
18. Berkano: A rigorous and well-practised programme of runic practice brings magical abilities, as related by Woden in the third part of the Havamal.
19. Ehwo: The rune of Woden's horse Sleipnir. The initiate now undertakes shamanic travel on the world tree. The horse is one vehicle for doing this. Also the rune of partnerships and sex magic embodying deities.

20. Mann: A reification of Rune 10. There is rarely such a thing as the 'lone sage', hence the importance of a community of humans and other beings. The rune poem hints at death: the shaman must die (enter trance) in order to access the tree, and many indigenous shamans describe entering trance as a 'death'.

21. Lagu: Entering the tree, entering the otherworld, passing through the watery area of altered consciousness: many indigenous shamans describe the entering of trance as submerging underwater and even akin to drowning. The rune is also related to feelings of trepidation, with regard to the spiritual journey, as described in the rune poem.

22. Ing: Recognition of the cycles of life/the universe. The beauty of these cycles is appreciated and celebrated.

23. Daeg: Travelling the tree produces insight and wisdom. The 'sage' is emerging. Where Ing is the cycle of natural life, Daeg is the cycle of cosmic life and Wodenic paradox.

24. Odal: Odal is the rune of returning 'home' from the spirit world to waking consciousness. The numerology refers back to 6, but the potential now is for dissolving individuality, rather than forming it.

### Skuld/Death Phase:

25. Oak: Resilience and strength is developed to the extent (a reification of and refinement beyond Elksedge) that deeper shamanic experiences can be successfully engaged with, and the Runester may be resilient against malevolent spirits.

26. Ash: The direction of the spiritual path is now straight and the will of the adept resolute. Ash as a spear: the spiritual weapon:

27. Weapon: The weapon (bow) of war and the spiritual weapon for killing shades and challenging death. Thunor's axe-hammer Mjollnir inverted, the scales of justice metering out death (of humans and others) appropriately, where necessary. The Heathen shaman might also wield Woden's ash spear Gungnir in this process, referring back to the previous rune.

28. Beaver: Earthly comforts and contentment, and the spiritual bliss which can be experienced in deep altered consciousness, especially Aesiric trances (see Chapter 4: Trance).

29. Grave: The fully initiated Heathen shaman can now enter ecstasy and, outside the circles of space and time, 'return to the source' – that is, 0.

## From 'Raggedness' to Majesty

LODDFAFNIR WAS GRIM – A PROSPECT-LESS YOUTH
UNREMARKABLE IN COUNTENANCE, ILL FATED, UNCOUTH
YET COURTED-HE BOLVERK 'PON FAIR CHALKLAND-HEATH
SOUGHT-OUT HIS WISE COUNCIL – DARED EMBRACE BELIEF

TO 'RAGGEDNESS' 'TIS TRUE 'LODDFAFNIR' IS IMPUTED
YET LODDFAFNIR, LODDFAFNIR, LODDFAFNIR DISPUTED
AS BOLVERK, A-ROUSING, SPAKE FORTH-THEN HIS 'SOOTH'
LO BECAME LODDFAFNIR, REMARKABLE, COUTH!

"WISE IN THE GROWING, WELL-CRAFTED BY LORE
MOST NOBLE OF DRAGONS RISE-UP, TILL YE SOAR
AND MAJESTIC AGAINST THE NIGHT-SKY BE
CAPUT DRACONIS – ETERNALLY"

THUS DID STOUT BOLVERK, THAT 'SIRE' OF OLD
MASTER OF LORE-CRAFT AND SECRETS UNTOLD
RAISE-UP ONE LODDFAFNIR TO HAVEN'S FAIR GATE
TO BECOME THENCE IMMORTAL AND GLORIED IN FATE

Loddfafnir implies: Lodd, 'rags', and Fafnir, the name of
the dragon killed by the hero Sigurd. The combination
'Ragged-dragon' is most likely a mocking term for
someone not yet versed in arcane lore – a 'tyro', a learner.
Thus we all start our journey into Heathen lore as a
Loddfafnir – a 'Ragged-dragon'. Loddfafnir can perhaps be
compared to the 'fool' in the Tarot deck. He denotes the
innocence of the beginner, who may want to reach-out and
touch the very stars themselves. We leave the identity of
Bolverk as a riddle for the reader.

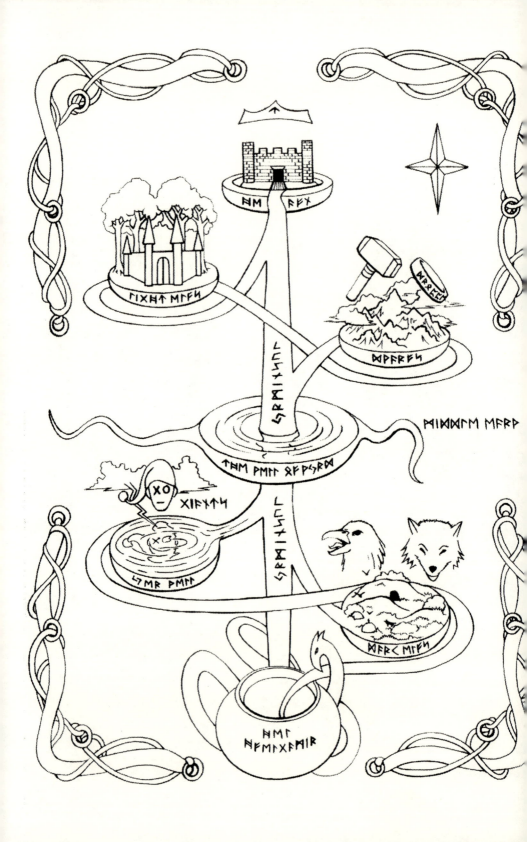

# – Chapter 3 –
## Cosmology - The Realms and Beings of Yggdrasill

In a wood someone must from a high tree
fall wingless – he will be in flight nonetheless,
dances in the air until he can no longer be
the tree's fruit. Onto the roots he then
sinks in dark spirits, bereft of his soul
he falls to earth – his spirit is on its way

(Old English Gnomic Poetry from the 'Fates of Men',
alluding to shamanistic flight on the world tree
Yggdrasill: translated by Pollington 2000:67)

At the outset of the previous chapter, we suggested that the Heathen shaman must embark on the task of being proficient in lore. In so doing, connections are made between the various elements which go to make up cosmogony. Some of these connections have resulted in the coherent and systematic approach we have taken in our task of producing Galdrbok's cosmogony. The same sort of proficiency in lore is required for cosmology, for cosmogony and cosmology are, of course, intrinsically linked. With the assumption that you are now well versed in the cosmogony of Galdrbok, it is time to introduce the subject of cosmology – the realms and beings of the world tree Yggdrasill.

'Cosmology' refers to the way we describe, map out and understand the universe and our own place in it, alongside other beings including stones, plants, birds, animals, and otherworldly beings. This 'map' is in many shamanic cultures planned in the form of a tree; in Northern cosmology this is the world tree Yggdrasill. In the previous chapter detailing cosmogony, we discussed how the cosmology (Yggdrasill) is brought into being: it is anticipated at the stage of the Hagalaz rune, produced through the dismemberment of Ymir at the Nyd rune, and itself manifests at the Yew rune.

The Yew rune itself 'symbolises' Yggdrasill and the arrangement of the worlds on that mighty tree. Simply put, there are nine worlds on the tree (or, more accurately, seven worlds plus the polar opposites of Muspelheim and Nifelheim). Joining these worlds are eight directions and six main paths. The paths can also be extended to 12 and 14 if all the worlds are joined to one another. All aspects of this cosmology, including the reasoning for this particular map, are elaborated upon in this chapter.

It is important to bear in mind that in many ways this tree-map is not fixed and unchanging, but transient and morphic. It is a plan of the otherworld, a place where the senses are disrupted, and where little girls follow white rabbits down burrows and may shrink and grow in size! As Alice knew only too well, no territory is entirely certain in the otherworld. Yggdrasill can, then, be mapped-out only for convenience. It is therefore not surprising that different people have produced different maps of the Yggdrasill world tree based on the same Eddic sources. Compare those maps suggested by Aswynn, Crossley-Holland, Gundarsson, and Linsell, for instance – they are all very different, yet based on the same evidence available to us. When trying to clarify things, it does not help when the sources themselves often disagree! They even describe things which are not physically possible: how is it that Helheim and Nifelheim can be both 'down' and 'to the north', for instance? One answer is that nothing is fixed in the spirit world; there are no 'physical' rules (such as gravity) as we have in 'the real world'. Thus, any map of it, including our's, can only be based on certain 'signposts'.

## Yggdrasill and other World Trees

Shamanisms manifest in many different cultural guises and diversity is a key factor to understanding shamans and their communities. These cultural differences and other factors such as socio-political location/history and environment, give rise to a variety of shamanistic and shamanistic-influenced spiritual traditions of the world. These traditions are born from the ways different societies come to understand their world and mark different ways of recording and relating spiritual phenomena, as well as expressing their effects. In essence, this is what 'traditions' are: indicators, signposts and records. The Yggdrasill tree is one such signpost. Consistent with various shamanistic traditions, it records a profound and holistic view of creation and the world(s) we live in (amongst other beings). Many cultures, including those as disparate as the Yoruba of Northern Nigeria and the Sami of Scandinavia, have versions of the world tree. They are culturally very different, but they also have similarities and consistencies. The basic framework of Yggdrasill is outlined in detail in this chapter, and in a summary at its close.

## Limitation and Structure as a Key to Shamanic Wisdom

While the map of Yggdrasill may be difficult to pin down, it is important to recognise that structure (constraint) includes its opposite – inspiration or freedom. For example, one needs to be thirsty to enjoy drinking, hungry to enjoy food, and the nicest bath taken is the one you ached for. Polar opposites are necessary for the modern Western ego to define itself in space-time. Thus we commonly encounter the terms 'over here – over there', 'male-female', 'positive-negative', and so on. One common experience for someone altering consciousness, however, is the (temporary) dissolution of these opposites. Ultimately, there is no 'good and bad' for indigenous shamans. This is not meant to imply that shamans are immoral. Buddhists, for instance, among other monks and nuns, also seek to eradicate perceived dualities, and they are, generally speaking, intensely ethical people. Polar opposition simply marks out the 'field of play': ultimately Heathen shamans aim to transcend these binaries. The Haven (not Heaven) and Helheim (not Hell) on Yggdrasill are differing ends of the same stick, like two ends of the same magnet. Runesters aim to reconcile them both. The way to do this is of course to have a 'plan', a systematic practice; in this case Galdrbok's system of Heathen shamanic initiation based around the 'map' of Yggdrasill.

## Plan Your Work, Work Your Plan

We need hardly say that there is far more value and empowerment to be had in travelling the world tree than simply entertaining oneself with TV. But because Heathen shamans are effectively engaging in an ongoing programme of growth, experience, repair, and both personal and group development, it is important that an otherworld scheme is consistent (see the narrative of Otherworld Geography in Chapter 6: Ritual). There is little point in each of us having our own maps of the otherworld and going to different worlds, for then there is little point in fostering a community. Such eclectic world trees do exist and may serve certain purposes, but one way or another, to be 'real', lived and truly effective a world tree needs to be schematic and it needs to be worked! Only by working consistently with a structured 'map' can we move purposefully and meaningfully from point to point, interacting with worlds and beings which are categorised using a consistent language.

Although it often takes some time to learn such a structure or language, it is important to do so. Without this structure, one is vulnerable to the chaos of the otherworld, and while there may be important lessons to be learned from such experiences, structure more usefully leads to freedom. The world you visit in spirit may not be quite like the one you see on the map, but that is part of the fun of it! Perhaps the darker parts of the otherworld are no more than the chaos of one's so-called 'subconscious' mind (as in a nightmare for example) or the negative aspects of the individual 'ego'. However, we suspect that this psychological model is rather too simplistic. Using a structured otherworld map allows the user to connect experiences meaningfully together (both personally and communally) and to identify patterns, much in the same way as we do when recognising letters and words on a printed page. Then the experiences of the otherworld(s) become meaningful, useful and repeatable.

In a psychological framework, the otherworld map is a map of the mind, a mind-map – your mind-map. So it could be said that the otherworld region is your region, your world. This does not make it a subjective fantasy and need not reduce it to psychological archetypes, since we are all human and what we experience 'inside' can profoundly influence what we do (and therefore affects other people and beings) 'on the outside'. So even if you are uncertain that the 'otherworld' we describe exists, you could begin practice by simply psychologising the map and experiences. With time, your experiences may, we suggest, lead to acceptance of a complex Heathen world-view which has less need for simplistic psychological language!

## Woden and Yggdrasill

We have much used the term 'Yggdrasill' so far, and by now you will know that according to various sources the term Yggdrasill refers to the Northern world tree. As you will also know by now, Yggdrasill is Old Icelandic for 'terrible steed', perhaps referring to Woden's horse Sleipnir – that is, Yggr's or Woden's steed. Concomitantly, Woden himself is the 'classic' Heathen shaman-god who travels the worlds of the tree, in search of wisdom, riding Sleipnir. Later we will look at traditional methods to emulate the travels of this cloaked, wise, wandering, wonder-worker. For now, here is an apt quote from Brian Branston's book

'The Lost Gods of England' (1957), evocatively describing the Anglo-Saxon Woden.

If a West Saxon farmer in Pagan times had walked out of his bury or ton above the Vale of Pewsey some autumn day, and looking up to the hills had caught sight of a bearded stranger seeming in long cloak larger than life as he stalked the skyline through low cloud; and if they had met at the gallows by the cross-roads where a body still dangled; and if the farmer had noticed the old wanderer glancing up from under a shadowy hood or floppy brimmed hat with a gleam of recognition out of his one piercing eye as though acclaiming a more than ordinary interest, a possessive interest, in the corpse; and if a pair of ravens had tumbled out of the mist at that moment, and a couple of wolves

howled one to the other in some near-by wood; and if the
stranger had been helping himself along with a massive spear [or
staff] larger by far than normal; and if all this had induced in the
beholder a feeling of awe; then he would have been justified in
believing that he was in the presence of Woden trampling the
world of men over his own Wansdyke (Branston 1957: 93)

Woden is able to shift his shape, leaving his body still as
though deep in slumber or dead. He is able to assume
animal and other guises in order to travel the otherworld
and gain experience and esoteric lore. Woden is the
'archetypal' Northwest European wizard. He is Tolkien's
Gandalf and from where Tolkien almost certainly gained
his inspiration; in Old Norse Gandalf means 'the magic
working elf' (Simek 1993: 99). He is wise, cunning,
resourceful and restless. Woden travels between the
worlds, a master of disguise, a trickster, a psychopomp, a
healer, and as such, he, like the goddess Freyja from whom
he learned Seidr-magic, is a shaman.

The Havamal tells us that Woden, in typical shamanic
fashion, undergoes an otherworldly initiation which
culminates in his discovery of the runes (the Anglo-Saxon
term 'run' meaning whispered secret). These runes are
represented by mysterious glyphs carved, scratched or
marked onto lots, slips of wood, bone, metal or other
materials: runes for divination, runes for magic, and runes
for shamanic journeying. Even the gods themselves 'shake
the twigs' (cast lots, runes) as told in Ymir's Poem in the
Poetic Edda (verse 1, line 3): 'they shook the twigs and
looked at the augury' (Larrington 1996:78). This indicates
that the gods are human-like and indeed many of their
exploits relate their fallible nature. Do not look for a

transcendent, perfect and singular (male) 'God' in Heathen Runecraft – Heathenry is far more nuanced and complex than that! Thanks to their human-like natures, we can associate with the gods. As such, the Heathen deities are also manifestations of the original Tiwas (Deva/deity), manifest in the worlds of 'things' (Yggdrasill), and require oracular guidance as we do.

In the Eddas, Woden undergoes his shamanic initiation and seizing of the runes, thus (Havamal 138-145):

> I know that I hung on that windswept tree for nine long nights, pierced by the spear, dedicated to Woden, myself to myself, on the branch of the tree of which nobody knows from where its roots run. They offered me neither bread nor mead from a horn. Then I bent over, downwards I peered, took up the runes, took them up screaming, and fell back from there... Then I recovered, began to think, grew, and felt well; word out of word gave word to me, work out of work gave work to me. Runes you will find and meaningful glyphs, staffs of advice; very strong runes, very mighty runes, which the mighty sage stained, and the powerful gods made, and the runemaster of the gods carved out (based on Larrington 1996: 34-35)

This extract is a vital key to Heathen shamanic initiation. Not only does the Heathen shaman replicate this initiation (see Chapter 6: Ritual), but also, when we pick up the runes we connect with the mythical figure of Woden. Woden and his counterpart Freyja are the shamans in us all. A parallel in Woden's use of the runes can be seen in the Nigerian Yoruba Ife religion which is based on the teachings of the prophet Orunmila. Orunmila introduced a method of divination known as Dafa, and the Ife priests believe that when Dafa is cast, it represents direct communication with (the spirit of) Orunmila. Clearly, shamanic gods and divination are not exclusive to the Old North, but are consistent across other indigenous cultures.

## Yggdrasill and Its Worlds

The Yggdrasill tree is depicted as a large yew (and/or ash) tree with many branches and roots. Situated upon the roots, trunk and branches are a number of otherworldly locations or 'worlds'. These realms include the lands of Giants (Jotunheim), Light Elves (Ljosalfheim), Dark Elves (Dokkalfheim), Dwarfs (Svartalfheim), Asgard (home of the gods), and of course Helheim, location of the seething cauldron and home of the fearsome Nidhoggr serpent/dragon. The Yggdrasill tree is surrounded by a huge wyrm, the Middle-earth (Old Norse 'Midgard') serpent called Jormungandr (Old Norse 'huge-monster'), the serpent of life and death which (like the alchemical Ouroboros) eats its own tail.

It must be noted that Helheim is not similar in conception to and does not operate in the same way as the Christian Hell. The only connection is that the term Hell may derive from or is a later corruption of the Heathen 'Hel'. While the term Helheim does not exist in the sources (only Hel), this alternative spelling allows us to make a clear distinction between the Heathen and Christian concepts, since there are no elements of damnation or punishment with the realm of Helheim – it is merely the underground world of the dead and location of Hvergelmir, the seething cauldron, a kind of melting pot where humans are aggregated and disintegrated after death and prior to a 're-cycling'.

Haven

Light Elves                           Dwarfs

The Middle Enclosure

Giants                                Dark Elves

Helheim

## Nine Worlds or Seven?

There is much confusion amongst Northern mythologists as to whether there are seven worlds on Yggdrasill, as for the Anglo-Saxons (according to Branston and Linsell), or nine worlds as depicted most famously in the later Icelandic mythology of Snorri's Prose Edda. This is all rather confusing, but fortunately there is a practical solution to this huge conundrum, and we think it is good to clear up any potential confusion as early as possible. As we have said, Yggdrasill is also known as Yggr's eight-legged steed Sleipnir, and this is our clue to solving whether we might best approach Yggdrasill as having seven or nine worlds. But does not an eight-legged horse simply confuse the issue of nine or seven worlds even further? How can a world tree with seven or nine worlds be represented by an eight-legged horse?

Well, let us begin with Tony Linsell's (1994[1992]) suggestion of an Anglo-Saxon (Old English) world tree consisting of seven worlds: Accordingly, Brian Branston argues (1957:169) that the Anglo-Saxons had terms corresponding to Aesir, elves, humans, giants, dwarfs and the dead, but they left no reference to the Vanir or Vanaheim, or the sons of Muspell (from Muspelheim). In contrast, and basing their accounts on later Icelandic sources, Thorsson, Aswynn and other recent authors on runes put forward Yggdrasill trees which include Vanaheim and Muspelheim as discrete worlds, thus arriving at a total of nine worlds. In Norse myth, Vanaheim is said to be the home of the Vaniric goddesses and gods of peace, plenty, and fertility, yet some Vaniric functions seem also to appear among the Aesiric gods and goddesses. Indeed, the mythology informs us that the Aesir and Vanir inter-marry, so it seems the idea of discrete Vaniric and Aesiric worlds is too simplistic. If all of the deities are, by their nature, 'divine' (again, do not associate this with the lofty nature of divinity in Judeo-Christian mythology), what is the need for two separate 'havens'? A further complication when it comes to disentangling (or not) the Aesir from the Vanir, is that the Vanir are described in the myths as Earth deities, in which case should they not be found in Midgard? There is further confusion as well: we have mentioned the worlds of Nifelheim and Muspelheim, the fog/ice and fire homes, respectively. Are these worlds akin to the others, or, if they are simply homes of fire and ice, more appropriately termed elemental forces? If they are included as worlds, this makes the total number of worlds nine, but if excluded, then there are seven worlds! Which is it?

One useful way of solving these cosmological issues is this: in his book 'Norse Myths', Kevin Crossley-Holland suggests the nine worlds are most easily represented as being distributed on three levels (Crossley-Holland 1980: xxii):

1. Asgard, Vanaheim and Alfheim on the top level.
2. Midgard, Jotunheim (Giant world), Nidavellir (given by Crossley-Holland as dwarf home, but there is some confusion among scholars between dark elves and dwarfs) and Svartalfheim (given by Crossley-Holland as Dark Elf home) on the middle level.
3. Helheim and Nifelheim on the bottom level.

Thus, Crossley-Holland excludes Muspelheim from his cosmology. But to take another angle, we could argue that Helheim and Nifelheim are one and the same, and include Muspelheim as the ninth world. In addition to all of this confusion, there is also a mysterious region called Utgard (outland) to try and situate.

Are you horribly confused yet? There is more! But do not lose heart – we are reaching a turning point! As mentioned, there also appears to be confusion between Dark Elves and Dwarfs in the various schemes portrayed by authors to date. Some claim that the word Dwarf derives from 'Svart', (swarthy or dark) hence Svartalfheim or Dark-Elf home. Others argue the term derives from the Sanskrit Dhvaras ('demons'). Finally, according to some authors, the Yggdrasill may be an Ash tree, not Yew. Such confusion can be unsettling, but as we stated at the start of this chapter, the territory of the otherworld is difficult to pin down – indeed it might be argued that since the otherworld lies outside the conventions of 'this' world, so we might expect such confusion as appropriate.

Our responses to these issues are as follows. These suggestions are of course our own and they are not intended to be 'the truth'. They do offer a sensible attempt to resolve the confusion. We suggest that the Dark Elves and the Dwarfs are two independent categories of being. We also think there are seven, rather than nine worlds, but do not exclude Muspelheim and Nifelheim from our cosmology. Furthermore, we can also accommodate and reconcile the numbers seven, eight and nine in one tree. And, we even suggest that Yggdrasill can be both a Yew tree and an Ash tree. How? Well! We demonstrate each of these points in turn by showing how a well-balanced tree can be produced, and how that tree can be represented by an eight legged horse, corresponding to Sleipnir and the literal translation of Yggdrasill as Yggr's Steed (also resonating with other representations of eight, such as the classic eight-spoked Dharma wheel of the Buddhists, or the eight limbs of Yoga).

## Seven Worlds, Nine Realms

Let us first deal with the problem of seven versus nine worlds, and the problem of Muspelheim and Nifelheim. In Norse mythology, the meeting of the polar opposites Muspelheim and Nifelheim – fire and ice – triggers creation (see Chapter 2: Cosmogony). We argue that rather than being worlds, they are just that, polar opposites, cosmic forces, or 'realms', representing a splendid Northwest European equivalent to the Chinese Ying and Yang. In as much, they are perhaps rather unlikely places for a shaman to visit, and our precedent lies in the fact that unlike the other seven worlds they are not visited anywhere in the mythology! It seems to us most apt to avoid concerns over visiting these realms since they are actually the polar opposites which comprise the creation and the known 'world', rather than worlds in themselves. In this sense, it is impossible to visit them! Following this reasoning leaves us with seven worlds, with the two extra realms of Nifelheim and Muspelheim. In this way we can deal with both nine and seven; the best, as it were, of both worlds!

On the matter of dwarfs and the dark and light elves, we choose to differentiate between all three. This is unlike those contemporary Heathens who, following Snorri's descriptions, regard dark elves and dwarfs as the same category of being. One reason for our decision is that the Old English language has a clear differentiation between elf ('aelf/ylf' [male elf] or 'aelfen/elfen' [female elf]) and dwarf ('dweorg'). Furthermore, Snorri – despite being the main recorder of Northern mythology and to whom we accordingly owe a great debt – wrote of these matters rather late in the history of Heathen traditions. It is not unlikely, taking etymology into account, that elsewhere in the Heathen world and well before Snorri's time, such as among the mid-first millennium CE Anglo-Saxons in England, dwarfs and dark elves were actually considered separate classes of being. Only later, perhaps, did the literature relegate them into the same arena, to avoid confusion or in an attempt to 'clear up' any discrepancies.

In this regard, our notion of dark elves accords with
Gundarsson's concept of Dokkalfar, meaning 'mound
elves' (Gundarsson 1990: 245). Thus our dark elves are
associated with burial mounds, shades, barrow wights and
ancestors, and we position dark elf world close to Helheim
and the ancestors (see also the discussion of otherworld
geography in Chapter 6: Ritual). Gundarsson's dark elves
(Svartalfar) are therefore dwarfs in our system. The 'dark'
colour may well refer to the dark nature of their abode –
caves in mountains – rather than their skin colour (Orchard
1997: 20). Gundarsson describes these Svartalfar as sometimes
being 'miserly and grudging' (Gundarsson 1990: 247). This
description is fitting considering that the 'materialist' side of
dwarfish behaviour would promote such attitudes, while the
flip side of the coin leads to altruism and conscience in our
system. Indeed, dwarfs can be wise and inspirational, such
as those who brew the mead of the skalds made from
Kvasir's blood, and who created the marvellous weapons
of the gods.

Snorri's subsuming of two separate beings into one is, in
our view, a later invention. So it is no wonder that the saga
material follows Snorri's precedent with gusto. In these
sources there is an even greater homogenisation of the two
categories. Indeed, we no longer hear of dark elves, but the
dwarfs are very popular. And there are further
'corruptions' since rather than being important and wise
beings, including Nordri, Austri, Sudri and Vestri who
support the sky, they become comical, ugly creatures in the
later sagas. Prior to this negative transformation, and well
before Snorri, it seems that perhaps the dwarfs of the
Anglo-Saxon era were more notable for their wisdom than
their comical appearance. Wisdom is that characteristic

which Simek argues is far more relevant to dwarfs than 'being small and usually ugly' (Simek 1993: 67).

In summary, we argue that before the later literature demoted the dwarfs into rather comical creatures, and subsumed dark elves and dwarfs into the same being, the Anglo-Saxons regarded the two as being very different. Indeed, this would accord with Branston's belief that the Anglo-Saxons acknowledged a slightly different cosmological order than the Old Germans, Scandinavians and Icelanders, in that there were seven rather than nine worlds. The best evidence we have for this is the mention of seven worlds in the Anglo-Saxon Nine Herbs Charm (see, for example, Griffiths 1996: 178-183). While it is difficult to clear up discrepancies like this because the literature is rather fragmentary and contradictory, choices must be made, particularly when producing a practical, workable cosmology. Our choice is to prefer the (probably) earlier Anglo-Saxon precedent to the later Icelandic. This resolves any issues over the differences (or not) between dark elves and dwarfs, and over nine worlds versus seven. With this problem addressed, what next of the Vanir and Vanaheim?

According to the Nordic sources the Vanir, in contrast to the Aesiric sky gods, are Earth-based deities – of nature, fecundity and earth-magic. As ever, things are not purely binary, since, as we have said the Vanir and Aesir inter-marry. All this makes it rather difficult (and impractical) to try and locate Vanaheim, the home of the Vanir, on Yggdrasill. Do they have a home of their own, or are they most comfortable in Midgard as earth-focused deities? Then again, since they marry with the Aesir, should the rightful place of the Vanir deities be Asgard? Branston suggests the Anglo-Saxons had no concept of Vanaheim, and Simek states that 'Snorri unquestionably invented Vanaheim as a counterpart to Asgard' (Simek 1993: 350). It seems to us most likely that the Vanir, as Earth deities, must be acknowledged to be a part of the earth, though they, like all the beings of all the worlds, may make journeys into other realms. So, we firmly identify the Vanir as being in Midgard.

## Yggdrasill as an Eight Legged Horse

Imagine next, if you will (and see diagram, below), Yggdrasill with six of its seven worlds depicted as enclosures, discs, or realms, with Middle Earth shown as a disc with a horizontal line passing through it. This line can be said to pass from east to west (or north to south since this is the ephemeral and ambiguous otherworld!) so that the two polarised directions at either extreme could represent Muspelheim and Nifelheim, and outside Midgard (also known in Old Norse as Innangard) as 'Utgard' or 'the outland'. Turning full circle, west becomes east, represented by the serpent encircling Middle Earth, with its tail in its mouth – Jormungandr, the Midgard serpent. The image of the Middle Earth serpent can be extremely useful in dealing with the mental image of an infinite cosmos. Our minds may balk at such a concept, perhaps because it tends to make us feel so insignificant. The Middle Earth serpent conceptualises cyclic-return, circularity, repetition, containment, ecological biosis/symbiosis, and how a world, though infinite, can be conceived of as a cycle or replication of itself.

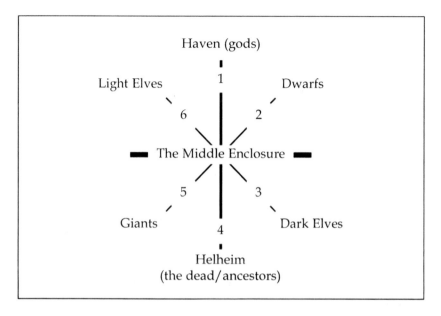

If we go on to count the directions on the tree-scheme given in the diagram above, they would match the compass points, that is, the eight directions of north, northeast, east, southeast, south, southwest, west and northwest. This is how our seven-world, nine-realm Yggdrasill also encompasses Sleipnir, the eight-legged steed of Woden – represented here by the spider-like branches of the sacred Yew tree, ever-green with roots in Helheim and branches in the Haven. The eight legs of Sleipnir can also be seen in the paths between the worlds. They extend 1) from Midgard to Asgard, 2) to Light Elf world, 3) to Dwarf World, 4) to Giant World, 5) to Dark Elf world, 6) to Helheim, and in both directions (7&8) along the plain/plane of Midgard.

Inadvertently here, we arrive at another discrepancy, often discussed but not resolved by other scholars of these mysteries: that is, whether Yggdrasill should be represented by a Yew tree or an Ash tree. The Icelandic Elder Edda (written down by Snorri) explicitly talks about an Ash tree, but it also refers to the world tree as 'evergreen' or 'needle-ash', which makes it sound more like a Yew. And, the Anglo-Saxon sacred tree was almost certainly a Yew rather than an ash (see discussions by Linsell and Branston) – yet both trees appear as major components in the Anglo-Saxon rune poem (alongside thorn, birch and oak)! As our discussion is dealing with the mythological 'symbol' of a tree, however, indeed the tree of all trees, we have no hesitation whatsoever of attributing both Yew and Ash!

Significantly, unlike the Yew tree, the Ash grows tall and straight. We argue this represents the Irminsul pillar, the 'gigantic pillar' or 'pole' (Simek 1993:175), comprising the worlds of Helheim, Middle Earth, and Haven. Ash wood was traditionally used to make spear shafts because it grows straight and copes well with impact – and it is associated with Woden's spear Gungnir (see the Anglo-Saxon rune poem and Chapter 2: Cosmogony). The Yew tree, on the other hand, with its masses of tangled, twisted roots and its numerous branches, represents the entire Yggdrasill tree with its many windy paths to the seven worlds. Thus, the problem of Yggdrasill being yew or ash is resolved – it can be both at the same time!

## The Six Paths to/from Middle Earth

Thus far in our cosmology, we have seven worlds with two realms, which adds up to nine, and eight 'spokes' on the tree. Taking Middle Earth as the centre of the tree, we can see that there are six paths which can initially be taken away from Middle Earth, or back to it, on any shamanic journey. To travel, for instance, from Light Elf world to Dark Elf world one would pass through Middle Earth. Similarly we can see that Middle Earth is between Asgard and Helheim. There are therefore six main paths on the tree (for kennings on this number, see rune six, Ken, of the cosmogony), as well as seven worlds, eight spokes, and nine realms.

The six worlds emanating from the central point of Midgard can also be viewed as points on the compass. Indeed, the tradition of midnight being the 'witching hour' is not without foundation. In the Northern hemisphere (outside the arctic circle) at midnight the sun is invisible, being at due south, or Helheim – and Helheim is an appropriate location for 'witchy' activities. At midday (noon), the sun is at its most visible, being at due north, The Haven. Interestingly, north is the sacred direction in Heathenry, and the direction at which a shrine should be placed – directed towards the gods. In this scheme Middle Earth remains constant. From this plan of the directions and positions of the sun, it can be surmised that there are effective times to invoke deities, or to visit the various worlds. This is based on the position of the sun, the time of day (connected to the circadian rhythms, and the patterns and rhythms reflected in the human physical economy), and in a wider time frame according to the movement of the planet(s). Facing the right direction at the appropriate time may therefore increase the efficiency of a rite. The extent to which you go into detail is left up to your own aims and objectives!

A plan of the world tree Yggdrasill according to Galdrbok, with its six paths, seven worlds and eight directions, is given on page 177. The two realms (making nine in total) of Muspelheim and Nifelheim can be positioned at the opposite poles of Midgard.

## The Seven Worlds and Altered Consciousness

We next present some practical and working suggestions for visiting the seven worlds. We also identify useful and meaningful reasons for doing so. Furthermore, we suggest clear definitions of the beings which inhabit these worlds and the states of consciousness they represent.

Simply put, the gods live in the Haven (Asgard), the light elves in Light Elf Home (Ljosalfheim), the Dwarfs in Dwarf World (Svartalfheim), Humans (and Land Wights and Vanir) in Middle Earth (Midgard), Giants in Giant Home (Jotunheim), Dark Elves in Dark Elf Home (Dokkalfheim), and the Dead or ancestors in Helheim (Hel). So, each world is home to a type of being, and we suggest that among other qualities each being represents a specific type of consciousness (see also Chapter 4: Trance). Our kennings on such matters may be different to other writers on Heathenry, but do not forget that there are many ways of reaching the same goal. We do not intend to pigeon-hole or dogmatise what each world is, or how each being in each world is constituted, but encourage you to reach your own kennings in these matters.

At this point in your reading and practicing of Galdrbok, it is important to familiarise yourself with the cosmology and beings in the worlds (including yourself!). Just as you did for the cosmogony, use the runes and scrying to internalise the cosmology, to make it part of your vision or worldview. For example, you might use the stone to descry the worlds. Sit in Midgard, the realm of the 'ordinary', and from this vantage point use the crystal to look from this world into the other worlds. You may be able to 'see' into giant land, for example, a realm of vast mountains and chaotic forces. You may also directly engage with giant beings – as indeed you should also with all the beings in the worlds. For inspiration regarding Jotunheim, read such parts of the Poetic Edda as Vafthrudnir's Sayings (Vafthrudnismal, see Larrington 1996: 39-49) and Hymir's Poem (Hymiskvida, see Larrington 1996: 78-83). And in such scrying you may also see and reflect on the 'giant' parts of yourself (as described in the section on giants, below).

The idea of internalising the cosmology is once again to enter into the spirit of the thing and not get bogged down with intellectual considerations. Too much time can be spent on trying to intellectually work out the specific details of what a dwarf 'is', for example; how old it is, how it walks and talks, what it is wearing, and so on. To find out, go to the world and engage with its beings! Specific details do emerge with time, practice and patience. But if you decide to wait until you have mastered such details before practising, you never will practice because you can only master such things through experience, and you can only gain experience by practising!

## The Haven, Aesir Deities and Aesiric Trance

The Haven is the home of the Aesir (and some Vanir gods and goddesses) who have 'deity' status, but they are also like us by virtue of their human-like exploits or 'personality complexes' (to use the psychological jargon). The Haven is at the top of the tree and it is significant that tree-sap rises. The sap in esoteric terms is the 'Ond' or life force in us all, situated or stored at the base of the spine. In cosmogonical terms, Ond is given to us by Woden (see rune 7: Gebo, in the cosmogony). And in cosmological terms, this sap/Ond is situated within the seething cauldron Hvergelmir, located in Helheim. These Northern themes are reflected in the Kundalini serpent, of Tantric Yoga, which is situated at the base of the spine, and raised in order to achieve 'bliss'. A further comparison is the 'Uachit' serpent of Khemitic (Egyptian) Hermetica. These consistencies across cultures attest not only to the neurobiological basis of some spiritual practices, but also to the importance of applying the human body in trance practices for spiritual work.

Gaining an experience of Aesiric consciousness involves raising the sap up the tree (body), unhindered, by accessing Aesiric conscious states. In states of altered consciousness, practitioners may control and guide the Ond so that shamanic ecstasy can be attained. The haven is characterised by a state of absolute freedom: the 'bliss' of Yoga, the Buddhist Nirvana, the Taoist's Tao – or 'shamanic ecstasy' (see also comments on the Grave rune in the chapter on Cosmogony). Indeed, the description of '!kia' among San (Bushman) shamans in Southern Africa, resonates with the shamanic ecstasy we describe – and, interestingly, Austin Osman Spare uses the term 'Kia' in a similar way in his system of atavistic resurgence, to refer to 'the Atmospheric I', 'Cosmic Spirit/Consciousness', or 'pure/preconceptual energy' (see Grant 2003).

The Haven is reached by crossing a bridge named Bilrost, the 'fleetingly glimpsed rainbow'. Bilrost (not Bifrost – see Simek 1993: 36) is etymologically related to the Old Norse 'bil' – moment, or weak point. The Bilrost is therefore that instant moment when, beyond time and space, the fleeting moments of shamanic ecstasy are experienced. This is the altered state of consciousness we call Aesiric trance or waking trance. As such it is different from deity possession (more on this below and in Chapter 4: Trance).

## Helheim, Ancestors and Disiric Trance

Helheim is a region which contains the Nidhoggr ('the one striking full of hatred', Simek 1993: 231), the 'wyrm' who regenerates that which has become 'inert' (the dead). Helheim is the polar opposite to the Haven. It is also the region of Hvergelmir, the 'seething cauldron', a melting pot

and the source of raw Ond, the vital animating power of all
things. Ond is chaotic and powerful, residing as it does in
Helheim, and as such must be dealt with or controlled very
carefully. But it is also subject to control, the guidance of
Aesiric consciousness at the polar opposite of the Haven.
As such, Ond can be encouraged to rise, and guided as it
does so. Helheim is the region of primary power, inhabited
by the dead and some Disir (related to Valkyries, who
choose the slain). Helheim is the region of dispersion,
where the husks and shells (shades) of the dead exist.
It is also a place with which the Heathen shaman, in the
role of necromancer (speaker with the dead), becomes
intimately familiar.

A great deal has been written about 'trafficking with the
dead', most of it in fiction. Unfortunately, the term
'necromancy' is often viewed negatively and is typically
depicted (often in lurid detail) as involving the exhumation
of human remains, preferably from a spooky old gothic
graveyard, and subjecting them to diabolical rites – none of
which would be complete without the obligatory young
virgin to sacrifice! Such imagery seems to be part of the
popular and misguided film-inspired baggage connected
with rites involving 'the dead' and the 'occult' in general
(occult simply means 'hidden' rather than 'evil' or other
such nonsense). In direct contrast, indigenous shamanic
practices involving communication with the dead fulfil
important social and spiritual functions. Among the Sora
people in India, for instance (see Vitebsky 1995),
communicating with deceased relatives allows the living
and the dead to resolve their differences. The dead may
then, we suggest, be 'free' to move on, while the living too
are 'free' to get on with their lives.

In the West, we tend not to venerate ancestors; often, living relatives are at best only 'tolerated'. After a lifetime of hard work, all our grandparents are afforded in remembrance is a photograph or two in an album which only comes out during infrequent, self-indulgent nostalgic reveries. Besides these issues, the Modern notion of 'progress' mistakenly considers our remote ancestors to be 'primitive' and our more recent ancestors to be ill informed, over religious, superstitious, or just plain old fashioned. No wonder ancestor communication is not on the agenda of the major Western religions – a trend we contest.

'Raising the dead' means to contact 'that which was' (temporally speaking) in order to obtain otherwise unobtainable information. Or, in other cultures, it can mean to admonish, placate, or even drive away the dead. Modern Westerners may find it difficult to grapple with who or what 'the dead' are, in a largely atheistic, secular society. Some contemporary Heathens engage in a shamanistic practice called Oracular Seidr which undertakes communication with the dead, enabling a dialogue with the dead in a way which is much like indigenous shamanistic practices (see, for example, Blain 2002, Wallis 2003, and discussion of oracular Seidr in Chapter 4). We discuss a different Heathen practice involving communication with the dead, here.

The dead in Helheim are not necessarily 'evil' in the Christian sense of the word. And by the same measure they are not intrinsically 'good' either. Such dualisms are of little use in Helheim. The dead are merely reflections or shadows of those who were once living, breathing human beings. It is difficult to speculate much further. Perhaps the condition of some of the dead reflects unfulfilled human desire, expectation, disappointment, instincts, and drives. Perhaps other dead humans also need to overcome traumas experienced in life or at the moment of death. Perhaps the condition of the dead reflects that which they were in life – indeed, their 'characters' can be pressed, examined or otherwise engaged with so as to apply themselves to new problems. They can even advise on problems which they never faced whilst alive! In this sense one can usefully seek advice from the dead – Helheim holds the records, eternally.

The Northern myths inform us that certain members of the Aesir undertake travel to Helheim. In Balder's dreams (Baldrs draumar in the Poetic Edda: see Larrington 1996: 243-245), the Aesir send Woden to Helheim to seek an explanation for Balder's disturbing dreams. Woden halts at the edge of Helheim's kingdom. Using his skills as a shaman, he awakens a dead prophetess from her grave. This grave is probably a burial mound, since standing-proud it would attract the attention of the rain and snow she complains about in verse five: 'I was snowed upon, I was rained upon, dew fell on me' (Larrington 1996: 243). There is a further link here, to Woden's classic association with burial mounds and the practice of Utiseta ('sitting out', often on such mounds: see Chapter 6: Ritual). Common sense suggests to us that the prophetess in the grave is none other than the seeress from the Voluspa, who may herself be Heidr (linked to the shamanistic deity Freyja), and it is no coincidence that Woden, in his capacity as a shaman, undertakes the task of raising her.

In the case of communicating with (close) genetic relatives, certain 'drives' might well be similar to one's own, so caution is definitely in order: it might be difficult to communicate with an ancestor to deal with your own or someone else's issues when they may be rather similar to your own. So, a problem, which might emerge in ancestor communication, is that you may experience pain when a particular relative is considered. This is part and parcel of the deal. The important point is that not only can we communicate with the dead, but we can also learn from the dead and their experiences. These experiences are, after all, some of the 'vital principles' or 'seed experiences' of many humans, some of the essences and drives of those who once strove to be human and who may strive to be so again. After all, the dead remain our ancestors, our predecessors. Although we may resemble our parents and relatives in the ways we look, behave, and so on, we remain unique individuals, capable of reconciling hereditary and non-hereditary limitations and (personality) conditions. This is the crux of it – to transcend the hang-ups in our personal and cultural baggage. Nothing on the tree is wasted; all is re-cycled and as such rises like sap from the seething cauldron (Hvergelmir) at the roots of Yggdrasill.

The proper approach to ancestor communication is not connected with one's personal difficulties with a parent, aunt, uncle or whomever. In the widest possible sense, it is through one's ancestral line that one is connected to the primary, cosmogonical time, and ultimately to the first division of cells, and thus to the primal giant Ymir. This 'genetic link' is in no way a racial or ethnic thing, for such notions all too easily fall foul of right wing politics, racism and ideas of 'folk'. We speak in the broadest sense of the link that every human being has with each other. But this link does also refer to specific ancestors, particularly those within the landscape you occupy. If required, you will have to decide yourself on how to deal with the issue of (even inadvertently) interacting with other indigenous people's ancestors in 'postcolonial' lands.

There is another very important role to the function of Helheim, which, far from making it a place to be shunned, makes it a place of vital significance, to be engaged with regularly. Helheim, or the Hall of Death or waiting, has to be experienced, has to be passed through by the questing Heathen shaman, for whom it is vital to 'die' to this world in the shamanic death of entering trance. The act of transcending one's natal personality and experiencing 'death in life' is central to the Heathen mysteries and to the shamanic experience of sacrificing 'self to self' on Yggdrasill. This process requires that we probe who and what we are, beyond name, age, likes and dislikes, comforts or pains. This is the supreme sacrifice, willingly relinquishing the ego-person, the part which dies anyway, to discover and experience 'a good death'. This is the 'vital self made new': freed from the bonds of personhood, the new you, in escaping the comfortable 'prison of slavery' constructed by the ego, can experience ecstasy, can shape-shift and travel in many guises. You can travel throughout the realms of Yggdrasill of which nine (the key number concerning the Yggdrasill tree) becomes a mathematical convenience: into timeless infinity the winner of Heathen wisdom may go!

## Miðgarð, Land Wights and Vaniric Trance

To enter the realm of no-ego, the Seidrmadr becomes accomplished at altering consciousness. Altered states facilitate a radical and dissonant reordering of the senses (known as synaesthesia) and an experiencing of the polar opposites of Helheim (the 'death' of Disiric trance) and Haven (the 'fleeting' rainbow Bifrost/Bilrost of Aesiric trance). Seeking a glimpse of the fittingly named Bifrost/Bilrost, to let alone cross that 'swaying road to [haven]' (Simek 1993: 36), is no easy task. Fortunately, Vaniric trance lets us 'see' into this world, indeed all worlds – and it is Vaniric trance which is induced when scrying, a basic practice introduced at the start of Galdrbok.

A crystal ball (and rune casting) is very useful in the production of the required 'open' mediumistic trance associated with Vaniric trance. Simply put, Aesiric trance provides access to the Haven, but memory of the visit and how much one can take away is limited by one's 'magical memory'. By this is meant how well all the other elements of the tree are integrated to produce not only a very familiar map of the otherworld, but also the power of 'in-sight'. This is the in-sight of the sort which enables us to see within, to truly see with Woden's 'Eye', the eye he sacrificed at Mimir's well in order to gain esoteric wisdom.

Middle Earth, we argue, is the home of the Vanir, thereby resolving the issues of 'where' it is – as discussed in greater detail above. It has been claimed that the Vanir represent

an ancient clan of female-centred (matrifocal) earth-loving
pacifists, or the non Indo-European cultures of pre-bronze
age 'old Europe'. This claim, primarily by the
archaeologist Marija Gimbutas and others since (e.g.
Gimbutas 1974; Eisler 1987; Gimbutas & Robbins Dexter
1999), is much challenged by current archaeologists since it
is a rather sweeping generalisation, to say the least,
ignoring the diversity of culture and gender perceptions
cross-culturally, and imposing our own heavily political
and binary gender divisions onto the past. Gimbutas and
others tend to conflate the anthropological terms
matrifocal, matrilineal and matriarchal, which do not all
mean the same thing. While inheritance along the female
line suggests some of our Heathen ancestors were
matrilineal, this does not mean they were matrifocal. Such
confusion over terminology exemplifies how such authors
mistakenly over-generalise and universalise the past.
Besides this, there is the issue that women and men were
conceived of differently in past cultures, as they are in
many contemporary indigenous communities – again, a
point we marked earlier.

Hand-in-hand with such problematic interpretations of
the Vanir as matrifocal, peaceful deities, has been the
suggestion that the Aesir are simply 'war gods'. Gimbutas
argues that during or just before the Bronze Age, nomadic
patriarchal warriors who worshipped male sky gods
swept down from the Russian Steppes and conquered
the indigenous matrifocal cultures they came across.
Accounts of a war between the Aesir and the Vanir appear
in both the poetic and prose Eddas, and according to
Gimbutas these accounts may be based on historical facts;
hence the hybridisation of cultures and mythologies.

Avoiding Gimbutas' contentious and sexist narrative of the past, and dogmatic imposition of historical fact onto myth, it seems the relevant cosmological teaching is that some of the (apparently earthbound) Vanir are able to travel to and indeed live in Asgard as partners or hostages of the Aesir (and vice versa). This is enabled through the machinations of the less than perfect Aesiric gods who blunder their way through several episodes of conflict, including warfare, bargain-making, hostage-taking and oath-breaking.

Mythologically speaking, the (Aesiric) Skyfather (sometimes named Woden, sometimes Tiw or Thunor) is consort to the (Vaniric) Earthmother (sometimes named Nerthus) – who was also named 'Erce' in Old English, found as 'erce, erce, eorthen mothor' in the Land Ceremonies Charm (see, for example, Griffiths 1996: 176). In this respect we think the basic categories of Aesir and Vanir are useful as a representation of the joining of gods and people. The 'Gods' and 'Goddesses' can, therefore, be revered as (divine) ancestors (as the king-lists demonstrate among our ancestors). This provides us with a useful working model for the Earthmother(s) (below, of the earth) and Skyfather(s) (above, of the sky). Of course, being above or below does not make either family of deities any 'better' than or more superior to another (though of course the deities in question might argue otherwise!). They are all deities and have different qualities – ask them, and you'll see! But also, we reiterate again that the Yggdrasill 'map' we outline is merely an outline. It does not dogmatically consign the Vanir to Midgard and the Aesir to Asgard since the Aesir and Vanir intermarry and migrate to each other's worlds, and all the beings travel all the worlds – especially

Woden. So, the otherworld is transient and our map must be flexible. How else could Helheim be down and to the north? How else could the Vanir be in Vanaheim, but also be Earth deities, but also in some instances be married to and living with the Aesir?

Middle Earth is the mid-point where all the worlds meet. In Middle Earth, (Vaniric) humans have choice – the humanist's concept of free will – but are limited by 'conditions', from the sociological and political, to the genetic, and so on. Humans have the ability through their dual consciousness/reflective action to reflect on the worlds, including Haven and Helheim. The Vanir can also, by choice, journey to the Haven. Middle Earth consciousness (that is, waking consciousness, not Vaniric trance) is the type of consciousness demonstrated by everyday people. It is the ordinary mind of all of us when we are late for work, bored, happy, scared, tired, hungry, in love, and generally pre-occupied with everyday living.

Midgard consciousness is not restricted to humans, however. Animist Heathens understand that all beings have consciousness of some sort, stones and trees included, and we respect the beings we share Middle Earth with. The Heathen shaman in Middle Earth, then, uses Vaniric trance to engage with these beings, as 'wights', shamanic helpers or 'spirits' (though not all are helpful – note the barrow wights in Tolkien's mythos), in a living landscape. In your own practice, you may find that there are particularly 'powerful' helpers in Midgard, from wolves and ravens to hedgehogs and slugs. You may first recognise these beings as 'helpers' in a variety of ways: they may visit you in dreams, they may present themselves to you in unusual ways in the 'ordinary world', or you might journey into Yggdrasil with the explicit intention of finding a helper. Observing and studying these beings, in their 'wild' environment wherever possible, is important. Engaging with them in altered consciousness is vital in order to be able to 'speak' with them.

When dealing with plants, especially when wishing to use parts of their 'bodies' (leaves, roots, branches, seeds, flowers, etc) for incense, talismans or other magical work, it is important to establish a reciprocal relationship – as we discussed when making your own wooden rune set (should you choose to use wood, that is). Some plants are, in the lore, especially powerful and extra caution is required – in the 'Way of Wyrd', Brian Bates details how an Anglo-Saxon shaman carefully 'hunts' various plants so as to negotiate their 'help'. The Anglo-Saxon 'Nine Herbs Charm' (see Pollington 2000), which also mentions Woden, lists important herbs that the Heathen shaman might usefully associate with the nine realms of Yggdrasill. In this poem each of the herbs is addressed personally, returning us once again to the theme of animism.

## The Skyfather(s) - Earthmother(s) Conundrum

The following scheme further interprets the 'Skyfather(s)'-'Earthmother(s)' cosmology, drawing on our previous discussion of cosmogony and cosmology. It presents creation as a kind of biotic (cellular) division, emphasising, accentuating and disrupting (more Wodenic paradoxes!) our contemporary Western polar sex-gender distinctions.

Tuisco, the Mythical ancestor to (all) the Germanic peoples is related to Ymir the hermaphrodite giant,

Tuisto meaning 'hermaphrodite' but perhaps also 'two' (thus phonetically related to the Anglo-Saxon 'Tiw' as in 'Tuesday', the second day of the week). This is Tuisto as the Allfather-Allmother. The term 'Tivar' was also used to refer to the 'plurality of gods', stemming from the one. Tuisco is ambisexual, s/he then polarises into Tiwaz, the generic Germanic version of the Old Norse Tyr and Anglo-Saxon Tiw. This is the Skyfather god of war who presides over the 'Thing' (legal meeting). Tuisto also polarises into Nerthus, the Earthmother who (in some guises) comprises the goddess of the sea, the primal womb-like waters. Thus we have in result, the Aesir (sky gods and goddesses), and the Vanir (earth goddesses and gods). While the former might be argued to be 'male dominated' and the latter 'female dominated', it is also clear that the diversity of the deities disrupts these classifications.

The Aesir and the Vanir, then, can be usefully approached as 'intermediaries' between Haven and Midgard, who jointly administer the worlds as intermediaries (a role fulfilled by the Deva or Angels in other traditions). As such, this classification might make it easier for us to engage with them, since these intermediaries are not the prime cause of creation/cosmogony, but are some of its effects and machinations. There is little need for speculation about an 'absolute creator' in the Northern traditions. Rather than waste valuable time intellectually pontificating about the 'creator', we can just get on with ritualising – including invoking the gods and goddesses!

Having now discussed the Irminsul Pillar of Haven, Midgard and Helheim, it is time to explore the other beings of Yggdrasill: Dark Elves, Giants, Dwarfs, and Light Elves. We suggest how these beings are constituted for the Heathen Runester and how they are engaged with when raising Ond in shamanic practice. Notice that each world and its inhabitants are entities in their own right – 'spirits' which can be encountered – but that on an easy-to-engage-with level, they might also represent aspects of human psychology. The giants, for example, may in psychological terms represent the 'subconscious' while the dark elves represent the 'unconscious'.

Each world and its inhabitants are not inherently 'good' (white) or 'bad' (black), but live 'grey' lives, as do we – they have both positive and negative elements. A giant can be both unpredictable and chaotic, and wise. And a dark elf can be constrained by drives and instincts but also possesses the means to be free from them. Simply being 'lower' on the tree than giants does not indicate that

dark elves are less important. As we have stated, the
otherworld, which Yggdrasill represents (and 'is'), is in
this sense beyond measure. All beings in all worlds have
positive and negative aspects – there is no rigid 'good'
and 'evil' in Runecraft, for what may be 'good' for a giant
may have unfortunate consequences for a god (and vice
versa, for example Thunor's giant crushing)! Heathen
shamans must traverse all the worlds in order to gain
shamanic wisdom and to 'harmonise' the parts of
themselves (and others) which go to make up their being
(see Chapter 7) by working with Ond. Thus, engaging
with the beings and the worlds may be viewed as a
psychological exercise, a means of crafting Ond, an
inducing of consciousness-altering experiences, and
literally 'talking' with 'spirits' (of elves, dwarfs, etc). How
you interpret your experience depends on your point of
view (discourse).

## Dokkalfheim - Dark Elf World

The Dark Elves, or Dokkalfar, are associated with burial
mounds, barrow wights and ancestors. Their 'dark' nature
is not 'evil', but derives from the way in which Dark Elf
World is situated close to Helheim and communes directly
with it. In some ways, Dokkalfheim shares some of
Helheim's characteristics: it is a 'dark' and 'shady' realm,
the mounds are those of ancestors and also resident in this
world are some Disiric entities which do not reside in
Helheim. Some of these are encountered in the form of the
famous Valkyries – these are not the buxom beer-serving
wenches who wait on tables in the Valhalla of later Icelandic
mythology! The Valkyries are 'those who choose the slain'
and are led by Woden, who simultaneously opens the way
to shamanic travel (up the tree) and guides the souls of the

dead to the nearby Helheim (down the tree) during the wild hunt, passing through Dokkalfheim as they do.

In terms of the raising of Ond, the Ond residing in Helheim has at this point risen to a free and unpredictable state. The Ond in Dokkalfheim can be used to fire up and empower yourself and others (in healing). It can also be used to face the shadows or 'shades' inside yourself (and others). This world and its associated state of consciousness can help to free one's self from artificial and unrealistic repressions, hang ups, and emotional and intellectual wants, thereby putting us back in touch with our spiritual direction.

The unpredictable and 'free' state of the Ond in Dokkalfheim means that this world may also be associated with visceral appetites and instinct. It is therefore a suitable location for the practice of some forms of magic, particularly 'dark' magic (the term 'elf-shot' comes to mind), and some forms of sex magic. Magic can be effectively practiced here because the 'ego' or 'self' can be 'left behind' in Midgard so that the 'subconscious' can work actively without restriction. But remember that it is easy to get beguiled by the dark elves and to disrupt social convention to damaging extremes. Be too unpredictable, create your own ethics (in spite of everyone else), and you too may not be able to exist in Midgard.

There exists a tremendous sense of freedom among the mounds of the Dark Elves, resonating with the feelings of freedom we might associate with wild animals and children. Animal spirit-helpers can run, fly, jump, swim, mate, and perform a whole host of other physical activities in the freedoms of Dokkalfheim. Given the associations, we link wolves and ravens, Woden's animal helpers, with this dark realm. Journey with your own helpers to this world and see for yourself.

## Jotunheim - Giant World

Situated in the lower half of the tree, Jotunheim, the land of the giants, is linked to Midgard and Dokkalfheim. Giants are thus linked to the middle enclosure of land wights and the lower world of ancestors. There are four types of giants which the Heathen Runester may have to deal with: the Etins or Wisdom Giants, the Risar or Mountain Giants, the Thurses or uncontrollable 'nature', and the more general Troll. All are subsumed under the title 'Etin-kind' (see Our Troth online, Chapter XXIV).

Thus, Runic shamans may have to journey to Jotunheim in order to come to terms with their own or someone else's uncontrollable Ond, or to deal with the vast natural forces which create havoc in Midgard: the Thurses. Giants are synonymous with 'sheer power' – a power which can be manipulated in the process of magic (see Chapter 7).

Specific immense spirits of nature (and here Etin-kind begins to cross over with other land wights) may need to be contacted to gain power and strength, such as the Risar or the more general Trolls.

The world of giants is also an ancestral world. Aesiric genealogies in Northern mythology seem to have an intimate association or connection with the Giants. For example, Thunor's name refers to giants ('Thurs' meaning giant), despite his being their arch-enemy. Woden was also born from a giant and indeed the ancestor of us all is the giant Ymir.

Contrary to (some) popular opinion, giants do not necessarily lack intellect. The Eddic sources repeatedly refer to wise giants such as Mimir (perhaps meaning 'memory' [Stone 1989: 11]), Vafthrudnir and Hyndla. In Ynglinga saga, Woden consults the preserved, severed head of the giant Mimir for divination (Ynglinga saga 4). Note also that Woden sacrifices one eye to gain wisdom from Mimir's well. A visit to Jotunheim might, then, involve the quest for wisdom among the Etins. But as the tales about giants attest, intellect is a creator as well as a solver of problems.

The simplest classification of Jotunheim and its Etins is that they dwell in Utgard, the Outlands where humans cannot exist (hence the Wodenic shaman can only go there in spirit form), and they symbolise all those things over which you have no control, be it psychological states or natural forces. Giants can therefore be used for positive ends in the taming of such forces. They are also balancing forces, keeping the gods in check just as Thunor keeps them under control. Without giants in the world(s), the balance of existence would be disrupted. Giants are well known for being manipulative and unruly. The world of the giants is characterised by a state of consciousness which is filled with the force of Ond but cannot translate it holistically so that it is prone to becoming disruptive.

Giants are not inherently malignant beings – no more so than deities are inherently 'good' – it is just that part of their nature is uncontrollable or unruly. Just as human action can be 'grey', rather than black ('bad') and white ('good'), so all the beings in all the worlds have their positive and negative points. In many respects, giants are across the corridor from dwarfs – both have considerable power, and in the Eddas, the Aesiric Gods seem to love pitting their wits against them both.

## Svartalfheim - Dwarf World

The Dwarf World is the world of materialism and making, situated above Midgard in the upper half of the tree – synonymous with caverns and mountains. By consciously utilising resources, Dwarfs make utility objects/items. Interestingly, they make items for the Aesir (Freyja's necklace Brisingamen and Thunor's hammer Mjollnir, for example), but it is significant that Dwarfs do not use such items themselves. The utility thinker has no use for a crystal ball, rune set, or rune-carved dagger or Gandr (wand) except as an ornament or trade item. Dwarfs are prone to greed and the love of wealth for its own sake.

Yet, the level of the dwarfs, like those 'below', is not to be disparaged in favour of 'higher realms' (since, as we have said, 'up' and 'down' are erroneous terms in the otherworld) but integrated. This is accomplished by utilising the skills of the Dwarf smiths, if they are willing, to smith the Ond being raised up the tree. Thus Dwarfs are a necessary element of the tree since it is their skill that can craft you towards shamanic ecstasy. There is a close association between smithing and shamanism in many cultures: in the Old North 'Wayland the Smith', while 'laughing', 'rose in the air' (Volundarkvida [Larrington 1996:108):

> [M]etal-making and magic-making can easily go together as, for example, in the story of Wayland the Smith (also Volundr, Wieland)… a cunning swordsmith – who is able to fly with wings he has made himself (although this motif is often referred back to the Daedelus myth, it is better connected to visual narratives in northern metal iconologies depicting shamanistic flight) (Budd & Taylor 1995:139).

Dwarf world is characterised by a state of consciousness which generally believes only in the here and now, and utility functions (particularly the gold-encrusted and ornate). Dwarfs (like all inhabitants of all worlds) do have a sensuous nature however, which is part of their natural urge towards ecstatic wisdom. For example, both Dwarfs and Giants desire to kidnap Frigg/Freyja.

## Ljosalfheim - Light Elf World

The Light Elves, like the Dwarfs, are makers of things, yet these do not necessarily serve utility purposes, nor are they for self-glorification or for fiscal return. The Light Elf World is in some ways associated with altruism and conscience, which manifest in the ability to exercise free will even at the expense of Dark Elf, Giant and Dwarf instincts, which are themselves not to be scorned but smithed and integrated. The Heathen shaman strives to be 'whole', to have balanced the worlds so that corporeal existence is celebrated.

But there are dark sides to all the worlds. In the sources, the light elves are also known for their trickery. And, a major risk of light elf world is to 'have one's head in the clouds'. To be with the light elves all the time is incompatible with everyday thought and action. This negative aspect of light elf world compares with the negative part of the dark elves. Too much dark elf Ond and you can teeter on the abyss of insanity with an inability to live a 'normal life' with the rest of your human community. And too much light elf Ond without the preparatory experience provided by previous initiatory work can bring misguided beliefs of spiritual ability and attainment which verge on ego-emphasis rather than ego-transcendence. The light elves have a 'dark' side and dealing with them can be just as treacherous as dealing with the dark elves!

## Further Significances

Heathen shamanic practice consists of exploring (getting to know) the landscape of the worlds and establishing allies among the beings within them. Regarding Ond, the aim is to waken the Ond in Helheim through Disiric trances and to smith this Ond towards shamanic ecstasy as represented by Asgard. Psychologically, it might be said that each world is a 'part of our consciousness' so that the task is to steer consciousness towards a willed result or wholeness. Of course, the most direct route to ecstatic states is via the Irminsul Pillar, a direct route suggested by some major world religions. This approach caters for the simplistic 'religious' process in many sects of Christianity, as well as the swift but treacherous 'left hand path' of Tantric Yoga and Kundalini Yoga, and the mystical route of Buddhism. But these paths are only suitable for some people.

We modern Westerners tend to be people who want to be able to 'get out there' and 'do something'. Such hastiness may not always be the best plan, but the initiatory, shamanic 'route' supplied by Galdrbok is suitable for the active seeker of wisdom. Rather than following the direction of the pillar then, the Heathen Runester travels the whole tree. This involves traversing Thunor's lightning bolt, which plummets from Haven to Helheim in the creation of the worlds; and back again, from Helheim to Haven, as the unfolding of shamanic, ecstatic consciousness. A diagonal, zigzag, lightning-bolt-shaped line is thus formed, from Asgard to Light Elves, to Dwarfs, to Midgard, to Giants, to Dark Elves, and to Helheim. By way of comparison, this lightning bolt resonates in various ways with the lightning flash of the Qabalah, the raising of the Kundalini serpent in Tantric Yoga, the Khemitic 'Uachit' serpent, as well as descriptions of '!kia' among San (Bushman) shamans. In the Heathen traditions, the lightning strike is also the ejaculatory impregnation of the Earthmother by the Skyfather.

A summary of the cosmology of Yggdrasill, its worlds, beings, states of consciousness and the raising and smithing of Ond, concludes this chapter. In addition to a summary of the cosmological lore we have presented, we also offer correspondences between each world and an associated colour and metal – for instance, red and bronze for Svartalfheim. You might elucidate further associations yourself, from suitable plants to specific planets. In all, this lore-hoard for each world has practical applications when engaging with the seven worlds of Yggdrasill. These connections are linked to the seven days of the Anglo-Saxon week and each day's corresponding deity, and, as will be made clear, these correspondences are significant when it comes to the invocation of deities (Chapter 5: Galdr). Having now set out the maps of cosmogony and cosmology in the previous and current chapter, we next present the scheme of trance states, mentioned only briefly so far, which facilitate shamanic journeying.

## Cosmology Summary

Asgard: The Haven. Aesiric deities. Risen Ond (the raised Kundalini serpent of Tantric Yoga). Shamanic Ecstasy. Aesiric trance. Colour: Yellow/Gold. Metal: Gold.

Ljosalfheim: Light Elves. Altruism and conscience, listening to the wisdom of the heart. Wisdom of the light elves. But experience too much light elf, too early in your practice, and illusions of grandeur may result. Light elves are known for their trickery. Colour: White/Silver. Metal: Silver.

Svartaflheim: Dwarfs. These wise smiths are capable of smithing Ond towards shamanic ecstasy, but they may be blinded by greed and swayed by the shiny reward of material wealth. Colour: Red. Metal: Bronze.

Midgard: Middle Earth. The middle enclosure. The earthly realm of humans, land wights (spirits) and the home of the Vanir deities – Vanaheim. Fertility and growth. In-between Helheim and Haven on Irminsul. The potential for growth towards shamanic wisdom, and the growth and demise of material wealth. Colour: Blue. Metal: Mercury.

Jotunheim: Giants. Unpredictability and disruptiveness. Wisdom of ancestral giants. Risen Ond reaches workable proportions, but there is the potential to get out of control – the smith is required to forge this energy. Colour: Purple. Metal: Tin.

Dokkalfheim: Dark Elves. Wisdom of the mound elves. A dark and shady realm. Facing shades and hang-ups. Ond begins to rise. 'Freedom' is felt and the potential for transformation. It is important at this stage to free-up the Ond in the right way, using the guidance of animal spirit helpers for instance, traveling by flight and shape-shifting. But the energy could also get out of control in other ways, such as the constraints of drug addiction and the dependency on false ideals. Colour: Green. Metal: Copper.

Helheim: Hel. Realm of the dead, of the goddess Hel, and of the seething cauldron Hvergelmir. Wisdom of the ancestors. Necromancy and oracular Seidr work. The Ond is manifest in the cauldron, but not yet risen (the dormant Kundalini serpent of Tantric Yoga). It requires the seething of Disiric trance to let it loose. Colour: Black. Metal: Lead.

# – Chapter 4 –
## Trance - Entering Ecstasy

A characteristic feature of indigenous shamanism is that its practitioners alter consciousness in order to accomplish specific (community-related) tasks. Most often, shamans undertake these tasks by travelling in the spirit world, but trance may also involve being an instrument for spirit incarnation, undertaking deity and ancestor communication, and deep contemplation. There is much evidence that our Heathen ancestors entered such 'altered states of consciousness', particularly through the chanting or singing of magical charms (Galdr – see the next chapter): for example in Erik's saga, the singing of a charm by Gudrid during a Seidr séance.

In the last chapter, we drew attention to three altered conscious states which enable shamanic practices, termed Aesiric, Vaniric and Disiric trance. These three trance states are associated with particular worlds on Irminsul, corresponding with Haven, Midgard and Helheim, respectively. The three worlds, their associated altered conscious states, and the three corresponding levels of the human body – head, heart and belly/groin – are vitally important elements of Galdrbok's system of shamanic Heathenry. We attribute three classes or types of existence to/on the Irminsul pillar, as well as three corresponding parts of the body, and three specific trances and their practices, in the following way:

Asgard – The Head – The Aesiric Level – Waking Trance &
   Deity Invocation
Midgard – The Heart – The Vaniric Level – Mediumistic
   Trance & Divination
Helheim – The belly/groin – The Disiric Level – Seething
   Trance

## Yggdrasill, Irminsul and People

In the last chapter we associated the Irminsul pillar, the
huge central post or pillar of the world tree, with the
straight and tall Ash tree. The Irminsul Pillar is the 'straight
and narrow' which links the polar opposites of Haven and
Helheim. These polar opposites are balanced in the middle
by Midgard, which is characterised by Nerthus (the Earth
Mother) and other earth goddesses, and her people (us)
who depend on her bountiful gifts.

We can usefully consider the human body as a personal
representation of a fully functioning world tree. Using
the Irminsul pillar as a metaphor, the head is Aesiric or
deity-like, while the heart is Vaniric and representative of
the Vanir, conscience and altruism. Finally, the
belly/groin is Disiric and is associated with ancestors
and the seething cauldron, the level of sexual excitation
and human reproduction. It is also the level where
'excrement' is ejected: the dead are 'recycled' in Helheim.
The 'dead' things we wish Nidhoggr to consume are
shades, hang-ups, and other aspects of ourselves we wish
to slough off. The human spine thus represents the
Irminsul Pillar, and our two arms and two legs become
the worlds of the Light Elves and Dwarfs, Giants and
Dark Elves, respectively. In a further kenning, the three
worlds on the Irminsul pillar might also be usefully

shown to correspond with the so-called triune brain: the 'R' or reptilian brain complex being Helheim, the mid brain Midgard, and the cerebral hemispheres the Haven.

Other aspects of human experience also accord with Yggdrasill's worlds: the creation of a human life through sexual intercourse, for instance, and the progression of that person through life. Sex involves partial seething of the boiling cauldron in Hel, corresponding in the physical realm with the rising and ejaculation of semen in males. This relates to the raising of Ond which peaks in orgasm (for both sexes) and is represented by Asgard. Ecstatic trance and ecstatic orgasm can both give fleeting glimpses of the Bifrost/Bilrost rainbow bridge, and both take the experient outside the space-time continuum: hence, in certain esoteric traditions, orgasm is named the 'little death'. The raised semen meets the female egg at the level of Midgard, where a foetus is produced, gestates (the pregnant Earth Mother) and is born. From Midgard, the phases of human existence itself then follow Thunor's lightning bolt from dark elf world to light elf world. The child corresponds to the dark elves, being impetuous and playful. The giants relate to rebellious adolescent teenagers, and the dwarfs to the desire to work and gain wealth, or the smithing of the self towards spiritual rather than material ends. The light elves represent the knowledge and wisdom which may come with old age, and Asgard corresponds with death – at which point the path is directly back down the tree to Helheim. With these thoughts in mind, you might like to explore other kennings on your body, your life, and Yggdrasill. In all such explorations, remember that these are not absolute models but merely additional layers of kenning.

# Aesiric, Vaniric and Disiric Trance in Detail

## 1. The Aesiric Level: Waking Trance and Deity Invocation

A deity is an office, a spirit, a 'non-human person', a force in nature, a function – and many other things besides. Each deity is a manifestation or representation of the whole (of Haven), even if s/he acts (or appears to act) independently. Aesiric altered consciousness is characterised by 'waking' trance, a trance in which one is fully awake but not present in the world of 'ordinary' senses. Essentially, experiencing this state involves a profound state of shamanic ecstasy. Aesiric trance is attained by invoking a deity, by being 'possessed' by it, and thereby assuming the deity form. The practice involves chanting Galdr and is discussed in greater detail in Chapter 5.

In many cultures, past and present, someone who invokes a deity (or a spirit) seeks to be 'possessed', yet 'deity possession' conjurs all sorts of stereotypes. To use the term 'possessed' may invite religious-based associations with possession by demons, as famously portrayed in the film 'The Exorcist'. However, we are interested in the shamanic rather than Christian worldview here. The process of invoking a deity in this way involves, taking a psychological approach, suspending ones normal ego-personality-complex (natal personality) and assuming the qualities and characteristics of the deity being invoked. This is by no means a simple cerebral exercise or a mere performance or drama. The effect we are after, in vibrating in harmony and sympathy with a deity-form, a force in nature, is far from demonic. Indeed, possession by spirits is a standard practice for many shamans. We should not fear the lack of control which 'possession' might seem to imply, despite our culture largely stressing the importance of 'control' (over money, one's career, etc). But, this does not mean such practices should be regarded carelessly, since any induction of altered consciousness has the potential to profoundly affect the subject. The practices outlined in this book aim to safely guide the initiate through the otherworld. Taking responsibility and care in such actions is up to you.

Aesiric trance is represented by the deities in Asgard, a state in which the aspirant assumes the guise of a deity by a temporary loss of self. This is represented by the eternal sound Au-(ng) the sound of the Aesir gods (see Chapter 5: Galdr). This sound represents, indeed actually vibrates, the point in the eternal circle of Wyrd where Skuld (the future), through Orlog (fate/destiny/karma), joins with the past and the pre-existing life of deities. In short, this is a transcending of the space-time continuum, in the no-space where Wyrd, Metod and Skuld meet. Cosmologically, the meeting of the three Wyrd Sisters occurs at the Well of Wyrd on Yggdrasill, which is situated in the sky. As described in the Edda, the Aesir also meet at Wyrd's Well, to discuss the affairs of the world(s). This Well is therefore an apt place to symbolise the otherworld location of Aesiric trance since in this trance you are, in a sense, in council with the gods!

As an aside, and with reference to the transitory nature of Yggdrasill's map, the location of Wyrd's Well is another example of how the map can only be based around certain, unfixed, principles. How else could it be that the Well of Wyrd is both where the Gods and Norns meet in council, away from the world of human people, but also potentially near Midgard. It is also found at the foot of one of Yggdrasill's roots, indicating that is should be 'beneath' the tree! To reiterate again, any plan of Yggdrasill is purely a set of pointers rather than a guaranteed map of fixed territory.

## 2. The Vaniric Level: Mediumistic Trance and Divination

Vaniric trance is represented on Yggdrasill by Midgard, and hence the Vanir deities, wights and humans. The emphasis is on people who are alive now, in this moment, not the dead who reside in Helheim. Vaniric trance operates at the level of Midgard, and by implication, Metod, the present time. Metod is associated with the moment and living in the moment, in the midst of things, in Middle Earth. Represented by the sound Va-(ng), this is the fluid, emotional state of living humans.

This 'mediumistic' trance state is characterised by a relaxed, reflective trance, mid-way between Disiric and Aesiric trances, reached through crystal gazing and rune casting or other oracular and divinatory techniques (see Chapter 6: Ritual). In this way, all the worlds of Yggdrasill can be 'descryed' or 'seen' through the use of the crystal ball, while present in Middle Earth – but they are not necessarily participated in or 'visited'. Vaniric trance resonates with the Peorth rune in the cosmogony, with its links to the lot box and rune casting. It also refers to the Eh (Horse) rune wherein the Vitki has, via shamanic sacrifice, accomplished the means (Sleipnir, symbolising the ability to shape-shift and travel) to travel into the spirit world – but at this point patiently stands 'on the threshold' looking in, content to descry the worlds.

Humans, in the present, are the inhabitants of Middle Earth, whatever 'world' they are close-to during shamanistic practice. That is, while in mediumistic trance your physical body is alive in Midgard, yet your otherworld body, the Hamingja (see Chapter 7), is in another place (or no place!) – the otherworld. Mediumistic trance is a state which people can and do slip in and out of, in daydreams, for instance. On return from such a dream it is common to hear someone comment 'you were miles away' or to be asked 'where have you been?'. It is the level at which many magical practices are conducted, including oracle readings and light meditations (in between the head and belly, on Irminsul). Without condemning or condoning them, we think that the use of alcohol and other entheogens (also known more pejoratively and erroneously as mind altering 'psychedelics' or 'psychoactives') may effectively contribute to Disiric trances, and perhaps to Vaniric trances, but most often not to Aesiric trances.

In terms of the raising of Ond, Vaniric trance and the Vaniric level on Irminsul correspond to the 'opening of the heart'. When scrying or rune casting, you may notice that your heart Hvel (chakra), positioned at the level of Midgard, 'opens', as mentioned earlier in Galdrbok. This is characteristic of Vaniric trance and is associated with the conscience and/or altruism discussed in the cosmogony (see Chapter 2). Note that the chakras, termed Hvel in the Runic worldview, also neatly 'fit' the plan of Yggdrasill, since there are seven chakras, just as there are seven worlds – indeed, the number seven is significant in many cultures. 'Speaking' with trees and other beings (land wights) in Midgard is also facilitated by Vaniric trance, so most practitioners prefer to be 'in the woods', or 'sitting out' (Utiseta) when inducing Vaniric trance. Utiseta at burial mounds with Vaniric trance may facilitate communication with the ancestors too. But a more intense engagement with ancestors is achieved during Disiric trance.

### 3. Disiric Level: Seething Trance and Ancestor Communication

Disiric trance is represented by the dead in Helheim and the Valkyries or Disir (Idis in Old Saxon), female otherworldly beings associated with death, ancestors and the battlefield. There is a link here to the three Norns, since one Valkyrie name is 'Skuld', and of course it is Skuld 'by her decree, who commits the wretched flesh to the earth' (see Linsell's translation of the rune poem). Key words for the Disiric level are 'the dead' and those to be 'renewed' or 'reborn'. In one respect, this level concerns the ancient or the Ur-d (Wyrd) dead ancestors, who in cyclic fashion will later become the Skuld (freed), with Metod or Verhandi in the middle.

The dead were formerly, or still are (time and space are disrupted in the otherworld), the deceased (note the 'dis' prefix also appearing in Disir) or dis-eased, no longer enjoying the ease or free-will of life in Middle Earth. This trance state is reached though what Jan Fries calls (1996) 'seething', produced by Galdr, chanting, ranting and raging, drumming, dancing and other external methods. Fries associates seething with 'Seidr': Seidr is a shamanic practice in the source literature and most contemporary oracular Seidr practitioners reconstruct the séance described in Erik's Saga (see Magnusson & Palsson 1965: 81-84, and the works of Blain and Paxson in partiuclar, and also Bates and Lindquist). Considering the increasing popularity of oracular Seidr among contemporary Heathens, to neglect brief discussion of it here would be remiss.

In Erik's saga a seeress, 'volva', or seidkona performs a séance for a Greenlandic comunity suffering a famine during the tenth century CE. Many features of the tale are shamanistic. The volva eats a strange porridge before the ritual, containing the hearts of various creatures. She perhaps wears items associated with her spirit helpers: a black lambskin hood lined with cats-fur, catskin gloves, and a pouch at her waist perhaps containing shamanic power objects. She holds a long staff – topped with a brass knob, studded with stones – a staff which may symbolise the world tree Yggdrasill itself. And, she sits on a ritual 'high-seat' with a cushion of hen-feathers beneath her. The verses which enable the spirits to be present are then sung

or chanted, and in communication with that realm, the volva prophesises a better future and answers questions posed to her by each member of the community.

The contemporary oracular Seidr session or séance is inspired by this and other sources, and is orchestrated as follows: two main figures are prominent in the proceedings, the volva and a 'guide' who sings and chants the volva and other Seidr-workers into trance. The text of the songs is based around Northern mythology and the tune is based on medieval sources. The guide keeps a precautionary and watchful eye on the proceedings. The guide's singing takes everyone to the gates of Helheim where the volva communicates with ancestor spirits (the geography of the road to Helheim is described in Chapter 6: Ritual). But only the volva enters a deeper state of trance in which she enters the realm of the dead.

The format of the Seidr songs means that at a specific point in the chant the volva, and only the volva, enters Helheim. Once accustomed to being in Helheim the volva vocalises descriptions of the territory so that the ritual can then move on to the oracular prognostications. The other members of the community gathered, who are currently gathered at the gates of Helheim, put questions to the volva – who experiences visionary imagery influenced by her/his presence among the dead. The intensity of many 'beginner' experiences requires vigilance on the part of experienced Seidr workers. 'Watchers' are present at all times to ensure the ritual proceeds safely.

In light of this discussion of oracular Seidr, Fries' (1996) reading of Seidr as a 'seething' or 'boiling' trance is rather unconventional. However, we argue it is not incompatible with the aforementioned reconstructions of oracular Seidr, since in our experience, oracular Seidr can involve a combination of both Vaniric (mediumistic) and Disiric (seething) trances. Furthermore, the ancient sources indicate that the description in Erik's saga is only one form of Seidr-work. Thus Fries' interpretation sits well with our notion of Hvergelmir being the seething (boiling) cauldron. Incidentally, the metaphor of 'boiling' compares with the 'boiling' Bushman (San) shamans of Southern Africa experience in their bellies when the supernatural potency called 'n/um' stirs and they enter trance or '!kia'. Furthermore, this is a type of practice potentially similar to Tantric Yoga, when raising the fire serpent.

It is through the seething Disiric trance that the Nidhoggr is wakened and Hvergelmir boils. This process of wakening and raising Ond may be accomplished by using the goddess Frigg as a power matrix. Frigg is the Heathen equivalent of the Roman goddess Venus, the maiden of desire and love (there are also links to Freyja). Simply put, the Frigg power matrix works because if you perceive your work as exciting and 'sexy', you will enjoy it and want to experience it repeatedly.

Kundalini practice is well known for its cleansing aspect and its ability to destroy. In Northern traditions, the Yogic Kundalini serpent is symbolised by the Nidhoggr, the serpent or fire-dragon which is wakened by the aforementioned 'sexy', 'passionate' and desirable quality of Frigg/Freyja. To raise the serpent/dragon is to awaken (invoke) the fire in one's belly. But a caution is in order here. Sufficient enthusiasm for anything, right or wrong (depending on your ethical system), can be easily raised. In raising the serpent/dragon one must ensure that one is doing so in conformity with a structured spiritual system and within an ethical framework – in this case the Heathen code of conduct, the relative morals of which seekers must establish for themselves.

If care is not taken, one is in danger of raising truly dreadful shades and other entities – in psychological terms, old repressions, lusts, hang ups, and ancestral negatives, hereditary or otherwise – from Helheim and Dokkalfheim. Nidhoggr can be destructive in its consuming and fiery nature, also known as the dragon's breath! Properly used, it can destroy ignorance, the rotten, and the non-functioning. During the seething Disiric state, the force of negativity is consigned to the seething cauldron, its energy re-employed in a positive way. This is not a practice to be dealt with carelessly or frivolously. Indian Yogis train for many years, strengthening their bodies, before even considering waking the Kundalini serpent.

The system we advocate here is consistent, sound, and practical: with the cosmogony, cosmology and altered consciousness explained, and clear, systematic connections between them discussed, we next approach what may perhaps be the most difficult of chapters for 'sticklers of tradition' – the forging of Galdr from the Northern wordhoard and powerful 'Indo-European' root sounds.

# – Chapter 5 –
# Galðr - Deity Invocation

G aldr as we have made clear thus far, is an Old Norse term meaning 'sung spell' or 'magic chant'. Galdrbok means 'Spellbook', and this volume provides the essential Galdr and other shamanic tools for the practicing Heathen Mage. 'Galdr' may derive from the term 'gala', to crow, and 'galan', mad or obsessed. Galdr may be used to invoke (or negotiate) the presence of deities. Shamanic operations may also require the practitioner to 'assume' a god form – requiring the entering of Aesiric trance – in order to be effective. By becoming the god/spirit, we can avail ourselves of its power (qualitatively not quantitatively). But how is this done? One powerful technique of invocation is to 'invite the deity in', by vibrating one's inner and then outer being at the same rate as the deity itself. Current physics has only recently informed us in scientific terms what diverse ancient peoples had known thousands of years ago: everything has a vibration!

Indigenous shamans in various parts of the world, including Northwest Europe, had/have worked out how to approximate some of the essential vibrations of nature, and how to emulate them. This provides us with a technique of deity and spirit invocation, a 'mastery' of essential forces in nature, which induces shamanic ecstasy and, hence, self-transformation. It is the gods (or one of the 'natures' or 'spirits') which the Runester must first invoke before a shamanic operation can be properly conducted,

as it is essentially the gods/spirits (natural forces) who
excel in this.

## Vibration and Galdr

Vibration is the essential energy matrix which holds
individual things together. When it breaks down, decay sets
in, and the essential oneness of any 'thing' dissolves.
Newtonian physics postulated that matter could ultimately
be broken down into minute but fixed building blocks, but
this theory has long since been discredited. Quantum
physics involves manipulating particles in nuclear
accelerators: these experiments, which are ultimately putting
quantum mechanics into an almost mystical category,
demonstrate the peculiar and unpredictable behaviour of
particles. At the atomic level, for example, the atom itself
contains vast space – synonymous with Ginnungagap.

All things have a vibration, and if we are seeking
sympathy/harmony with a force in nature (a deity/spirit),
we must cause our inner environment to 'vibrate' in the
same way as that force in nature (the deity/spirit) we are
invoking. The sacred sounds were elucidated by well-
known ancient peoples, in India and Egypt for example,
who left records. These sounds represent the essential
vibrations of various forces in nature. Consider that
Runecraft, like other contemporary Paganisms, does not
embrace the concept of a god outside his/her creation, so
these forces exist inside us as well. This makes it all the
easier to resonate with the frequency of the force. Science
must ultimately be a practical subject, so rather than
challenge the truth of the 'sacred science' recorded by the
ancients, try these sacred sounds, or 'Galdr', for yourself.

'Galdr' has the plausible meaning of 'magic chant' (Simek 1993: 97) or 'sung spell'. These spells are used 'to set into motion the magical powers which the person in question wants to bring into his service through the power of the rhymed word' (Simek 1993: 300). The play on etymology and sound or word associations in the Galdr which we use here is designed to imbue certain words with associated, connected and practical meanings. We have integrated the classic sounds of Mantric Yoga with the Northern wordhoard and its emphasis on rhyme. Before discussing these Galdr in detail, our reasoning for this integration requires explanation.

## On 'Tradition' and Cultural Exchange

Communities rarely 'stand alone', without contact with other communities, and societies are continually undergoing change. There have been attempts by some cultural (not to mention racial) 'purists' to conceal the influence of one culture on another, and this is applicable in the Northern context. The Celts and their Northern neighbours were much alike, for instance. It is evident that Northern European communities were indeed 'indigenous', but they also imported, borrowed and adapted from a variety of other cultures, ranging from the Scandinavian Sami and Greenlandic Inuit, to Mediterranean and Asian communities (and probably beyond, as the find of a statue of the Buddha in one Norse burial indicates). This does not mean Northern religions were eclectic, it does mean their customs, deities, rituals, burial techniques, words, and so on were influenced by other cultures. Some of the borrowed material was 'Northernised', to coin a term, and perhaps even exported back to where it came from.

Hence, we remind the reader of the angle we took in the introduction to Galdrbok: the system offered in this book is neither the 'true', 'authentic' tradition of the hoary runemaster-shamans of old, nor is it channelled speculation. It is a practical, working system which, as an unfolding tradition, is indigenous and ancestral – for Heathens today. Northern traditions were passed on and changed via an oral record, with aspects of them being written down only latterly (since around 1000 CE). Much has likely been lost, destroyed, and altered, and much of this, if we had it to hand, might reveal far more intimate connections with other cultures than we have hitherto discovered or even imagined.

Conversely, perhaps much was added late. Both the Roman Empire and Christianity had their effects on the Old North – our seven days of the Anglo-Saxon week refer to specific Heathen deities, yet the correspondences also extend to specific Roman gods. Material culture, customs, stories, words and a myriad of other human attributes have been exchanged, bartered, borrowed or even stolen, across the globe, for millennia. Deities appear in distinctly culture-specific groupings complete with unique rites of worship, devotion and/or negotiation. Yet, as we have seen, many 'deities' from a variety of traditions have parallels in other cultures, whether borrowed, lent, or discovered independently through common human experience.

## The 'Indo-European' Wordhoard

With these thoughts in mind, we have usefully connected the time-honoured, tried and tested, and widely accessible 'sacred sounds' (of ancient Khem and Mantric Yoga), with their North European counterparts, to generate sacred

Galdr. Indeed, our discovery is that the Galdr we present provide striking connections between existing 'sacred sounds' and the North European wordhoard. In the most obvious linguistic sense, Audhumla, for example, is comprised of 'audr' meaning 'riches' or 'wealth', and 'humala' meaning 'hornless'. But it is also striking to us that the 'dhum' of Audhumla is comparable with the Hindu mantra for the cosmic cow 'dhum', or when sacralised, 'dhung'. And, while we also suggest that the 'Va' part of Vanir denotes their feminine qualities (as also in water, or 'va'-ter), it is also rather eye-opening that when sacralised with the -ng sound, the 'va' becomes the Mantric 'vang' sound which is associated with both water and femininity.

These findings hint at cross-cultural consistencies, which can be usefully understood, we suggest, in the light of academic linguistic studies on the so-called 'Indo-European' language groups – though we by no means claim to be expert linguists or scholars of this approach. One caveat is due: just as we are not proponents of Gimbutas' monolithic interpretation of 'goddess culture' and its alleged clash with Indo-Europeans, so we recognise that the concept of the 'Indo-European' has been exploited for political ends in the past (also, see Anthony [1995] on the links between the Nazi culture-historic approach and Gimbutas' eco-feminist interpretation of the Indo-Europeans). We assert that our interpretations of the Heathen past are not nationalist, bigoted, or otherwise chauvinistic in intent. For us, hand in hand with an appreciation of diversity there is open-mindedness, liberality and tolerance, all expressed from within a specific indigenous Heathen standpoint.

'Indo-European' is a linguistic construct for addressing similarities and differences in various languages across Euro-Asia. We think it no surprise that there is a resemblance between the sounds and meanings of some of the Norse wordhoard and those of yogic mantra, since they may be from a common Indo-European root. It is from the Indo-European language group that our modern languages have developed and it is therefore not unreasonable to argue that 'Indo-European' is a useful term in this context. Having come across these striking connections between these Indo-European languages, we have linked the components of certain Northern terms with the time-proven, trance-inducing, vibratory Mantric sound associations which bring such names to life. In this way, Audhumla for instance, is not simply a word meaning (broadly) cosmic cow, which is important in itself – but furthermore, with the link to sound vibration, it is now possible to harmonise yourself with that cosmic being, and indeed with all the major deities of Heathen cosmogony/cosmology.

In the seven Galdr we present in this chapter, we have associated the appropriate vibratory sound for that deity with corresponding images, colours, deity functions and magical items (such as Woden's spear or Thunor's hammer). In a coherent and systematic approach, these correspondences clearly refer back to aspects of the cosmogony, cosmology and trance states introduced in preceding chapters. In effect, simply using a given deity Galdr will thereby invoke attributes which a practitioner has 'loaded' it with. So, the chant becomes a non-intellectual mnemonic device, a short-cut to re-membering, invoking and embodying a set of principles, correspondences, forces and associations; the external and internal facets of nature-gods.

## Vibrating Galdr into Ginnungagap

The great Ginnungagap is the place or space – the eternal 'gap' – into which the Galdr are 'pushed'. This is the great animated and fecund space or womb of the mother, and the eternal space (outer and inner) into which the Galdr vibration is projected. The projection is effected by adding the '-ng' or '–ing' sound to a given vibratory word. Thus the famous 'Om' (or more correctly 'aum') sound of Mantric Yoga is actually projected as 'au-ng', and it is projected into Ginnungagap – hence 'gin-aung-a-gap'. The Om is 'the primordial sound of timeless reality which vibrates within us from the beginningless past' (Johari 1986: 35). Essentially, Om is the primal word of divinity. Thus the 'Aung' vibration is a component part of all the Galdr (excluding Tiw, for reasons explained below), and all the Galdr are projected into 'gin-aung-a-gap'.

Interestingly, it is the god Ing, Yngvi, or Yingvi-Frey, the 'Green man', who brings everyth-ing to life in the Galdr, as he does in Middle Earth. As the -ng (Ing) sound is the sound of the animate and fecund Ginnungagap itself, so it is a sacred 'bringING-to-life' sound. It is important to not associate mundane things with this sound. Approach the sound as 'sacred' and therefore only appropriate for vibrating (speaking) in sacred contexts. Therefore, when learning the Galdr or discussing them, substitute the -ng (Ing) sound for the 'M' ('em') sound to avoid activating the Galdr (use Aum instead of Aung, and Vam instead of Vang, for instance). This makes the Galdr all the more potent when used in sacred contexts.

It is also important to avoid other improper associations with the Galdr. For example, if one feels embarrassment in the company of others whilst learning a Galdr, then one might inadvertently and unfortunately associate that Galdr with the discomfort of the experience, raising negative memories and experiences each time the Galdr is practised or used. By substituting the 'M' sound, one can experience the effects of the Galdr almost, but not quite, during the learning process. This 'almost' experience is enough to differentiate between practice and discussion, and the magical and transformational effects of actual use from the sounding of the Galdr in mundane instances.

A group of Heathen Galdr practitioners can either all vibrate the same Galdr externally (vocalising the Galdr) or vibrate a different Galdr independently from one another internally (without vocalising). The latter provides the opportunity for a group to invoke many different gods at the same time with each member being involved with a single deity, without the confusion of many Galdr being sounded all at once. This is particularly effective when each person requires ritual for independent means yet the group wishes to work together, for 'group power'. Of course, internalising the Galdr can also be practical when working alone and one requires an element of privacy.

## Invocations for the Seven-Day Gods

It would be a difficult if not impossible task to propose Galdr for every known Heathen deity. The various manifestations and regional varieties of Woden, for example, number in the hundreds. After all, which Woden would we choose, and from which Germanic language group? Therefore, in Galdrbok, we account for (and engage with) many deities by subsuming them under seven main gods and goddesses and seven principle Galdr. Our precedent for this is the seven days of the week – referred to a number of times earlier – which are, of course, named after seven Anglo-Saxon deities. The number seven is significant in Northern cosmology, for not only are there seven days in the week, but there are seven worlds, the seventh rune is Gift (synonymous with Woden and shamanic sacrifice), and there are also seven notes in the musical scale, seven colours in the light spectrum, seven planets, and so on. The seven planets make up our seven day week and each deity corresponds with one specific day/planet – Sun for Sunday, Moon for Monday, and so on.

The Roman influence on this correspondence between day, planet and deity is of no concern to us, since we are more interested in practical application than purely academic interpretation. Either way, the system clearly worked for the Anglo-Saxons. Indeed, the Saxon deities 'fit' with their Roman and other Indo-European equivalences, so that Wednesday is Woden's-day, and the day of the Roman Mercury, the Greek Hermes, the Egyptian Anubis, and the Ancient Sumerian / Neo-Babylonian Marduk-Kurious ('curious' – the ubiquitous, questioning and questing Wednesday deity). These cross-cultural correspondences perhaps make the connections all the more interesting and possibly all the more potent.

The seven Anglo-Saxon deities and their days of the week are:

Sunday or Sun's-daeg – Balder

Monday or Moon's-daeg – Freyja

Tuesday or Tiw's-daeg – Tiw

Wednesday or Woden's-daeg – Woden

Thursday or Thunor's-daeg – Thunor

Friday or Frigg's-daeg – Frigg

Saturday or Siter/Sitr/Sitter's-daeg – Disir/Ancestors

Invoking deities according to the Heathen initiation system of Galdrbok is effected in two stages. Reciting the 'mundane poetry', presented first below, is the first stage – these chants are used to invoke the presence of the deity and to link yourself with the aspect of nature around you which each deity represents. Thus, Woden's poetry will resonate with the wind, Thunor's with rain, thunder and lightning, and so on. In a ritual, it may suffice to simply chant the poetry for the deity, since enough of the deity's presence may be felt for the required effect. But for a more potent practice you may employ the second stage of the invocation in which intonation of the Galdr with its sacred sounds will follow recitation of the mundane poetry to take-on the spirit of the deity and effect Aesiric trance (deity possession). Simply put, incorporate the poetry into rituals so that they precede the use of the main Galdr, which invokes the deity itself. These Galdr are listed and some explanation of their wordhoard provided, following the presentation of the mundane poetry.

# Mundane Poetry for the Seven-Day Deities

### 1. SUNDAY – BALDER

ATTEND, LOOK, LISTEN AND FEEL

THE SEVEN-DAY GODS ARE MANIFEST, REAL.

SUN, GOLDEN JEWEL IN THE SKY-FATHER'S FACE

YOU EMPOWER THE EARTH WHILE THE WOLF GIVES CHASE

### 2. MONDAY – FREYJA

MOON, SILVER GEM, SO HIGH AND SO BRIGHT

YOU COMMAND THE SKY, BUT ONLY BY NIGHT

EVEN NJORD AND HER TIDES, WITH ALL OF THEIR MIGHT

ARE SUBJECT TO MANI 'TIL HE'S PUT TO FLIGHT

### 3. TUESDAY – TIW

OF THE SKY-FATHER TIW, I PROCLAIM

PRIZED 'NIGHT STAR', GUIDE-ARROW OF FAME

PLUNGED INTO THE ARMS OF NERTHUS, EARTH-MOTHER

YNGVI-FREY-FRIG – EARTHLY LOVER

### 4. WEDNESDAY – WODEN

OS-WODEN, WEDNESDAY'S ONE EYED WONDER

WANDERS WILFULLY WHITHER WHO KNOWS?

TAKING HEALING AND WORTCRAFT, STARCRAFT AND

CUNNING, LORECRAFT AND MAGIC WHEREVER HE GOES.

A WHISPERING OR RAGING WIND IS HE

THAT GRIM HOODED RIDER OF YGGDRASILL TREE

GOD OF THE CROSSROADS, TO YOU AND TO ME

5. THURSDAY – THUNOR

THUNOR MUST I SPEAK OF NOW

GOD OF WEATHER FOR FARMER WITH PLOUGH

BY SKY-FATHERS SEED, THE RAIN ON THE GROUND

CARRIED BY THUNOR, DOES PROSPERITY ABOUND.

YET BY THUNDER AND LIGHTNING OAK-WILL-HE-FELL

AND CLEAVE AND CRASH MOUNTAIN FROM ASGARD TO HEL

KEEPING ORDER IN HAVEN, THAT BRIGHT LUSTY MAN

KEEPS ORDER ON EARTH, WHEREVER HE CAN


6. FRIDAY – FRIGG

FRIG-FULL, RIPE, GODDESS ELECT

ING GREEN MAN WITH PHALLUS ERECT

MAN AND WOMAN BE HEARTY AND HALE!

UNFASTEN CLOAK-PINS AND LET LOVE-MAKING RAILE


7. SATURDAY – DISIR/ANCESTORS

SITTER'S DAY IS STILLNESS OF HEART

A DAY TO REMEMBER FROM THIS WORLD WE PART

WYRD-COME-VALKYRIE HAS A GRAVE FOR US ALL

BE WE KING, QUEEN, BEGGAR, THANE OR THRALL.

BALEFUL DAY OF EVIL EYE

OF DEATH AND GLOOM AND GHOSTLY CRY

IS PART OF THE CIRCLE – AYE, BY-THE-BYE

YOU CAN SPEAK WITH THE DEAD IF YOU DO BUT TRY.

## Galðr of the Seven Northern Deities

The following Galdr are written in a loose form of 'Galdrlag' – a stanza with a particularly strict stave-rhyme-connection, emphasising parallel verse-form. This follows the tradition of Northern 'skaldcraft', the poetic craft which used Galdrlag for the composition of 'magical verse'.

The Galdr consist of three basic devices:

### 1. A specific number of words:

This numerical device connects the Galdr to the cosmogony presented in Chapter 2, in a holistic, symbiotic way, by acting as another form of mnemonic device. The integrity of the numerical system is based solely on this relative framework.

### 2. Carrying words:

These consist of nouns, verbs or other words resonating with various attributes of a given deity. These might include 'totem' animals – wolves for Woden, for example. Carrying words also describe various 'magical' artefacts such as Woden's spear Gungnir and Thunor's hammer Mjollnir. In some cases the persona of a deity is expanded by the use of other names of that deity – for example, 'Gondlir' in Woden's Galdr. These names, attributes or artefacts are re-called/re-membered and used as mnemonic devices. In this way, the mere mention of Woden's eye, Tiw's severed oath-hand or Thunor's hammer Mjollnir, will recall an entire body of 'lore' instantly, which floods in, in feelings and images (image-magic) – caused by the

Galdr, without linear thinking! The task is to empower the mythology by packing the chants with power, letting the carrying words evoke complete myths (all connected back to the cosmogony and cosmology) and the sonics transform you.

### 3. Indo-European sonic (Mantric/sacred) vibrations:
The sonics can be used alone or repeated for rhythmic or repetitious (trance) purposes as the user sees or feels fit.

## Practicing the Galdr
There are no hard and fast rules, but by and large the rhyme, rhythm and alliteration should come naturally, just as when one recites aloud a poem, nursery rhyme or a part from a play. The Galdr are entirely effective if chanted without a 'tune', so the out-of-tune amongst our readers can feel quite safe! However, Since Galdr may mean 'sung spell' from the verb 'galan' meaning 'sung' or 'twitter' (Simek 1993: 98), you may want to sing the Galdr. We have not provided musical notation, though it can be used. An element of 'performance' or 'showmanship' certainly adds to the potency of a ritual, since the more you put in, the more you get out. And Northern European folklore is replete with the potency not only of special words of power, but also entrancing melodies sung by elves and other otherworldly beings. No doubt the appropriate 'tune' for each deity will present itself to you.

## 1. Balder's Galdr

Day: Sunday
Deity: Balder
Planet: Sun (the son)

### Galdr:

BAALDHUR'S ANCIENT FEH

ELF-DISK SON, YNGVI-FREY

HODDER THREW, HE COULD NOT SEE

GIVE STRONG BREEZE TO HRING-HORNI

EIGHT SPOKES GUIDE THE FAIR WHEEL FAR

AUNG H(E)RING HERAUNG H(E)RA

AUNG H(E)RING H(E)RA

### Kennings:

'Feh' describes the 'fee' that Balder and we also must pay.
This is the debt of physical death owed for living a life, and
the shamanic death induced in order to alter consciousness
and achieve shamanic ecstasy/wisdom.

'Elf-disk' is a kenning for the sun (see Skaldskaparmal in
the Prose Edda). For Yngvi-Frey, see below.

The line on Hodder refers to the mistletoe dart thrown by the blind god Hod (Hodder) which kills Balder, and the fact that Hod's actions were not intentional.

'Hringhorni' is Balder's ship (funeral pyre). According to Simek, the ship carries a ring on its stern, giving the ship its corresponding name. The depiction of ships together with 'sun' like images are common in ancient Scandinavian rock engravings. 'Hringhorni' is also an amalgam of Skidbladnir, the sun/fertility ship of Yngvi-Frey (or Freyr) and Naglfar the death ship ('nail ship', 'corpse ship' or 'ship of the dead' – Simek 1993: 226). Thus Balder's mode of transport for shamanic travel might be inferred as the sun ship to get to the otherworld and the death ship to return. It is of course strikingly fitting that the Hring of Hringhorni reflects the sonic vibrations associated with this deity (and Tiw – see Tiw's Galdr, below).

'Fair Wheel' is a kenning for the sun (see Skaldskaparmal in the Prose Edda).

Sonics: A protraction of the sonic 'Aung' with 'Hr' sound differentiates Balder's Galdr from Tiw's Galdr (see Tiw's Galdr, below). Aung is both the divine sound (Om/Aum) and the method of projecting (-ng/-ing) that sound and the rest of the Galdr into Ginnungagap. The Hring and Hra sounds connect with the eagle, hawk and falcon sounds found in Tiw's Galdr (again, explained below). As the son (sun) of the Allfather in his manifestation as Tiw, whose totem is the eagle, these sounds are fitting for Balder. The Heraung sound is the 'her' sound of the 'hero', which is pushed into the gap.

This is a Galdr of sacrifice, forgiveness and of shamanic wisdom – of Balder 'only good things are told: he is the best of all [the gods]' (Simek 1993: 26). He goes to and remains in Helheim, effectively remaining in an ecstatic (dead) state (until Ragnarok). The same sonic vibrations appear in both Balder's Galdr and Tiw's Galdr, modified only by the 'Aung' sound. In Tiw's Galdr the sounds are polarised (he is the polarised Allfather) to challenge shades ('Hering Hera'), but in Balder's Galdr the sounds are no longer polarised ('Aung Hering Hera'). This is because Balder represents the two becoming the 'One'. It is also the three main male gods becoming the 'One', the function and totality of the trinity Woden, Tiw and Thunor (or, as in the cosmogony, Woden, Vili, Ve). It is the Galdr of becoming complete, free, totally functional and awake (Aesiric trance), perhaps mirrored in other traditions by individuals including Christ, the Buddha and Krishna. This condition can be termed 'Balder-nature', which marks a return to the Allfather as an ecstatic being.

Balder's Galdr has 34 sounds. 34 is 2 x 17, or twice the number of sounds in Tiw's Galdr. Balder has double because there are seventeen sounds for the Father/Mother and seventeen for the Son/Daughter. Furthermore, 3 + 4 = 7 and the seventh rune is Gebo, with associations of sacrifice. In one sense, Balder is the Aesir's sacrifice since he is relegated to Helheim until after Ragnarok. But he is also Woden's second sacrifice (after the first which is himself to himself), since despite Hermod's efforts of riding to Helheim to bring Balder back to Asgard, Woden must give up his son to Helheim until Ragnarok.

## 2. Freyja's Galðr
Day: Monday
Deity: Freyja
Planet: The Moon

### Galðr:
FREYJA FLIES IN FALCON GUISE
AUDHUMLA SEIDR-WISE
BRISINGAMEN HILDISVINI-SYR
AUNG VANG DHUNG VANIR
MANI VANG DHUNG

### Kennings:
Freyja (like Frigg, and the connection is not coincidental), has a falcon garment which is associated with shape-shifting, magical flight and, by implication, Seidr (and) shamanism.

Audhumla is the 'noblest of cows'. Audhumla can be said to mean 'the hornless cow with lots of milk'. The image of the 'holy cow', Magna-Mater or Earth Mother is a common motif in many religious traditions. Audhumla is an important feature early on in the creation/cosmogony, and Freyja's Seidr (seething magic), as a form of shamanism, is most likely just as old.

Brisingamen is the necklace of the Brisings, the shiny necklace of Freyja. Hildisvini is Freyja's boar, her totem animal or spirit-helper. Syr, similarly, is Freyja's sow-name. The pig/boar seems especially to be a Vaniric totem.

Sonics: Vang refers to water, the element which moves in accord with Mani, the (male) moon. Dhung refers to Audhumla. Mani is the 'man' in (of) the moon. In Anglo-Saxon, the term 'man' is not gender specific, but the moon is male in Northern traditions (according with some of the older religious traditions elsewhere, such as the Sumerian). Living by, and measuring 'moons', Mani co-ordinates water (linked by some to emotions), tides, and (monthly) fertility cycles. Years are measured by the 12/13 month cycle.

There are 18 sounds, tying this Galdr into the cosmogony and rune 18, Birch. The Birch rune and tree are linked to Freyja in the cosmogony. Numerologically, 1 + 8 = 9 and the ninth rune is Hagalaz, a form of frozen water. Sing this Galdr in a 'lullaby' or spat 'witchy' fashion. Use it in acts of passive divination such as crystal gazing, in healing, seething Seidr, and other practices associated with Freyja.

## 3. Tiw's Galdr
Day: Tuesday
Deity: Tiw
Planet: Mars

## Galdr:

HAFRAKEN-SKY, ALLFATHER LORD

OATH-HAND SEVERED, GLEIPNIR CHORD

EAGLE HIGH

HRASVELGR CRY

H(E)RING H(E)RA

TIW H(E)RA

## Kennings:
Hafraken is a kenning for sword from the Skaldskaparmal (a treatise on the poetics of skaldic poetry. See Faulkes' translation of the Prose Edda). The sword is a characteristic weapon of Tiw. Allfather refers to Tiw's role as Skyfather and Allfather.

The oath hand was used for making pledges and oaths. The innocent Tiw lost his hand in the fettering of the Fenris wolf. Interestingly, the Irish God Nuada and the Indian God Surya are similarly one-armed. There is also a Roman legend in which the Hero sacrifices his hand in order to prove his innocence. Gleipnir (Old Norse 'open one') is the cord with which the Fenris wolf is finally bound after the failure of two other fetters (see Gylfaginning 33 in the Prose Edda). Interestingly, Gleipnir is constructed with things which essentially do not exist, for example, the roots of a mountain and the breath of a fish.

The Eagle alludes to the Skyfather, whose totem is the eagle, as well as to the eagle, named Hrasvelgr (Old Norse 'corpse eater'), who sits at the top of the world tree – whose tip is in the sky. 'Hra' was a battle (hunting) call which may later have degenerated into the more polite and useless, Hip Hip Hooray! The 'call' should have been He (Hay) He Heraghhh!

Sonics: The first sound, Hri-ng, is the name of the father of a number of Hodbrodd's warriors in the Poetic Edda (in The First Poem of Helgi Hundingsbani, stanza 51, line 1: see Larrington 1996: 121; and also Orchard 1997: 90). The connection between this name/sound and warriors (human and deity) is significant in the context of Tiw's Galdr since he is both All-father and a warrior god. This sound also relates usefully to Vedrfolnir, 'wind-witherer' (see Gylfaginning 16 in Snorri 1998 [1987]: 18), the hawk (or falcon) who sits between the eyes of the Hrasvelgr Eagle, because all falcons cry the 'hri' sound. Associate Vedrfolnir with the Ond force raised to the top of the tree. Hring-Hra combines the eagle and falcon/hawk sounds. 'Tiw H(e)ra' is a protraction connecting the noun 'Tiw' with the eagle sound. The eagle sound is also fitting with Tiw since it is an animal associated with battle and mightiness. Unlike Balder's Galdr, Tiw's Galdr does not use the Aung sound. This is because Tiw's Galdr remains polarised while Balder's does not (explained under Balder's Galdr, above). Furthermore, Tiw's Galdr is not projected into the gap in the same way. It is a harsher, more immediate vibration which works best when the eagle is emulated. As such, Aung is an inappropriate sound for the martial vibrating of this Galdr.

There are 17 sounds, relating Tiw's Galdr to his rune, the seventeenth in the rune row. Tiw's Galdr is vocalised as a hunting sound, so sing the Galdr in a voice which rises and falls, like a bird of prey. The Galdr is used to gain clarity, wisdom, justice and to hunt/combat shades and shadows. Tiw is invoked for guidance, particularly in finding the martial spirit to wage war on ignorance and negativity, and on those shades from Helheim/Dokkalfheim which would defeat us and bend us low. Tiw is also the god of righteousness, justice and balance – qualities which may result from regularly invoking him.

## 4. Woden's Galdr

Day: Wednesday
Deity: Woden
Planet: Mercury

## Galdr:

GUNGNIR DRAUPNIR WODEN'S EYE
SLEIPNIR, HANGATIR, GONDLIR'S CRY
GALDR FATHER, VARDLOKKER SING
AUNG AING, WODEN AING

## Kennings:

Gungnir is Woden's spear, the initiatory tool in 'side grazing', and dedicating self to self. Draupnir, 'the Dripper' is Woden's (and later Balder's) arm ring, probably an oath-ring. Two dwarfs forged Draupnir: Sindri 'the spark sprayer' and Brokker 'the one who works with metal fragments', seemingly Sindri's assistant. Together they are also responsible for forging Freyr's golden boar Gullinborsti, his ship Skidbladnir, and Thunor's hammer Mjollnir. Woden's eye refers to the sacrifice of one of his eyes at the well of Mimir to enable 'second sight'.

Sleipnir is Woden's eight-legged horse, alluding to the Yggdrasill tree itself. Hangatir means 'hanging god', referring to Woden's self-sacrifice (Havamal 138, see Larrington 1996: 34). Gondlir is a Magician-sorcerer, a name for Woden in Grimnismal (stanza 49, see Larrington 1996: 59), referring to Woden's knowledge of magic.

Galdr is of course the 'spoken spell', or shamanic chant, of which Woden as a shaman-god is the master or father. Vardlokker is the 'tempter of the soul' otherwise known in the Landnamabok as seidlaeti or 'magic tune'. The 'seid' part refers the 'tune' explicitly to shamanism; it is therefore a form of Galdr and hence shamanic song (Simek 1993: 353). While Woden learnt Seidr from Freyja, he is said to be the Seidrmadr (master) par excellence, so it is fitting that he is also the Vardlokker, linked with seidlaeti.

Sonics: The 'Ai-' sound has both letters pronounced, so that 'A' and 'I', are sounded. 'A' relates to the 'Aah' sound in the Ansuz (Woden's) rune, and the 'I' refers to the 'Ae-' sound in 'Aesir'. Together, the 'Ai-' connects Woden with the ecstatic 'cry of making', and the '-ing' suffix is the bring-ING to life of the sound (A)ing, which is vital to the development of insight. Such insight helps to balance, control and engage with the negative aspect of Loki, Woden's blood brother, shadow and nemesis. These sonics are protracted into Ginnungagap with the Aung sound.

Woden's Galdr is used to invoke the cunning, skill and wisdom of the shaman god Woden. Intone it sonorously. This Galdr represents the Ond of the Aesiric Woden deployed in understanding – standing under (the tree) – and it is indeed Woden's eye which sits under the world tree, at Mimir's well. It is also the in-turned eye, the inward looking eye, the eye which can see into the (other) world(s) – and is therefore linked to scrying. A kenning for the crystal ball, then, is Woden's Eye and the Head of Mimir (which in an alternative telling of the myth, is preserved by Woden and used by him for divination).

There are 16 sounds in Woden's Galdr. In the cosmogony, rune 16 is Sowilo, the point at which the initiate has the strength to begin re-climbing the lightning flash to Woden's realm, Asgard. Sowilo is also the rune of magical abilities, and Woden, as the Northern Mage par excellence, relates some of these in his 'Sayings of the High One' (Havamal). Note that 16 is 1 + 6 = 7, referring to the rune Gyfu, Gebo, or Gift. Woden's gift to us is the runes and the second part of the cosmogony wherein he has provided the tools to enable shamanic wisdom. It is also the rune of sacrifice and the ultimate sacrifice, or shamanic initiation, was of course Woden to himself.

## 5. Thunor's Galðr

Day: Thursday
Deity: Thunor
Planet: Jupiter

### Galðr:

THUNORAD AND LIGHTNING CRASH, CLOUD HIGH ABOVE

THUNOR RADDING CHARIOT GRIPS MJOLLNIR IN GLOVE

HRUNGNIR OR HRIMTHURS, AT SUCH WILL HE FLING

HEARKEN NOW, AUNG HUNG (HOONG) SH(E)RING

THUNOR-THURS AUNG HUNG SH(E)RING

### Kennings:

'Thunorad' is Anglo-Saxon meaning 'thunder-road', or 'thunder's-travelling' – thunder is the noise of Thunor's chariot, and lightning occurs when Mjollnir is flung. The 'lightning' and 'cloud' also allude to the thunder god.

Thunor radding refers to the 'riding' of the Rad rune. Mjollnir is Thunor's hammer (lightning) which returns like a boomerang when thrown. As well as possessing aggressive and defensive properties, Thunor's hammer is associated with fertility, and is used for blessing, consecration, and other ritual and initiatory actions.

Hrungnir means brawler or rioter, a giant (Skaldskaparmal 17 in Sturluson 1998 [1987]: 77). Hrimthurs(ar) are the 'hoar-frost giants' (e.g. Havamal 109 [Larrington 1996: 29], Grimnismal 31 [Larrington 1996: 56], see also Simek [1993 :159]). These giants are the arch-enemies of Thunor, and they also represent the giant forces in ourselves (and in the world) which can be dealt with using Mjollnir.

Sonics: the sacred sounds here first send out Mjollnir (line 1), then call the return of the hammer (line 2) – thus Mjollnir behaves like a boomerang. The Aung sound propels Thunor's Galdr into Ginnungagap. The Hung and Shring elements of the Galdr refer to Thunor's propensity to 'measure' out justice. The 'hu' link in HUng and THUnor is consistent, and Thorn is Thunor's rune. In Shring the 'sh' sound (see also Tiw's Galdr and Disir/Ancestor's Galdr) is fired with the might of Thunor's giant skull-cruSHing hammer, Mjollnir. When inverted, Mjollnir is a pair of scales and it is this form of balanced justice which Thunor metes out when crushing giants with the hammer. Thunor brings equilibrium among Giants and the Gods by forceful means when it is required. Notice how when held with the handle downwards, Mjollnir becomes a Tiw rune, the Tiw of justice. Here again is a connection between the triune Allfather of Woden, Tiw and Thunor (see the section below entitled 'The Polarised and Triune Allfather').

Project Thunor's Galdr forcefully! The 32 sounds take us right through the Futhorc and back to Thurisaz (Thorn) again, Thunor's rune. Also, 32 is 3 + 2 = 5, the Rad rune, the riding motion mentioned in the second line of the Galdr. In this case, this motion is Thunor's chariot, which is itself thunder.

## 6. Frigg's Galdr

Day: Friday
Deity: Frigg
Planet: Venus

### Galdr:

FRIGG-FIRE, FENSALIR'S FARE
IDUN'S APPLES, SIF'S GOLDEN HAIR
CELESTIAL COW
VANG KLING SAU
VANG KLING SAU
VANG KLING SAU

### Kennings:

Fensalir (Old Norse 'marsh halls') is Frigg's abode (see, for example, Voluspa 33 in Larrington 1996). The 'Fare' spoken of in the Galdr refers to the product – Frigg's fire – of her abode. Fensalir, as Frigg's home, is set deep in the (watery) marshes and its produce (fare) has to be coaxed out from its subterranean location.

The goddess Idun is the goddess of rejuvenation – linked to Frigg as a goddess of fertility. She will raise up the celestial 'cosmic-person', the ecstatic Heathen shaman, with the rejuvenating effects brought about through trance work. Like the Bast-Sekhmet conundrum in ancient Egyptian religion, the cat-headed Bast (Venus) conceives, but, the Lion-headed Sekhmet does the nurturing (despite the more common familiar role ascribed to her as a Kali-like destroyer, a bringer of pestilence, destruction and death). The same relational scheme between Freyja and Frigg appears in this book. The celestial cow mentioned here also refers to Audhumla, the classic incarnation of female deity, as exemplified in the cosmogony.

Sonics: These sounds are repeated three times, once for each of the triune aspects of the Goddess – Maid (Friday), lover/mother (Monday/Friday), and crone (Saturday). The 'Va-' sound refers to the feminine, and the 'sau' (pronounced 'sow') to the 'sow'. The 'Kli-' sound is similar to the 'Kri-' sound (see below), but unlike the harsh Disiric Galdr it is softened by the feminine Lagu rune and the letter L.

The Name Frigg may ultimately be connected to the Indo-European root word 'Prij', meaning love. Frigg is of course related to 'frigging' – love-making. Frigg is the 'darling' of the chief of the gods, Woden. Given that Fiorgyn (also the name of Thunor's wife) is probably linked to the goddess Jorth (the Earth) and that Frigg is the daughter of Fiorgyn, it often becomes impossible, as is commonly the case, to ascribe linear genealogies to the gods and goddesses. The Earth-Mother (Jorth) is said to be Woden's daughter and also his wife, making Frigg her own daughter! Clearly, linear thought in this case is not very productive and it is more useful to speak of various manifestations of 'Earth goddesses'.

One association of Frigg's Galdr, like Freyja's, is again to the 'sacred cow', linking Frigg to her role as consort/wife of the Sky-Father (of which Woden, Tiw/Tiwaz and Thunor are aspects). In this sense, Frigg is the excitement in the belly (groin), the surge of vital force, the 'Ond' which most often manifests (in the mundane world) as the sex-drive. Frigg is the vital force and mother of herself, meaning that she is her own energy, the source of her own creation, and consort to Woden as Allfather. Like the divine cow, she is not 'created' in the mythology; she simply appears, like the proto-cosmic giant Ymir.

Sing this Galdr, brightly/sweetly. It is used to raise Ond up the world tree (spine) in an emotive way, to empower an idea, for example, with sensual force. This encourages the Hugr (mind) to connect a selected idea/thought or a given oracular pronouncement, with something desirable/ sensuous. This is the aforementioned Frigg power matrix, an ancient technique for making changes in the Hugr in a way which makes them (sexually) appealing. It is a form of sex magic! There are 20 sounds to this Galdr, for the meaning of which, see the Cosmogony. The twentieth rune is 'Mann' and humans live 'on' the Earth Mother in Midgard. Further, $2 + 0 = 2$ Uruz, the huge bovine aurochs with all its connotations of immensity and (sexual) strength, referring again to the cosmic cow Audhumla.

## 7. Disir/Ancestor's Galðr

Day: Saturday
Deity: Ancestors; the day of the Vanadis/Disir/Idises
Planet: Saturn

### Galðr:

WOLF RUN, RAVEN FLY

CATTLE KIN AND COMRADES DIE

MOUND-WISE, THE VANADIS CRY

AUNG KRING

VAL-KRING

KRING KRING

### Kennings:

The wolves and ravens are very much associated with the
Valkyries who ride with Woden on the Wild Hunt. Wolves
and ravens are also, of course, Woden's spirit-helpers. The
Valkyries are linked with the Disir, Vanadis and Idises (see
comments above under Disiric trance). This association is well
put in Partridge's illustration of the Grave rune in the Futhorc
(Linsell 1994[1992]: 117, and see the Rune Cards). Simply put,
the Valkyries are intimately associated with the dead.

Cattle kin is a kenning for our fellows, both human and other beings (including animals, plants and other 'spirits' or 'wights'). All such beings must die, and become ancestors.

Connections between the Vanadis, 'sitting out' (Utiseta), and the ancestral burial mounds, have been discussed above (under Disiric trance).

Sonics: The first Kring is pushed and deified with Aung. The second Kring is shaped with the feminine Va-l, the Va from Vanadis and the L from the feminine Lagu rune. The 'kri' sound refers to the 'kyri' in ValKYRie, the shriek of death, of battle, and the sound of killing – for the Valkyries collect the souls of the fallen in battle. 'Kring' is repeated twice, once for 'this side' (the 'real' world', ourselves who will die) and once for the 'other side' (the dead, in the other world). Repeating them twice resonates with shamanic entrance to and exit from the otherworld. The repetition is also associated with the double (twin-aspected) canine-wolf-guardian(s), as expressed in Woden's two wolves Freki and Geri, and the hound at the gates of Helheim named Garm.

The Disir (Vanadis) and Valkyries are associated with the ancestors. The Disir are thus intimately connected with Helheim and Dokkalfheim, with burial mounds, long barrows, family shrines, and similar sacred sites. They are, simply put, akin to ancestral spirits. As an aside, Saturday also contains '-ur', perhaps referring to the past or ancient-time associated with the ancestors: the cosmic female cow Audhumla (Ur rune) derives from that ancient time. Associate Kri-ng with death, and the activities of the howling 'she wolves' and 'ravens' which run wildly in Dark elf world and Helheim.

The Galdr is used to invoke Disiric spirits, ancestor spirits who, whilst being elements of 'that which was' can be 'stretched' and extended into conversation with the living. They can teach us about ourselves, each other, and the world(s) in which we live. The Au-(ng) sound, associated with the Aesir, is used to control or pacify the potentially disruptive and hard to manage Disiric force, the rising of Ond, and during rites involving the raising of the dead. Intone this Galdr initially in a calm and dignified way. For Disiric trance increase the pace, complicate the rhythms and increase the volume, pronouncing the sounds harshly. The Heathen Seidrmadr is able to waken Nidhoggr with this Galdr, seethe the cauldron, and raise the Disir. Such a practice is not for the faint-hearted and should not be undertaken lightly. Only the well-practised are capable of controlling such forces. Caution is advised! There are 20 sounds, referring to the Mann rune. The Anglo-Saxon rune poem links this rune with death, and by implication, with the ancestors. Numerologically, 2 + 0 = 2 Uruz, which links this Galdr with 'Ur', the ancient (e.g. SatURn, SatURday). Ur is also linked phonetically with the Norn 'Urd' (Wyrd) who is a representation of the past or 'life unfolding'.

## The Issue of Deity Overlap

Having 'separated' the deities and trance states associated with them, it is pertinent to note that there is some dispute over the 'overlap' of deity attributes. It is hardly possible to divide the deities completely as can perhaps be done with greater certainty regarding the gods of Rome or Greece, when some of their characteristics resonate with others.

Neither can the trance states be categorically and absolutely separated; there will be fluidity – we discuss the fluidity of trance in more detail in chapter 6: Ritual.

With this idea, we must also be wary of giving deities 'lower' or 'higher' stations; a hierarchy hard to place on the gods. Surely, the notion of better/worse can hardly be appropriate to gods! The Gods should also not be separated on ability. While Tiw may be Skyfather and Allfather, this makes him no 'better' than any of the others. Woden, as the patron of shamans is no 'lesser' than Tiw simply because Tiw is Allfather. Indeed, in the sources both Woden and Tiw are Allfather. In an attempt to address this sort of deity overlap, we have suggested that the concept of Allfather brings all the gods together, principally in the triune aspect of Woden, Tiw and Thunor, as discussed in more detail in the section entitled 'The Polarised Allfather', below. All the gods are a reflection or aspect of Allfather (read also as Allmother, of course), and this includes the freedom to err. In the myths, gods may falter, but this does not incur a value-judgement; the purpose of their transgressions is for our kenning. Unlike the gods of other systems who are far 'beyond' human faults, the Northern gods are accessible and approachable for the Runic shaman. Furthermore, underlying and permeating all things is the Web of Wyrd, and with the gods 'subject to its power' we, as humans, can relate to the gods further. Wyrd is the way of the universe with the gods, ourselves and all of creation as a part of it.

All of the gods and all of the runes are in all of the worlds of the entire tree. Their attributes are fluid and not rigid. The multi-talented abilities of the deities are thus readily acceptable. Moreover, they are not hierarchically placed.

The presence of all of them makes up the whole. Their stories are there for our kenning. In as much as we can find kennings, this may be as far as we can go in finding 'authenticity' today. The evidence – archaeological, literary or otherwise – is limited and never entirely objective. What is important is that this system works for us today.

## The Polariseδ anδ Triune Allfather

An example of how deity overlap can be reconciled surrounds our concept of the polarised Allfather. The polarised Allfather comprises Tiw in his role of the ambisexual god (Tuisto), who is a part of the 'Great' Goddess, who in turn is a part of him. This is the nature of their sacred marriage. Tiw in his polarised aspect does equate with the Roman god of war, Mars (Tuesday), but this is only because polarisation/duality (the existence of two), creates strife (as well as balance) between parties with conflicting interests. Balance (Tiw) comes from the harmonisation of two (polar) competing opposites. Versions of Thunor's hammer when placed handle down, represent the Irminsul Pillar with a cross beam, akin to the scales of justice which are an emblem of Tiw, just as Yggdrasill is a motif of the tree-journeying shaman-god, Woden.

Tiw is also connected with the Pole Star. According to the Anglo-Saxon rune poem, Tiw is 'a clear dependable sign… is ever on course and never wanders' (see Appendix A). Pennick suggests this apex of Irminsul was named Tir (Pennick 1990: 57), and Fries that it is the 'need-nail… that holds the world in place and around which the heavens revolve' (Fries 2002[1993]: 232). The pole star and Irminsul are also associated with 'Woden's spear' in its role as the 'nowl' or 'nail' of the universe around which all else revolves. Thus a further connection emerges, with the triple manifestation of the Sky Father: Tiw (Irminsul Pillar), Woden (Yggr's steed), and Thunor (Sky chariot, double hammer, iron gloves to grip it, and strength doubling girdle/belt). In one sense, this balances well the triple manifestations of the goddesses as the Wyrd Sisters, or the maid, mother, and crone.

We might, then, conceive of first, Tiw as a judge, the holder of the 'law'. Second, we might consider Woden as a Lawyer (law operator), and third, we can view Thunor as a policeman (law enforcer but representative of the common people, the makers of the law). It is as law enforcer that we see Thunor keeping 'order' (see the poetry for Thunor, above) in Asgard and Middle Earth. The law needs strength to support it and enforce its judgements – thus Thunor is a justice-maker (killer of giants) and is associated with Thursday and Jupiter, the Roman day/god of justice. This need not be confused with the All-father's role of judge and the law of the universe. With creation and the manifestation of corporeality, we can only elucidate the Law by divination. In this respect, Tiw, in contrast to Thunor, becomes the powerful male god whom we invoke for 'guidance' (see aforementioned rune poem), particularly in finding the martial spirit to wage war on ignorance, negativity, and those shades from Helheim which would defeat us and bend us low (as mentioned under Tiw's Galdr).

The profound kennings bound into Tiw's Galdr illustrate how the gods can overlap, and how the issue of overlap can be empowering. We pinpoint here, the eagle Hrasvelgr which is prominent in the Galdr. This eagle is sitting at the top of both the Irminsul Pillar and Yggdrasill itself. In overlap, both Tiw and Woden have the eagle as one of their 'helpers' or shamanic forms. The Hrasvelgr eagle has a falcon sat between its eyes, representing the risen Frigg-force (Ond). But Freyja also possesses a 'Feather Form' which enables her to fly, so that there appears to be overlap between Freyja and Frigg. Furthermore, Freyja sometimes lends the cloak to the mischievous Loki, nemesis and antagonist of the gods and humans (see, for example, Thrymskvida 3 [Larrington 1996: 97]). Loki too can therefore partake of and direct the raising of the Ond, for mischievous or even destructive purposes. Frigg, as distinct from Freyja on the other hand, with her 'Feather Form', is called 'Mistress of the hawk's plumage' in an early kenning (see Skaldskaparmal 19 in the Prose Edda). This example of the eagle, the falcon and the feather form or cloak, again illustrates that there is much overlapping of deity attributes in the myths. Rather than balk at the complexity, we argue that it is possible to embrace the ambiguity and diversity of the mythology available to us.

## Deities, Ancestors, Totems and Spirit-Helpers

Issues of overlap also crop up when we consider the meaning of deities, ancestors, and 'totems'. The way we use 'totem' here coheres with anthropological understandings in some ways. Like shamanism, 'Totemism' is an anthropological construct used to describe how some indigenous communities (for example in Australia and on North America's Northwest Coast) have genealogies (a kind of family tree) relating humans to animals and/or other beings. In this sense, for Wodenic shamans, totem ancestors are the wolves and/or ravens of

Woden: in the myths, Woden is inseparable from these beasts – they are his spirit-helpers and their Wyrd is intrinsically linked to his. Furthermore, genealogies of our Northern ancestors trace back the family line to Woden. Thus, there is an intimate connection between Heathens today, deities as ancestors, and their totems as our totems. As will be made clear in the rest of this section, there are great similarities and connections between the deity Woden and the totem/spirit-helper wolf/raven – and other gods and their respective totems.

There are so many deities, spirits, spirit-helpers and ancestors that engaging with them all, or choosing which ones to work with, might seem to be a mammoth task. For example, which Woden do I use of all the hundreds named in the sources, which ancestor, which grandparent or great grandparent? We therefore subsume the multitude of deities under seven principles, these being the seven gods/goddesses of the week, discussed above. Thereafter, it is up to the aim of the Runester to decide which of these 'Wodens' (or aspects of Woden) is most appropriate to invoke – for example, Woden as Grimnir the masked god, or Woden as Hangatir, the hanging god.

Furthermore, to invoke and indeed be possessed by gods and ancestors is to understand that deities and ancestors are in many ways very similar. Historical precedent for approaching the gods as ancestors is found in, for example, the Swedish kings lists in which the ancestry of the kings is traced back to Woden. Just as in the cosmogony we all derive from the same primal giant, so, in line with the old king lists, we all have Woden as an ancestor. And just as our human origins lie with the early hominids in various parts of the world, so we are all 'one tribe' – in common parlance – of humans.

In engaging with the dead and deities, we might approach them, and at a psychological level, as personality complexes. In this way it is unnecessary to worry about waking a grandparent or Napoleon Bonaparte from the grave and the emotional or political turmoil that activity might incur! Staying with the psychological language for the moment, what we actually invoke and communicate with, then, is the archetypal (to use a Jungian term) representations (or principles) of all the ancestors and all of the gods. A vital point to add, however, is that we do not think ancestors, deities and totems are merely 'personality complexes', 'archetypes', or 'aspects'; the language of psychology is limited. Our experience suggests the ancestors, gods, deities, wights and other 'spirits' are entities in their own right.

Taking this process a step further, we have no need to rigidly distinguish between a deity and its associated animal spirit-helper, for they are connected. This is reminiscent of ancient Egyptian portrayals of gods with animal heads. Thus, when invoking Woden, we are at the same time invoking the wolf (and/or raven), and when invoking Freyja, the falcon (and/or cat/lynx). Undergoing a shape-shifting (Old Norse 'hamfarir') experience into a wolf or falcon then, is, at the same time, assuming the form of a deity. This idea gives us good reason for taking on the form of an animal, and helps us to avoid the problem of deciding what/who to invoke for a particular ritual –

whether to shape-shift into an animal spirit-helper, invoke a god with Galdr, or communicate with an ancestor. For all of these aspects can be invoked at once! At the same time though, it is possible to work with one being at a time, depending on the requirements of the ritual.

On a practical note, and in relation to communicating with the dead, our suggestions thus far mean that it is unnecessary to be concerned about waking your immediate family from the grave. When at the edge of Helheim, you will be met by your guide to that realm, and this guide will most likely be your animal-helping-spirit. If your helper is the Wolf, then you can, at the same time, be communicating with Woden, who is of course also your ancestor. The idea of trafficking with the dead does not have quite so many problematic or gruesome connotations as you might have imagined.

Decisions on shape shifting can be based on either the affinity you have for the spirit-helper, or on which 'totem' comes to you – indigenous shamans are more often chosen by the spirits than vice versa. Thus, for Thunor, if you do not resonate with the goat (Tanngrisnir [Toothgrinder] and Tanngnjostr [Toothgnasher] pull Thunor's chariot) it might be more appropriate to ride the chariot itself. The same applies to Balder's ship Hringhorni, the ship combining both life – the sun in the form of the ship Skidbladnir – and death (Balder's death) as represented by the ship Naglfar. A list of deities and their shape-shifting forms or otherworldly mode of transport might include:

Sunday/Balder: Ship

Monday/Freyja: Cat (Lynx), Falcon

Tuesday/Tiw: Eagle

Wednesday/Woden: Wolf, (also Raven, Eagle, Horse, though for consistency we associate the raven with the ancestors, and the horse with riding the tree rather than shape-shifting)

Thursday/Thunor: Goat, Chariot

Friday/Frigg: Falcon

Saturday/Sitr's-day/Ancestors: Raven

The overlap in forms here (e.g. Woden: Raven, Ancestor's-day: Raven) can be resolved at your own discretion. For simplicity and practicality, it may well be advisable to associate one particular form with one deity. (For a powerful ritual which utilises shape-shifting, deity invocations, ancestor communication and the three trance states, see Ritual 6 in Chapter 6: Ritual).

We would like to make a final note, to conclude this chapter, on the issue of overlap. An issue which often arises in the early stages of practice is that of deciding which of the seven deities to invoke. We argue that it is not always necessary to have a specific purpose for which an invocation is necessary. The initiate may simply wish to honour the deity, a ritual which would be similar to 'Puja' (yogic devotion). Considering the statements made so far, such a 'worship' (another difficult term, but one that we can not find a better/clearer substitution for – with the caveat that worship involves negotiation with, rather than surrender to a deity) of a deity could simultaneously involve a form of deity, and both ancestor and totem worship. At its simplest level, this is a ritual which involves going to / invoking a deity simply to be with that deity. For many people attracted to the spiritual path, this is like an 'itch which needs to be scratched': many of us simply feel and know that we want to alter consciousness and that when induced and used in certain ways, altered states of consciousness are good for us!

Perhaps the simplest way to choose which deity to work with is to cast the runes and follow their advice. There may, rather, be a particular need which steers the choice of a deity, such as invoking Freyja for a healing, Freyja or Frigg for a sexual practice or raising Ond, Woden for magic, Thunor for strength, Tiw for justice, and so on. There might also be a collective/group purpose which needs to be addressed, and the corresponding deity or deities can then be chosen and worked with.

Woden, of all the gods, is particularly permeable and tends to 'overlap' in many ways. As a shaman deity, a walker between the worlds, Woden is he who travels to all the worlds, who restlessly (like the initiate) seeks knowledge, especially knowledge of his own death. He is of both this world and the otherworld, standing on the threshold. His favourite haunt is, after all, the gallows! Incidentally, it is interesting that in Old Norse the gallows was termed 'horse of the hanged' (Thorsson 1984: 44), clearly connecting such a place to Woden. Woden's liminal nature is clear in the German day for Wednesday which translates as 'mid-week', that is midway between the three days either side of it. He also has two personalities. He is the strong, male warrior god who stands up to giants and tests his wisdom. But he also learnt his Seidr magic (women's magic) from the goddess Freyja, for which Loki accuses him of being 'ergi' (roughly translated as 'unmanly') – male seidr practitioners are also described as being 'ergi' in the sagas. Woden is a double-aspect deity, embodying both Aesir and Vanir characteristics. He also has two wolves which may be associated with the entrance to the spirit world, one wolf looking into that world, one looking into this (as noted in Saturday's Galdr, above).

For the Ulfhednr group, Woden is our patron deity. And, as the opening of the way ritual illustrates (see the following chapter), Woden is always invoked in our practices, whatever the ritual. It is also possible that a particular deity will call you, requiring a relationship and responsibility which should not be undertaken lightly!

# – Chapter 6 –
## Ritual - Guidelines for Practice

No shaman exists in an acultural vacuum – shamanism is culturally embedded and structured, as we have made plain. During shamanic practices, structure or 'ritual' is important, comprising a formula so that practitioners know what they are doing, why they are doing it, and 'where' they are going (in the worlds of the spirits). This chapter presents some guidelines for ritual practice for the Heathen shaman. In this way, we embed the themes discussed in chapters one to five into a practical sphere, elaborating particularly on the oracular practices introduced in chapter one.

Our suggestions here are only guidelines. We encourage you to experiment with ritual and elucidate kennings in your own way, in your own time. All rituals in Galdrbok can be rooted into rune and scrying practices, procedures with which you should by now be familiar. If so, you now have 'the basics', comprising familiarity with mediumistic trance, the runes, the casting of runes, interpretation and connections of the runes to the cosmogony, and the technique of scrying – making you now ready to progress onto more detailed and advanced ritual practices.

In the West we have reservations about such 'subjective' spiritual practices, particularly those rituals which involve ancestor communication, as we marked earlier. One reason for this is that our community relationships have broken down over the last century. We also lack major rites of passage, including the transition from child to adult, marriage, and death, as our modern 'rituals' become increasingly secular. All of these rites of passage are intrinsic to the life of the Wodenic Seidrman and we suggest that you prepare and standardise the basic format for such rites when the appropriate times arise.

The more advanced work of a Runic shaman requires the practitioner to move beyond passive mediumistic trances into more active forms of participation. For these rituals to 'work', consider that 'you only get out, what you put in'. It is vital that in these rituals you are 'moved' – including in some cases physical movement – in order to fuel your intention/will for the ritual to be a success. This may require some effort, which is one reason why shamanic practices, systems (spiritual technology) and tools (runes, staff, gandr, blade etc) are important. Guidance is required not just in what to do, what to believe, and so on, but also 'why' and 'how'! Galdrbok sets out an effective system of rituals addressing these needs.

## Initiatory Ritual Structure of Galdrbok

At its simplest, using the runes and crystal as a way of life, a way of everyday life, marks the starting place for all other ritual practices. Indeed, a Vitki could potentially reach a profound state of spiritual attainment simply through this practice alone. But there are, in addition, further rituals which facilitate a process of gaining greater insight and understanding of ourselves, the world around us, and the Way of Wyrd. The following ritual components can be seen as separate rituals in their own right; sometimes it is appropriate only to do one of these, at other times a combination of one or more. Following rituals 1-3 might well comprise a suitable method for opening any ritual, time and space permitting: set up a shrine, open the way, and perform a cosmogony mimesis; then complete any additional ritual needs. Scrying and Runic practice themselves, for example, might follow these three rituals. If time does not permit a lengthy opening, break the ritual down into smaller 'seed' parts, in which case the opening could take from five minutes to an hour, as time and circumstances permit.

## Ritual 1 - The Shrine

In Chapter 2, we wrote of the god Ve, whose name means 'shrine', and the way in which he figures in the cosmogony as one the trio of first gods, Woden, Vili, and Ve, and dismemberer of the body of Ymir in the process of creation. The shrine is therefore represented by the ninth (Ve) and tenth stages in the cosmogony (the onset of cosmology and birth of Yggdrasill). In one sense this element of the cosmogony, and Ve himself, resonates with the human body, and by extension the whole of middle earth – recall the maxims 'as above, so below' and 'man is a miniature macrocosm'. Cosmogonically, Ve is that part of the triune Woden which is materially manifest. These emphases on 'body' (giant, god, or human) suggest the shrine should be a significant and vital part of any Heathen's ritual work. The shrine also marks a starting point of initiation (we can only proceed from our own bodies), so it is the starting point of ritual. Numerous other religions worldwide stress the importance of the shrine, from Christianity in the West, to Tantric Yoga in the East.

As well as our own bodies as shrines in themselves (recall the over-used maxim 'treat your body as a temple'), the ritual shrine also consists of a representation of the world tree. A suitable example would be an image of Woden carved into Yew wood. Unlike the Christian crucifix with Jesus on it, and instead of having a tree pictured with Woden hanging on it, this might comprise the tree itself (a piece of Yew) with Woden carved in it (the 'image'). As the term Yggdrasill indicates, the tree and Woden are in many ways inseparable. Each time this 'idol' of Woden is produced and set up as the shrine in itself, a shamanic initiation is represented: not only did Woden hang on the tree in shamanic sacrifice, and not only is this ritual re-enacted by Heathen shamans (see Ritual 5), but also, in requiring altering consciousness, every ritual involves a shamanic initiation.

The idol is brought to life with the fertile and generating power and life force which is Ing – recall how the '-ing' sound brINGs the Galdr to life. So, in setting up the shrine, greenery (Ivy, Oak leaves, etc) representing/embodying Ing is used to activate the idol, enlivening and bringing to life or 'Ingifying' the Woden image. In this simple ritual of setting up a shrine, then, which only involves a carved piece of wood and some greenery, we find a multitude of potent symbols – Woden himself, Woden's shamanic sacrifice, our own shamanic sacrifices, the tree Yggdrasill itself, the 'material' world, and the human body – our starting point for ritual and our shrine for life.

## Ritual 2 - Opening the Way

With the shrine in place, all other rituals may follow. Though a shrine is not always necessary, nor is it always practical to raise one, it is desirable. Each ritual then proceeds by 'opening the way', that is, 'opening' the heart or spirit of the initiate (and therefore closing down the ego) in preparation for the rest of the proceedings. You may first like to make some sacred space by shaking in the spirits (appropriate to the ritual, and/or the local land wights) with a rattle, or mark the space with a Gandr, ritual blade such as a sword, or staff. Following this, the primary deity invoked – as the god of the threshold and opener of the way – is Woden. Accordingly, recite the mundane poetry for Woden and his Galdr, to open the way.

## Ritual 3 - Cosmogony Mimesis

The next important step in the subsequent stages of ritual is to replicate the cosmogony and reaffirm our place in it. That is, to establish our origins and the map of the tree, so as to situate the Heathen Magician in the otherworld. The dismemberment of Ymir and re-memberment of the body parts into Yggdrasill is reified in this ritual. Bread and mead can be sanctified (using rattles/wands/Runic symbols/rune charms), dismembered (poured into horns and broken into pieces), and consumed. Numeric symbolism can be useful here, depending on the number of people present, based on the 'eight' pieces of Ymir used to embody the cosmology: in consuming these 'body parts', the cosmogony and cosmology are effectively embodied by each person who is present. Ymir can also be dismembered in the form of eight twigs of incense (the stalks of the sacred plant Mugwort, for instance), which are burnt in a censer, on charcoal, or in a fire. The smoke thus represents the dispersal of Ymir into the worlds, and at a profound level, we can inhale Ymir into ourselves. Every act of ritualised cosmogony mimesis then, is a profound and empowering re-enlivening of the 'original' cosmogony.

We stress the importance of this dismemberment ritual because, as precedent, dismemberment is a common and important theme in many spiritual systems worldwide. In the long barrows, passage 'graves' and other Northwest European Neolithic 'tombs' (though they were more than mere graves or tombs), disarticulation and the re-ordering of bones in some way was a common practice. Some archaeologists think this process involved the breaking down of individual personalities, individual people, as they crossed over to the spirit world and entered the community of ancestors. Especially when working rituals at such places, our cosmogony mimesis resonates with this interpretation of ancestral funerary rituals. Following the legacy of Neolithic ancestors, then, the individual 'ego' consciousness is broken down when we alter consciousness and enter the other world – and also enter the ritual community (comprising the other human practitioners present and the 'ancestors', 'spirits', 'deities', and so on). When the dismemberment ritual is practised at such locations, it follows that dismembered ancestors whose remains once lay in the 'tombs' will be connected with all the more readily.

A short, punchy and direct poetic telling of the cosmognoy is powerfull during this ritual. The Cosmogony Lay marks a good example. Another good example is the short four-page telling of the Creation in Crossley-Holland's 'Norse Myths' (1980: 3-6). Various percussive sounds can empower the ritual further via aural communication. And rune postures can act as a mnemonic device to re-member and embody the rune, its associated cosmogony, and 'power'. In this way, each ritual utilises all five senses, in a kind of overload, to enable the entering of the otherworld. The shrine impacts sight, incense hits smell, bread and mead fire taste; Galdr, rattles and drums assault hearing, and dancing, and Stadrgaldr (rune postures) or other movement stirs touch. The main aim and consequence of this assault on the senses is to thrust yourself into trance, into the otherworld. Furthermore, it acts as a mnemonic device, for re-membering all past rituals and how their empowering potential inspires you to work more rituals. This is the 'desire' or 'passion' for Heathen shamanism embodied by Frigg/Freyja, the Frigg matrix. As the Galdr states, 'Frigg-fire, Fensalir's fare'!

With a simple, three stage ritual set-up, then, the shrine is raised, all present are made 'open' and the cosmogony and cosmology are reified. Everyone and anyone can participate in a ritual of this kind, albeit with different levels of kenning. In addition, it may be pertinent to honour specific gods and goddesses, wights (such as your own 'house wight') and ancestors, by hallowing a drink of mead or ale (or such like) and toasting the respective being – known in Heathenry as a 'Symbel' (pronounced 'sumbl'). The specifics of the sorts of rituals which can follow these initial ritual considerations are next presented – although of course a ritual might simply involve the setting up of the shrine, opening the way, cosmogony mimesis, a symbel, or whatever, in their own right.

## Ritual 4 - Rune-casting and Scrying as Midgard Vaniric Trance

We begin ritual at the shrine, which on Yggdrasill is Midgard, the realm of Vaniric deities and people. New initiates will, as mentioned, first obtain or make a rune set, and obtain a crystal ball. These are the basic tools for putting Galdrbok's Heathen shamanic system into practice. Runic shamans will then begin familiarising themselves with these mandatory tools. There are numerous rune guides and crystal books, some of which describe how to scry – examples are listed at the end of this book.

The practices outlined in Chapter 1 for rune casting and scrying induce Vaniric/mediumistic trance. By utilising the crystal sphere to descry the worlds (view the tree), and by using the oracle to 'get in tune' with Wyrd and negotiate the Web of Wyrd, Heathen practitioners take the first step in the system of initiation – affirming a Heathen lifeway and adopting regular practice of altered consciousness (with runes and crystal). In accordance with the cosmogony, this step on the path of initiation corresponds with rune 14, Perthro (the lot box).

At this stage the initiate is also required to get to grips with the cosmogony/cosmology; that is, internalise it. The process of inward looking/questing might be described as 'leaving one's eye behind' as a pledge, honouring Woden's own sacrifice in order to gain esoteric knowledge. Such work confers on the initiate the acquisition of the Wodenic eye. One eye will thus be left at Mimir's well (at the base of the world tree) as a pledge, a token of remembrance. The eye (your eye) symbolically sits there as a reminder of your otherworld experience, and you can, by memory (and vision), recall all of your otherworld journeys. The purpose of this practice is to establish within your Hugr (mind) a cosmic tree, under which you leave (as proof of visiting) your Wodenic eye.

A practical way of internalising the cosmogony and cosmology is outlined in the ritual entitled 'Voluspa', towards the end of this chapter. Furthermore, a ritual of oath-swearing, or making a troth-pledge on the ring Draupnir, is also provided, introducing another form of making a pledge. This is an initiatory ritual wherein the Vitki/group of Runesters swears on a rune ring, 'arm-ice' or similar suitable ring/bracelet.

## Ritual 5 - Hung on the Tree

At the next stage/ritual, which also starts out from Midgard (the Vaniric level), the initiate undertakes a mimesis of Woden's sacrifice on the tree. This is the shamanic initiation which requires dying to this world, in order to travel shamanically on the tree. Hitherto, the Runester has only looked into or descryed the tree using the stone sphere (rune fourteen of the cosmogony, Peorth). This next, most powerful ritual embodies Thunor's lightning bolt (the lightning flash through the tree) and marks the thirteenth rune of the cosmogony – Yew – since it is on Yggdrasill that the Heathen shaman emulates Woden's shamanic sacrifice. The shamanic sacrifice may also involve an experience of dismemberment. The perception of being dismembered while in trance is a common theme in indigenous shamanisms. In Galdrbok's system of initiation, there is the need (Nyd) for this sacrifice in order for the shamanic path to proceed, just as there is the need for Ymir to be dismembered, as represented by rune number ten – Nyd – in the cosmogony.

Hanging on the tree begins with the practitioner undertaking rituals 1-4. The Runester then descends directly to Helheim (the geography of this 'road' is described below). This is accomplished via Disiric techniques, using dancing, drumming and other seething ecstasies. The journey to Helheim may well involve frenzied seething to the point of physical exhaustion, perhaps followed by shape-shifting into animal spirit-helpers. Then, collapsed and in Helheim, the Heathen shaman travels through the other worlds: Dark Elves to Giants to Midgard to Dwarfs to Light Elves and to the Haven, thus for the first time actually entering each world in turn (rather than simply descrying them). In so doing, the practitioner is waking and raising Ond, and carefully steering it up the tree, gleaning a brief glimpse (Bifrost or Bilrost, the fleeting rainbow) of the Haven (ecstasy), before 'falling' (as Woden states in Havamal 139, see Larrington 1996: 34) once again to Midgard.

In undertaking this ritual, the Heathen Mage has undertaken the first major shamanic initiation, corresponding to runes 13 to 20 in the cosmogony. Having hung on the tree (rune 13, Yew), and accorded with Wyrd using the runes and crystal (14 Perthro), the Wodenic shaman gains resilience (15 Elksedge), strength (16 Sowilo rune) and direction (17 Tiw rune). The act of sacrifice may bring rewards in the form of magical abilities (18 Berkano), and the initiate is able to use the horse (19 Eh) as a vehicle to enter the otherworld. This 'journey' (also fitting the interpretation of the Eh rune) is taken alone and requires a shamanic death (20 Mann) in order to access the world of the spirits. It also requires submerging or drowning (21 Lagu) beyond the 'real world'.

As a result aspirants are now fully initiated Heathen shamans and have the where-with-all, having descried the tree and experienced the shamanic sacrifice – the lightning strike – to further explore, travel and raise Ond up the tree, in other ritual practices. You should repeatedly explore or 'visit' each world in turn in order to get to know the territory, establish allies, face enemies (such as shades), perform magic, and so on – to be fully proficient in cosmogonical and cosmological lore.

## Ritual 6 - Deity/Ancestor Communication and Shape-Shifting

In the previous chapter, we mentioned a ritual which utilises deity and ancestor communication, and shape-shifting – these three elements are intrinsically linked and, in the spirit of this overlap, this ritual can potentially incorporate all three trance states. While this was possible also in the previous ritual (Ritual 5), the aim there was to experience each world rather than work with the three trance states, per se. In Ritual 6 however, the three trance states are explicitly induced.

The Heathen Mage begins with Vaniric trance in Middle Earth, undertaking the first three rituals, as outlined above. The appropriate mundane poetry and Galdr for that deity is then chanted to invoke the shape the Runester wishes to assume, for example a wolf for Woden. As you chant the Galdr, you will feel yourself transform into the wolf, feel yourself run with the wolf – feel as the wolf. This process should involve the sort of 'movement' we described at the start of this chapter. As you run, swim, fly, fall (or whatever) in animal form, feel yourself descend to Helheim, down, down, down and to the north (the 'road' to Helheim is described below). Simply put, the Galdr thus becomes a shamanic tool for Disiric trance which enables shape-shifting. Furthermore, on reaching Helheim, the place of the ancestors, the Galdr has the potential to facilitate a swift rising up the Irminsul Pillar with the deity into its Aesiric form in Asgard.

One variation of this ritual is that instead of assuming the form of the deity, the animal shape (as a discrete helper experienced in the otherworld) can take you to the deity in order to communicate with it. Just because the deity and animal are intrinsically similar does not mean both cannot be encountered at the same time in the otherworld, after all, the deity may equally appear to you as voices in your head as much as a 'person' standing in front of you. In the spirit world, anything is possible and nothing too bizarre – just consider your dreams!

## Otherworld Geography: The Territory of Yggdrasill

When undertaking shamanic travel on the world tree it is obvious that you need to know where you are going and how to get there. Thus far, we have described the otherworldly beings resident in various realms of Yggdrasill (Chapter 3: Cosmology), and how to get to the otherworld via the trance states (Chapter 4: Trance). We have also offered a number of rituals which aid shamanic and other forms of journeying to the otherworld – but what of the 'geography' of the otherworld? Just how can you 'get' from the 'real' world into the Midgard of the otherworld? And how does one get from one world to another?

### Midgard: Two Worlds in One

In the 'everyday' 'waking' world we are in Midgard. The terms 'everyday' and 'waking', etc are convenient for distinguishing between 'ordinary' and 'spirit' worlds – but we use them in full appreciation of the fact that the boundary between them is fully permeable. Behind or within this 'everyday' Midgard is the 'spiritual' world of Midgard. Most people can not see this part of Midgard, most of the time, though parts of it sometimes slip through in visions and sightings of ghosts and other 'supernatural' phenomena. It is this spiritual side of Midgard which contains the Hamingja and Fylgja, land wights and other spirits, and which becomes visible when trance is induced. The movement from one side to the other is comparable with Alice's journey through the looking glass, which is itself comparable with the misty clouds of Nifelhel seen in the Vaniric trance induced through scrying practice.

We next offer an account of the otherworld geography which is encountered on the way both down and up the tree from Midgard. This we have gleaned from Eddic and other sources. Our accounts begin as description but end as narrative. Such is the way of the otherworld; it is hard to quantify and express in mundane terms. Let your initial readings of the description wash over you. Familiarise yourself with the geography before undertaking your own journey. And in those journeys, begin the process of mapping your own route to the worlds of Yggdrasill. What we provide are only guidelines, landmarks if you like, of how the Yggdrasill landscape appears to us. Yours may differ slightly, as informed by your own readings of the Eddic, Saga and other sources. It is the landmarks which interest us here, as handed down to us in the accounts written by our ancestors. And beyond the landmarks, the journey is unstructured – it is not a path-working or visualisation. What you experience in the otherworld, beyond the map, is your own personal (and/or communal) and inspirational (in the sense of ecstasy) shamanic journey.

## Entering the Tree

A useful exercise for familiarising yourself with the two sides of Midgard ('real' world and 'other' world) and the connections between them is to visualise (in the stone sphere or elsewhere) a yew tree which you know well in the 'everyday' world – all the better if you can actually, physically be there for this practice. If you are going 'down' the map of Yggdrasill, then a yew tree near a burial mound is perfect, or sitting at the roots of a tree, or even inside a hollow one. If going up, then sitting in the branches of the tree would also be effective, so long as you do not fall out!

You may start by conducting rituals 1-3, above. Next, begin scrying, either at your chosen tree or with the tree you know well 'in mind'. As you feel the onset of Vaniric trance, experience how this yew tree becomes a 'spirit' yew tree, in fact Yggdrasill itself in all its mightiness. Take some time to take in the magnitude of the tree from a distance and examine the tree close up, in detail – each branch and leaf. Ratatosk the squirrel runs along the branches carrying insults between Nidhoggr and Hrasvelgr, while four stags nibble at the tender shoots. Three vast roots descend into otherworldly realms, and the mighty branches stretch up so high, into Asgard, that you cannot see their tips for the bright golden light of the sun which forces you to turn your gaze.

The huge tree before you is hollow and a path enters it, well trodden by many generations of Heathen shamans who have walked this way before you. Tread that same path and feel the smooth bark at the entrance (note the etymology 'en-trance') where other travellers have steadied their way. Notice how the light dims sharply as you enter the tree. Within, there are two features to note. The first is a hole in one of the hollow roots below you, down which you can see only utter darkness. The second is a hole in one of the branches above you through which chinks of light warm your face.

Once accustomed to the interior of the tree, you might simply sit in this space and familiarise yourself with it. Then again, you may feel compelled to take one of the routes which lead to the worlds of Yggdrasill, the roots leading down the tree to Jotunheim and Svartalfheim, the branches to the upper worlds of the Dwarfs and Light Elves. From within the root you hear the yelps, whines and hoots of the creatures in the lower worlds. And from the branches above you hear the dull ringing of hammer on anvil, echoing from the realm of the dwarfs, set deep within high mountains. From even higher above you can just hear the faint singing of light elves, or is it the distant notes of birdsong – you cannot tell, but you wish to find out! The route you decide to take depends, of course, on the reason for your journey. Now it is time to make that journey.

**Helvegr: The Road to Helheim**

To embark on the road to Helheim, you crawl down the hole in a root which immediately seems much larger than it first appeared! You may begin crawling or walking down the root, but soon the mode of travel is running, or perhaps flying, swimming, falling, or simply floating. You might even feel as if you are riding a horse and we need not say which horse that might be or why it is that you ride it! Down, down, down you go, down and to the north, until you reach a cave. Within the dimly lit cavern it is damp and you hear the rushing water of the freezing cold River Gjoll ('loud noise'). Moving towards that sound you might find that your spirit-helpers are waiting for you in this cavern. On the other hand, you may have to call them or otherwise negotiate their presence. Be patient, and wait. In particular, those of the four legged, canine kind may appear, or those which feast on carrion, or perhaps other creatures of the night. With helpers close by, then, you take the path which follows the River Gjoll, into darkness once more.

As you fall, fly, run or swim, ever downwards, you are flooded with immense feelings and emotions which seem to well up from nowhere. There is sheer anger here, and sobbing tears. You feel as though these emotions are like vast natural forces. The roots of mountains press against your sides (in the form of the Rises), mighty hailstorms and winds batter your skin (in the form of the Thurses), information which is too much to bear at once swells around your head (the presence of the Etins), as if the freezing River Gjoll itself is thundering on your head (like Trolls). You are, of course, passing through the realm of the Giants, and it is a mighty and vast realm – but your helpers are with you, helping you retain your Hamr in spite of the onslaughts of giants.

Sufficiently strong, you may choose to remain in this huge realm with its mighty rivers and mountains, perhaps to pit your wits against the forces of giant land as Woden and Thunor have done before you. And you may need to tame and control certain forces and minds. Or you may feel pulled onwards, downwards, and to the north.

Your form is altered further as you travel – perhaps you shape-shift your Hamr into the Fylgja of your helpers. Or perhaps you are rowed along the River Gjoll in Naglfar, the ship of Death. It is particularly efficient for a group of Seidr-workers to join together and row themselves on this journey to Helheim in Naglfar, for the group otherworld experience is all the more empowering than the 'private' journey. A similar mode of group transport can be used when moving up the tree (see below).

Your falling flattens-out a little as you enter the realm of the Dark Elves and emerge from the darkness of the root into a faintly moonlit, shady land. It is a sparse landscape within which there are many shadows, often playful, sometimes menacing. The Dark Elves frequent lush green burial mounds, green being the only colour apart from dark grey and black in this land of night – and there are many mounds in this place, with only the River Gjoll to guide your way to Helheim between them. With your Hamr strong you can easily travel through this land and negotiate the Dark Elves, or perhaps it is time to sit a while on top of a mound and face the shadows. You are now close to Helheim.

You journey on, still following the lead of the River Gjoll until you reach a bridge, called Gjallarbru in the lore. Before the bridge is a ruin and from within the ruin emerges a giantess. Modgud she is named, and you must give your reason for passing this way before she will let you travel on. With an open heart you know the reason for your journey and tell the giantess. True to her word, Modgud lets you pass and you cross Gjallarbru. Before long on this path, in the darkness of the new moon, you meet a second bridge, Slidr, in which weapons of war clink and crash by in a torrent of blood. With an open heart you can cross this bridge without fear of falling into its depths, no matter how thin its path seems.

On the other side of the bridge, you do not travel far along the road when a high wall looms before you, visible in the pale new moonlight. You recognise it as the wall of Helheim, the residence of the Goddess Hel and home of the dead. You follow its wall to the gate, confident in the knowledge that Woden has trodden this path before you. At the gate sits a wolf which is larger than life. You know his name to be Garm and you tread warily past this guardian. Also by the gate is a burial mound, and you recognise that to be the resting place of a seeress who once told Woden of the making of the worlds, and of Balder's fate. You do not enter Hel through the gates, for those who enter rarely return. Like Woden, you sit atop the mound by the gates and call upon the seeress. You may have a power song which raises her from the grave, or she may simply appear at her own will before you. What you ask of her, and why you ask it, is up to you. But this woman may be Freyja herself, in the form of Heidr, so consider very carefully what it is that you ask – all the better if the reason for your questioning is for someone else rather than, or as well as, yourself.

Your questioning at an end, you graciously thank the
seeress who will then most likely (as she did to Woden)
retire, belligerently, determined that you will not wake her
again! You retrace your steps now, making sure to 'Hail'
Garm respectfully as you pass, and then cross the River
Slidr once more. Much easier now is the crossing, for with
the hidden lore you have gained from the seeress – whether
heartening or troubling – the bridge seems far wider in
your empowered state, and the weapons beneath less
threatening. Back now to Gjallarbru, and a 'waes thu hael'
to Modgud who will be there also the next time you take
the road to Helheim. Closer to Midgard you travel, past the
tempting shades, past the threatening but wise giants. Back
in the cavern you are now, and thanking your spirits for
their help. Then you are literally sucked back up the root,
as your body demands your Hamr and Fylgja, and the
tumultuous sound of the River Gjoll fades behind you. You
emerge from the hollow root within the hollow tree.
Sunlight showers through the entrance and you follow it,
tracing your steps back to Midgard.

The otherworld geography of the Road to Helheim is well
represented in the Eddic sources. For descriptions of Giant
land, there are many accounts, the most inspiring perhaps
being Vafthrudnir's sayings (Vafthrudnismal, see
Larrington 1996). Read also Hymir's Poem (Hymiskvida)
and Thrym's Poem (Thrymskvida) in the Poetic Edda. For
the territory of Svartalfheim we have depended on our
own otherworldly kennings since the Dark Elf world of the
Anglo-Saxons has not been recorded in literature. We
experience it as a place of burial mounds, shadows, and
playful but sometimes malignant spirits. For the road to

Helheim, read Woden's accounts in Voluspa and Balder's Dreams – again, in the Poetic Edda.

### Visions of Bilrost: The Fleetingly Glimpsed Rainbow

The journey towards the top of the tree also begins inside Yggdrasill, at the level of Midgard, where the hollow branch above you sheds warm light onto your skin. Recall the faint sounds of the Dwarfs smithing in their workshop caves deep within the high mountains, and the even fainter singing of the light elves. You are impelled to climb that hollow branch, and find neat footholds and gnarled stumpy steps in the hollow tree which take you there. You pull yourself through the opening and find yourself on a hefty branch of the mighty yew.

Below, far lower than you remembered for such a short climb, is the opening to the tree and the age-old path from Midgard before it, which you trod only a short while before. Birds twitter in the branches above you and you feel beckoned by the eagle Hrasvelgr and falcon (or hawk) Vedrfolnir, though you cannot see them. The branches feel as though they were laid out especially for you (and other Heathen shamans) to climb. But it is a long journey as you tread, ever upwards. You may feel as though, so fast do you climb, that soon your feet no longer touch the branches and you are flying, floating or otherwise moving ever upwards at a speedy rate. Your helpers appear around you, particularly those of the feathered kind, be it the mighty eagle or falcon, or the little wren, robin or black cap (a warbler which much loves the Yew). You might even feel yourself rowed up the tree in Balder's ship Hringhorni, or once again the riding is on horseback. Onwards and upwards!

The light of Asgard is calling you, but more intrusive and beckoning as you move upwards now is the increasingly indignant pounding of dwarfish hammer on anvil. Your path moves sideways, a little away from the light above you and along one of Yggdrasill's mighty branches until you find yourself at the entrance to a cave high up a mountain. The sounds of dwarfs, deftly crafting beautiful things, deep within the earth, charm you to enter the cave. But inside they bicker over who's hammer is who's, over who's making is the most skilled. Can you negotiate these short-tempered dwarfs? Perhaps the dwarfs even take a hold of you and begin to work their magic instruments on you, to smith your 'fibres' (as they did to Brand in Brian Bates' book 'The Way of Wyrd').

Back at the entrance to the cave you continue your flight through the branches, wanting to be ever closer to the sweet singing of the light elves and the welcoming warmth of the golden light. You feel as though the journey takes forever, but that it is a journey which does have an end. You feel the warming presence of the light elves wash over you. Perhaps you can not climb as far as you like because it is not yet your time to reach the heights. The pull of Midgard and its earthly wants are too strong and weigh you down. Perhaps a few of the elves who sit lower in the branches are prepared to share their wisdom with you for a short while. Perhaps they try to trick you in some way – take care not to fall out of the tree! Or perhaps in a moment of divinely inspired ecstasy you are fortunate to shoot up to the top of the tree and glimpse a bright rainbow.

If not, then it may be that the beauty of Asgard, the source of the bright light all around you, is far higher up the tree than you can see. Perhaps it is far too bright for you to look at for long, and you must turn back. But perhaps before you do, your effort in this hard journey is rewarded by the fleeting vision of the rainbow bridge. Blissfully harmonious are the sounds of its vibrating colours, glimpsed only for a moment; before you feel your body calling you. Back down at the centre of the tree, your mortality beckons you, and you plummet, cushioned by the prickly branches of Yggdrasill. The crafty wisdom of the light elves is fresh in your being as you pass the skilful sounds of dwarf-smiths and fall downwards, until you find yourself back on the branch at the entrance to that hollow Yew. You look down and slide back through the hole, to return to the inside of the Yew with its dark hollow root below and bright hollow branch above. Emerging from the tree you say 'waes thu hael' to the beings of Yggdrasill, to your helpers, and to the tree itself which sustains you.

Your crystal clears. And the sights and sounds of 'reality' flood in.

The upper world of Northern cosmology is far harder to chart than the lower realm. We know of the beings of these places, but the geography is less certain. In all these parts of Yggdrasill, in both upper and lower worlds, you must trust your own experiences and your own readings of the sources to elucidate the map. Trust in your own intuition, your own openness. And if otherworldly guides present themselves to you, to aid your journey, always question who they are and why they are present. If they will not respond, take care in whom and what you trust.

## Beyond Ritual: The Fluidity of Trance

Rituals 1-3, above, represent the early or basic stages of ritual experience. Just as Woden undergoes many shamanic initiations – from hanging himself on the tree to being hung over Geirrod's fire – these three rituals can and should be repeated many times, the more the better. However, these rituals are also preliminaries to deeper, more profound rituals. We have discussed the entering of Vaniric trance for divination and scrying, the entering of Disiric trance to awaken Ond and ascend the tree, and the entering of Aesiric trance by intoning Galdr and inducing deity possession. All of the rituals outlined above utilise one or more of the three trance states. In summary, the three trance states and their associated practices are:

1. Vaniric Trance: Runes and scrying open the way and facilitate communication with spirit(s)/deities/ ancestors via a 'tool', as well as descrying or viewing the world tree.
2. Disiric Trance: sensory deprivation facilitates shape-shifting, shamanic journeying, and the seething of Ond.

3. Aesiric Trance: Galdr facilitates taking on god-forms (or possession) in order to focus Ond towards the Haven and achieve ecstatic states.

It is important to point out that these three elements are not necessarily mutually exclusive or independent, and a single ritual practice is not necessarily limited to one or another of the trance states. Essentially, trance is fluid and our classifications of it are useful devices for the rational-ego mind to be able to understand; they are not rigid categories. While you may distinctly know that you have used or are going to use, for example, Vaniric trance, at other times more than one trance is entered.

Basic Vaniric practice, for example, includes a simple rune cast for a client in order to divine their Wyrd. However, there is nothing to stop the onset of other trance states during such a ritual. A Heathen Magician may suddenly become possessed by a deity, in such an instance, and therefore enter Aesiric trance. Or, Disiric trance may spontaneously occur, and the rune casting perhaps then develops into shamanic journeying and shape shifting, with the Runester returning to Midgard with valuable information for the querent. When scrying, on the other hand, mediumistic trance may accelerate into Disiric trance if you close your eyes and stimulate shape shifting. Or it may develop into Aesiric trance if the Galdr are employed. By and large, a Vaniric trance is a good first point of entry towards inducing the other trance states. It can also be a point of exit, since after a decent session of seething or deity possession, the Seidrmadr may use scrying to realign with Midgard and let prophetic kennings swim 'into view' before 'waking' into 'everyday' consciousness.

A good example of the fluidity of trance is the shamanic initiation (Ritual 5), which involves all three trance states. The starting point is Midgard with Vaniric trance, during which 'the way' is descried with the crystal ball or divined with a rune cast. From here the Vitki wakens Ond and seethes by dancing or by some other active method, in order to induce a Disiric trance and descend to Helheim by following the divined map. You then focus the Ond using Galdr (deity invocation and possession).

In another instance, Heathen initiates specifically embarking on a ritual of deity invocation may start in Vaniric trance (ritual components 1-3 above), then descend to Helheim to take on the god/ancestor/totemic form by reciting the Galdr, and then be raised to the Aesiric level. Other rituals might involve other combinations of trances and other ritual techniques. So, a healing ritual might involve seething to raise Ond for healing, along with a deity invocation (for example, Freyja). On the other hand, a healing might purely involve work in Midgard with the aid of the land wights. Spell casting, in contrast again, might involve other trances (see Chapter 7: Magic).

At more subtle levels of trance it may be difficult to distinguish which trance has been entered. This is the epitome of the fluidity of trance. In oracular Seidr for example, the Seidrmadr descends to Helheim but remains 'aware' in/of Midgard so that the advice of the ancestors can be voiced to the community. This is a mediumistic (Vaniric) state, but involves a considerable amount of seething; otherwise the advice from Helheim cannot be gleaned. It is a skilful balancing act between being sufficiently deep in trance to stay in Helheim, but at the same time awake in Midgard for the body to be stable and act as a human oracle. It is for this reason that many workers of oracular Seidr clasp a staff, for it is both a support and a means of staying in contact with both worlds at the same time. In such instances, you are in the archetypal shamanic role of 'walker between the worlds'. In all, remember that while we offer these rituals for your use, the potential for situation-specific ritual construction is limited only by the experience of each Heathen shaman!

## Ritual Work and the Edda

In companion with the aforementioned rituals, ritual work should, as mentioned, involve internalising the cosmogony and cosmology. As an extension of the shamanic initiation ritual outlined above, Runic Magicians can progressively and productively utilise the first four chapters of the Poetic Edda:

The Seeress' Prophesy (Voluspa)
The Sayings of the High One (Havamal)
Vafthrudnir's Sayings (Vafthrudnismal)
Grimnir's Sayings (Grimnismal)

The first four chapters are ideal because they reveal the exposition of Wodenic wisdom, including Woden's shamanic travels, as well as supplying mythological details. The remaining chapters of the Poetic Edda are concerned mainly with the exploration of heroic kingship, though do contain important mythological themes. The myth of Ragnarok, in the Prose Edda, can also be usefully incorporated as a metaphor for one's own death.

## Part One: Voluspa (Cosmogony and Cosmology)

The seeker of Wodenic wisdom reads the seeress' impressive account of the birth of the worlds, everything in them (it) and their collective fate, and learns of the entire scheme from beginning to end. In reading Voluspa it may not be apparent that it is indeed Woden who has called-up the seeress in the first place (or vice versa). So, using Vaniric trance one emulates that great Heathen shaman by internalising the cosmogony as an ongoing narrative which sometimes thunders, sometimes whispers, threatens and cajoles, but above all informs. Let these differing aspects of the seeress' voice run through your mind and see the events with an inner eye.

Pay particular attention to verse twenty-eight, concerning the hidden eye of Woden. Woden gave one eye to drink from the well of Mimir, a wise giant. The tale holds a kenning discussed earlier: the eye is the shamanic inward looking eye, no longer turned to the outside world. This is Woden emulating the 'Hag-sitter', the female hedge-sitter, who sits on the fence, able to see both sides. The process of inward looking and questing, culminating in a grasp of Voluspa (in spirit and not to the letter) confers on the initiate the acquisition of the Wodenic eye. The myth of Mimir's Well also provides good reason for visiting Jotunheim regularly – to consult Mimir's head!

## Part Two: Sayings of the High One

After fully aquatinting yourself with the Voluspa, after fully internalising the cosmogony and cosmology, you then begin to take the sayings of the high one into Vaniric trance, one verse at a time until you reach verse 138 (this might mean working with one verse a day, but the format is up to you). Verses 138 through to 145 constitute the narration of Wodenic initiation proper and should only be attempted after the onset of a decent Disiric trance (roughly corresponding to Ritual 5, above). This trance state places you in the very crisis required to break through the life-death barrier and die to the world. This is Woden as sacrifice, himself to himself. Woden has shown the way, and we can follow his lead. The purpose of this practice is to symbolically and powerfully experience the age-old shamanic rite of willingly dying to this world in order to enter the 'other' world.

Verses 146 through to 164 are statements of magical attainment. Some authors have connected these 'spells' with actual runes. Verses 146 through to 164 talk only of knowing the spells or charms which are named but not revealed. These curious 'spells' constitute a magical boast, a proof of magical ability acquired on the path, if you like. These are the magical abilities Woden has attained via shamanic initiation: having undergone the shamanic initiation (verses 138-145, ritual 5), the Heathen Mage can develop them also – corresponding in the cosmogony with the Birch rune.

We do not think these 'lays' (magic spells, Galdr, chants, or whatever) of Woden's are necessarily an attempt to encapsulate the scope or whole range or agenda of rune magic, as has been hinted at by other authors. Nor is there any direct reference to individual runes in the verses mentioned; such interpretations can only be conjectural, or inspirational. Indeed, the last direct reference to runes seems to have ended at verse 145. Besides, concerning 'spells', it is customary to create

Galdr as needs require it, using your own words and poetry. We do, however, consider Aswynn's (1994) interpretations to be quite effective, in which specific runes are associated with each spell. Learn the Havamal 'lays/spells' and by all means interpret them or associate runes with them; or, use these poetic statements as examples to create your own Galdr. One positive aspect of a non-dogmatic system is that the bare bones are provided, such as in Galdrbok, leaving readers to make rituals, Galdr and whatever, as they so intuit.

In addition to the Sonic Galdr specific to the seven-day gods and goddesses of the week which, in the syncretic method outlined in this book, etymologically connect various Northern deities with tried and tested Indo-European and Sanskrit holy sounds (see Chapter 5: Galdr), Galdr are also power songs. Essentially then, we have stipulated some Galdr containing the sonics, but there is still much room for creating other Galdr/spells as required, such as those suggested by Woden in the Havamal.

Your own 'power songs', based on Woden's account in the Havamal can be based on the runes or a rune-cast and associated with poetry plucked from an inspirational trance state. One could, for example, identify a problem and seek the answer in a vision. In this vision, induced using Vaniric/mediumistic trance, one recovers a 'power-song' which might include one or more runes. Such a power song could then be profitably sung as a 'spell' which affects the Heathen shaman in a profound and practical way. Poetics seem to have once played a significant role in Galdr or 'spell' magic – and indeed they still do. As we have suggested, the rhyming of the Galdr is a device which itself enables trance, and music can be effectively added to the rhymes. But, for the poetically uninspired, we recommend the practice of letting the mood or the moment seize you. Explore what you can come up with from the inspiration of a given rune. If all else fails, you have the rune and its strength, sound and vibration at your disposal, which might be argued to be more than enough!

## Part Three: Vafthruðnir's sayings

These sayings can be usefully internalised as an expansion of cosmogonical, cosmographical knowledge. Vafthrudnismal is a text imbued with the wilful wanderings of a cosmically intransigent Woden in his eternal quest for knowledge. The associated ritual practice, here, is to take a series of shamanic journeys into Vafthrudnir's hall (in Jotunheim) in your own search for hidden lore! This also makes for a particularly good 'scenario' with which to encounter giant land.

## Part Four: Grimnir's Sayings

In Grimnir's sayings, Woden undergoes 'shamanistic rituals' of 'torture, starvation and heat' (Larrington 1996:50, Grimnismal 1-2), by being suspended over the fire in Geirrod's hall. Despite being topped and tailed within a narrative framework, Grimnismal was most likely composed for recital. And that is what we recommend you address next – the recital of (ancestral) lore as described in Grimnismal. Such oration is a key to the showmanship which is an integral part of shamanship. In indigenous shamanisms, the most important aspect of a ritual is the healing/divination, but it is also important for the shaman to keep the audience 'entertained' (or en-tranced). We do not think shamanism can in any way be reduced to the idea of a mere 'performance', but performance is certainly a part of it. Grimnir's sayings can be internalised using the same process as in Part 1.

## Ritual and the Wheel of the Year

The practices discussed in this volume are intimately related to the land in which we live and its seasons (this applies wherever you live in the world, and to whichever seasons you have). Galdrbok follows the main eight (for number symbolism see cosmogony and cosmology chapters) annual festivals of contemporary Paganisms. In short, these are 'starcraft' meetings, festivals which mark and celebrate the seasonal changes in nature during the ever-turning 'wheel of the year'. There is a clear emphasis on the agricultural cycle in this scheme and these times can be used to connect with the land and wights in the landscape, reflect on how the changes in nature reflects changes in self and community, observe long-term patterns of stability and change, and to make ritual and celebration.

The following dates for each festival are somewhat arbitrary since they may depend on planetary alignments, the proximity of sunrise and sunset, and the festivals can (and should) last for some days. These eight festivals are:

1. Yule (Winter Solstice) 21st December
2. Thunor's blot (First day of Spring), also known as Imbolc (First Lambs), 2nd February
3. Eostre (Spring Equinox) 21st March
4. Beltane (May Day) 1st May
5. Litha (Summer solstice) 21st June
6. Lammas (Loaf-fest) 31st July
7. Autumnal equinox 21st September

8. Winter's Night (also known as Samhain and Halloween,
   the first day of Winter) 31st October

For full discussion of the meanings and history of these
festivals, we recommend reading Harvey (1997) and
Hutton (1996). Please note that while there are numerous
folkloric practices which mark the historic precedent for
these festivals, there is very little evidence to suggest such
a system of eight celebrations was in practice anywhere in
Northwest Europe. Indeed while some of them may be
Pagan in origin, much of what we know about them
derives from Christian times. The important thing as
that these festivals are relevant today. Note that some of
the festivals of our Norse and Anglo-Saxon forebears
also cohere with these modern Pagan dates, while there
are additional festivals as well, and some these are
discussed below.

According to the wheel of the year and the eight festivals
associated with it, appropriate rituals can be formulated
and specific gods and otherworldly beings
invoked/worked with. Specific deities fit with the
celebrations of the 'stations of the sun' (to use the title of
Hutton's 1996 book) since it is plausible to identify their
acting out the wheel of the year in the mythology, be it
specific to Nordic cosmology or to the actions of other
Pagan gods and goddesses. Major figures in the Heathen
wheel of the year are:

Ing (also Thunor and Frigg) – fertility, fecundity, nature,
   and growth
Balder – hero and son/sun
Freyja – fecund/ alluring maiden

Frigg, Erce and/or Sif – pregnant mother
Hel and/or the Valkyries/Disiric ancestors – crone

For Heathen shamans, the wheel of the year marks opportune times to work with specific trance states, deities and the beings of Yggdrasill. But, feel free to produce rituals specific to the festivals beyond those suggested here, and do not feel tied down by the guidelines we provide. We have come across interpretations of shamanisms which suggest shamans somehow honour spirit over matter, with the spirit journey being 'better' than the body from which it travels. This is a complete misunderstanding: shamans travel to the spirit world precisely in order to effect changes in the 'real', physical world. In short, celebrate the seasons, in both spiritual and mundane ways (if the two are separable, that is) through ritual and festivities – be rapturous Heathens!

## Yule

The festival of Yule (21st December) is derived from Anglo-Saxon times. The night before the winter solstice was Modranicht (Mothernight) on 19th or 20th December, as recorded by Bede. This is the night of the Disir as it is so close to the darkest point in the year, and is a time for remembering and contacting ancestors. It is a good time for journeying to Dark Elf world and even more so to Helheim, but beware for this is both the most powerful and therefore the most dangerous time for such questing. Yule itself is the longest night, a time for all night vigils over the Yule log. The most pertinent ritual for this night is shamanic initiation (see Ritual 5, above) for it was at Yule (according to Our Troth online, Chapter XLVII) that Woden was hung over the fire in Geirrod's hall (Grimnismal, see Larrington

1996). It is an ideal time for seething the cauldron and raising Ond in ecstatic rites. It is a time when 'wod-taken men' don ritual costume and become possessed by the god (Our Troth online, Chapter XLVII). This is the time par excellence for Disiric trance and the journey to Helheim, for Seidr work and prognostication of all sorts.

The Winter solstice, the time of most darkness, is when the spirits of the otherworld are most prominent. This is the time of death and darkness, of retreating within one's-self, a time of self-reflection. But it is also the time of birth and rebirth. As we know, spring will return, and so we also know that Balder will be reborn after Ragnarok and the hero will rise again. No Golden Age is this, but the real potential for the return of Spring and the possibility of shamanic wisdom and ecstasy. Thus, Yule is a time for planting new seeds (of the spiritual/magical sort), which will sprout in spring. Say 'waes thu hael' to such acts at this time of 'Wassailing' by toasting (the Norse 'symbel' ritual) with drinking and feasting – the term wassail perhaps deriving from the Anglo-Saxon words 'waes' and 'hael', meaning 'be whole' (Pennick 1989: 237, but see Hutton 1996: 13).

The term Yule may derive from the Old English term 'gehol' meaning wheel, perhaps referring to the wheel of the year (Linsell 1994[1992]: 148). So, it is a time for celebrating the rebirth of the Sun (son) with a large feast (for most non-Heathens/Pagans, simply the traditional 'Christmas dinner') and for giving thanks to the gods and wights for the year's (Earth Mother's) gifts – and, of course, to each other. Gifts can be laid around the Yule tree (an evergreen, symbolic of the Yew and the endurance of life) and the greenery of Holly and Ivy are brought in to 'deck' the home as further symbols of life in the darkness. These plants tell of the pre-eminence of the Holly King in the dark (death) part of the year. Mistletoe is also seasonal, representing the fateful dart which killed Balder, the son (sun), who is reborn at Yule.

The traditional Yule period was thirteen nights (rather than the twelve Christian days) ending on New Year's Eve/Day, January 1st. Throughout this time, the Wild Hunt, led by Woden, rages across the land bringing both terror and fertility. It has been argued that the popular but now mostly half-hearted 'New Year's resolutions' derive from the belief that this day of the New Year is a day of Orlog (see Our Troth online, Chapter XLVII): New Year's resolutions are the corrupted practice of oath-swearing, so this is an important time for rune casting to elucidate Wyrd's map for the coming year, and then swearing oaths to fulfil this map. New Year's day is also a time for 'chasing out the old' to 'bring in the new'. Use your magical tools to ward out all the bad thoughts, memories and energies of the old year and welcome in the new. Of course this is made all the easier if it turns out to be a sunny day because you can freshen the home with windows and doors open!

### Thunor's Blot and Imbolc

The feast of Thunor (Our Troth online Chapter XLVIII) celebrates the gradual return of longer days (i.e. Spring is on the way!). New growth is visible all around us, manifest first in the form of Snowdrops. At this time the Frost Giants are at their strongest in the form of rain, hail, and freezing cold. It is the worst part of Winter and therefore appropriate to have a celebration to cheer us all up, a

celebration to honour the might of Thunor which will drive back the Frost Giants and let Summer in. It is also a time for working productively with the Giants, since they are now waning in power and more easily dealt with, especially if Thunor has been invoked. Alternatively, simply use Thunor's Galdr at this festival.

For Heathens, Thunor's blot may be best honoured on the first Thunor's-daeg (Thursday) of February, while for other Pagans the 2nd of February is celebrated as 'Imbolc'. Imbolc marks the first day of Spring and the re-growth of Ing who has been 'sleeping' or 'dead' over Winter. It is also the re-growth of the Earth goddess, as a virgin/maiden, with associations with Freyja. It is also the time of the growth of the hero Balder into a boy, having been born at Yule. And, this is the ritual occasion to recognise Thunor's warding off of the Frost-Giants as the first growth emerges. Tend the magical seeds (spells and plans) planted at Yule by strengthening the magic.

### Eostre: Spring Equinox
Another major festival with Saxon and Germanic origins is Eostre at the spring equinox (21st March), the term and

date borrowed by Christianity for Easter. Eostre may be etymologically linked to the Old English term for East, referring to the direction from which dawn's light comes and therefore the coming of warmer Summer days. According to Bede, Eostre is a goddess (of Spring), but there are problems with this interpretation (see Hutton 1996). Hares are sacred to Eostre, linked as they are in the folklore to Easter eggs. Thus, Eostre is the celebration of new life (the egg symbol) and the ripening of the Earth. Eggs are eaten at this time as a symbol of strength and the growing strength of the year, and various folkloric practices involve painting and/or rolling eggs (as well as eating chocolate ones!).

Spring Equinox is the time of equal light and dark, an equality which is leading towards greater light, so it is conducive to work with the Dark and Light elves. At Eostre, Ing/Freyja/Balder have grown substantially, so this is the time of potential for further growth and for reproduction – as we see all around us manifestly in nature. Essentially, 'the sap is rising', so it is a good time to work with the 'springy' new Ond around you in nature and within you (especially symbolised by Dark Elves). At this time, if your magic has been effective, you will see how the Ond has prompted the shoots of your Winter magic to emerge – use the Ond of Spring to strengthen the magic further. Among the gods, Balder might be seen as a young man, and the goddess Freyja might be seen as the maiden/virgin (post-pubescent) at this time.

### Beltane and Walpurgis Night
Beltane or 'Walpurgis night' is the first day of Summer (May 1st). All around us, Ing is vibrant and strong. This

date in the year is when the 'bel-fires' are lit and people jump over them for cleansing and for ridding themselves of negative Orlog as best they can. Ask that any hang-ups be carried away by the dark elves in the smoke. Both Eostre and Beltane are certainly good times for working with these fiery spirits. In light of what is happening around us in nature, Beltane is a good day for love-making. Handfasting (marriage), sex magic, and the blessing of children are all appropriate on this day. Beltane is the time of the magical seeds planted in Winter coming to fruition.

### Litha: Summer Solstice

The Summer solstice has endured as a popular festival throughout Scandinavia (see Our Troth online Chapter LII), and according to Hutton (1996: 321) may have been a major ritual in Northwest Europe for fifteen centuries 'or more'. Stonehenge in Wiltshire is a common meeting place for this festival today. At sometime in June, perhaps at the solstice, the Anglo-Saxon festival of Litha took place (Linsell 1994[1992]:149). At the Summer solstice, nature is at its strongest for it is the longest day, but also at its weakest and most vulnerable, about to pass its peak. The 'green' everywhere will soon pass to 'burnt' earthy colours, due to the strength of the sun.

It is at Litha that the Oak king (the Summer manifestation of Ing) and Holly king (the Winter Ing) of folklore do battle. In the mythology, we speculate that this is the time at which Balder had his bad dreams (Baldrs draumar, see Larrington 1996) – dreams which prophesise his death. At dawn on the solstice, hail the light elves, for their strength is at its height and it is an ideal time to work with their magic and the rune of the sun. Be altruistic and giving on this day, and perhaps anchor your thoughts to the kennings of the Gift rune. Above all else, Summer Solstice, in contrast to Yule is the time for Aesiric trance and the use of Galdr, particularly the Galdr of Woden, Tiw and Frigg.

## Lammas

The Icelandic Freyfaxi or Saxon Loaf-fest is at Lammas (see Our Troth online Chapter LIII). Lammas, on 1st August, is the time of celebrating the 'first fruits' (as written in 921 CE in the Anglo-Saxon Chronicle), embodied by the ripening of arable crops and the harvesting of them – with one sheaf being sacrificed to the gods, and corn dollies being made. This harvest may be mythically embodied in the song of John Barleycorn (according to Pennick 1989: 249-251). These arable 'fruits' contributed towards the 'loaf', hence the Saxon 'loaf-fest' or Lammas – and, of course, to that sacred, celebratory drink, Real Ale. In our Modern industrial culture it is hard to see the relevance of such an agrarian celebration – until, that is, one ventures into rural areas and sees many combine harvesters cutting the vast fields of golden crops. And whether Lammas is this visible or not, the basic ingredients of much of our food are arable derived.

Lammas is a time of the Jera rune (the 'fruitful year', see Appendix A), of giving thanks to the Earth, and reaping the fruits of the magical seeds which were planted at Yule and tended since then; see your plans reach fruition. Great fairs were held all across Britain at this time to celebrate the harvest. While it was also named Lughnasadh, Lughnasa, or Lugnasa after the god Lugh in Ireland, it was not apparently a pan-British festival of the sun or of fire as is commonly believed (Hutton 1996: 327-330).

For some contemporary Heathens, Lammas is sacred to Sif and Thunor (see Our Troth online Chapter LIII). In Snorri's Skaldskaparmal (see Faulkes 1998 [1987]: 96), Loki cropped Sif's (presumably blonde or flaxen) hair, seemingly out of spite, a cropping which compares with the harvesting of corn. In repayment, Loki brings Sif golden hair (see Frigg's Galdr, Chapter 5) and also arranges the crafting of Thunor's hammer Mjollnir, Woden's spear Gungnir and ring Draupnir, and Frey's boar Gullinborsti and ship Skidbladnir. Sif's golden hair is a contemporary kenning for the cornfield as it is caressed by the breeze and makes gentle waves. Thunor can in turn be seen as the fertility god who ripens the grain with rain (see Thunor's mundane poetry in Chapter 5: Galdr) – and the lightning strike which 'impregnates' the earth with 'semen'. Lammas is also the time of honouring the dead Balder who is killed accidentally at this time by the blind Hod (see Balder's Galdr), and hence this is the occasion for lamenting the fact that the King has died: the Holly has now, over six months after Yule, triumphed over the Oak and the dark half of the year is underway.

At Lammas you will perhaps find yourself atop a burial mound which is surrounded by fields of ripe corn. You might journey into the mound and take the road to Helheim in order to question a seeress about the future, as Woden did when Balder went to that realm (Baldrs draumar, see Larrington 1996). The giants (note the reference to Thunor again) can also be advantageously worked with at this time, though like the summer lightning in August they can be unpredictable. And, so close to high Summer, the power of the light elves remains strong at Lammas so Aesiric trance can be well practised. It may also be a time for elucidating –

through rune casting and/or oracular Seidr – what the dark half of the year will bring, and for monitoring yourself and your community as the retreat 'inside' begins.

### Autumn Equinox
Later, at the Autumnal equinox, darkness equals light once more, and it is a suitable time for dealing with the elves. We prepare for Winter, and watch the land enter a period of slumber.

### Winter's Night
At Winter's night, the first day of Winter, also known more widely as Halloween, the veil between the otherworld and this world begins to grow thin. This is the traditional time of 'spooks' – it is dark elf time, without doubt, and a time for 'letting go' (Pennick 1989: 41) of the magical seeds and plans which you made nearly a year ago. But the veil between Midgard and spirit grows thinnest at Yule... and so the Wheel of the Year turns on.

### Other Annual Rites
Various Heathen organisations (and indeed groups in wider Paganisms) celebrate ritual dates other than those mentioned here, such as at the times of full and new moons and various remembrance days for heroes. We leave it up to you to decide which times are the most appropriate and significant in your own calendar. We follow the eight main festivals of the Pagan year and we encourage you to celebrate any other festival you deem relevant. One such example is Remembrance Sunday on 11th November, which to some contemporary Heathens marks the time of the Einherjar, the slain warriors dedicated to Woden.

## The Place of Ritual

Having decided when to conduct your rituals, be it at one of the eight major festivals, on an Anglo-Saxon sacred day, at a new or full moon, or simply on a day of the week which resonates with a particular deity or practice, it is important to decide on a location. Ritual can be undertaken just about anywhere if required, and the easiest place is of course at home. You will have a Harrow (shrine) in a suitable place at home, perhaps inside at the hearth, perhaps outside beneath a suitable tree. Regularly attending these shrines and making offerings and rituals, is a vital way of fostering a good relationship with the local wights of the house (including House Ghosts) and garden (Land Wights). The simplest ritual at the Harrow might involve tending the shrine itself and the sacred objects you keep there. Regularly 'reviewing' your personal shamanic tools is as important as the group's 'power show' (see below, under Oath Swearing). It is a reminder of the magical tools which connect you to Wyrd and help you on your path. Reviewing is also important because some tools may cease to be useful after a time, in which case it is time to thank them and let them go.

Like Woden, many Heathen shamans often feel the need to wander, and ritual may take you to locations beyond the local. Favourite places are ancient trees (especially hollow Yew trees, where it is possible to enter the spirit world as described above) where you may communicate with the tree wight. As you practice your Runecraft in the presence of different species of tree and plant, you will notice how each species and indeed each individual tree 'speaks' differently. In this way you will, over time, come to know which tree is most conducive to a certain sort of ritual, and which tree will benefit most from a particular rite (Yew for Woden, Oak for Thunor, Ash for Tiw, etc). Such rites are a reciprocal affair, benefiting both the tree (and land around you) and yourself. But beware: all is not fluffy and bright in the indigenous shaman's world – we stress the importance of responsibility and caution, for different wights respond in different ways. It is vital that you are well prepared and sufficiently guarded in such practices. Performing Thorsson's (1984) 'Hammer Warding' or a related ritual, chanting a rune row, invoking the dwarfs of the four directions, or simply rattling-in sacred space, are all ways of preparing ritual space.

Apart from Yew trees, the Northern Mage's favourite haunt among other sacred sites, is the burial mound. Utiseta (sitting out) is practised at such sites, which at its simplest consists of sitting atop the mound and inducing Vaniric trance by rune casting and scrying. Utiseta can also involve passive ancestor communication through the stone and runes, and active ancestor communication via Disiric trance. Again, these are powerful rites so caution and discretion are due. Do not forget to make sacrifices, offerings or libations to the ancestors, such as hallowing and pouring mead, ale or such like at a suitable spot. Hallow the mead by signing the hammer over it: Thunor's hammer Mjollnir is as much a symbol of blessing as it is of giant crushing; as we have said, place Mjollnir handle up and the scales of justice are revealed. Offering the mead in this way is a simple way of performing a 'Blot' (in no way etymologically related to 'blood'), the popular Heathen ceremony (past and present) of sacrifice, 'Blota' meaning 'to sacrifice' or 'to strengthen the god' (Simek 1993: 271). And the Blot is related to the 'Symbel', a rite of toasting the gods (and other entities including each other) using hallowed mead.

Offerings and sacrifices at sacred sites can take other forms, such as clearing up the litter left by thoughtless visitors, or engaging in conversation with someone who without really knowing it may be damaging the site. All too often these days, Pagan visitors to sites leave offerings which are no good to place or person. Ensure that any offering you leave will not sit around for long. Small pieces of bread will soon be eaten by the local birds for instance, and liquid feeds the grass, but large piles of food will rot, and coins wedged in trees or megalithic stones will cause damage. Make your offering with due thought and respect to the place and those who may visit after you.

Far too often you will reach a site to find candles and nightlights still lit, and the remains of charcoal and incense on the ground. Discourage such acts by removing these items, for the heat and wax from candles and nightlights can damage megalithic stones, burn scorch-holes in the grass, and are of course a blatant fire risk. If you use incense, place the charcoal in a heat resistant container and take the remains away with you. All these acts are a vital part of reciprocating with the spirits of a place. If you live close to a site and are able to visit it regularly, it might be possible to establish a strong bond between yourself, your community, and that place. In this way also, Galdrbok's system of Heathen shamanic initiation can be seen to be far more than solely a personal spiritual quest, for it is also a social and earth-orientated spirituality.

## A Heathen Community

We have stated previously that there is rarely such a thing as the 'lone sage' (see Mann rune in the cosmogony). Most humans seek companionship and the 'spiritual life' is not divorced from such matters. Indeed it is much easier to keep your practices going if you are a member of a group. You may sometimes feel that you are 'flagging' (we all have 'off' days, after all), and that you just do not feel like practising. What better way to boost you into getting on with it than a group of like-minded people who will be meeting at the appointed time? The last thing you want to do is let them down. And when you arrive, the ritual is likely to boost your spirits and you will be pleased that you went.

A communal focus is also intrinsic to shamanic practices in indigenous cultures. Among the Southern African San Bushmen, for instance, the trance or healing dance is entirely a group event and the purpose of it is for community healing, not simply healing yourself as is so true of some 'New Age' philosophy. Even 'vision questing' Native American shamans, while seeking their visions alone will return to their communities to seek guidance on their experiences.

So, it is all the better if you do meet like-minded companions while on your Heathen path. These friends, along with other 'helpers' from the spirit world, will keep the 'thing' (thing is Old English for a community meeting) going even if you are having a low point. Having community promotes a vital sense of belonging and helps individuals to avoid becoming too insular and private. Indeed, the Heathen shaman, in community, must be a negotiator – between the worlds and between people – and will inevitably be involved in resolving disputes and controversies.

## A Rite of Oath-Swearing

A pragmatic way of establishing and strengthening a community bond is to participate in an 'oath-swearing'. Oaths are far more than the mere 'promises' which many people half-heartedly make and so easily break in our modern culture. For our ancestors, breaking an oath was tantamount to a severe crime, and incurred some heavy penalties. This is unsurprising, since apart from the various social reasons that such bonds were made (ensuring communal reciprocity), oaths were sworn in the presence of the gods. Breaking an oath insulted the gods – not a good idea!

The most common sort of oath was a 'Ring Oath'. One recorded ring oath occurred when the Saxons and Danes made an oath swearing over a ring in 876 CE. In the Landnamabok, with its recorded oath swearing ceremonies, the words of the oath are taken on a holy ring reddened with the blood of sacrifice. In Iceland, the office of Gothard (both chieftan and priest) was responsible for the holy ring. The ring, called the 'altar ring', was probably kept in Thunor's temple and is described as having no join and about the size of an arm ring. According to Snorri, the priest evaded injury in battle by wearing this ring (Davidson 1993: 93-94).

The importance of the ring in Heathenry is neatly encapsulated by Woden's arm ring Draupnir (the Dripper), from which eight of the same rings drip every ninth night, and which Woden placed on his son Balder's funeral pyre.

For today's Heathens, a (usually silver) rune ring or arm ring ('arm-ice'), perhaps engraved with 'Draupnir' in runes, is an excellent ring on which to swear oaths. While all sorts of pledges may be sworn, from Handfasting (a marriage) to friendship, the sort that we mark out here, as of particular import, is the group oath – to undertake the Heathen system of shamanic initiation and support each other in times of need.

Borrowing from the various elements of ritual suggested in this chapter, you will be able to orchestrate the right kind of group ring oath for your circumstances. You may erect a shrine on which all the group's ritual wealth (from crystal balls and runes, to blades, Gandrs and other powerful objects) is gathered. This 'power show' affirms to all gathered that a similar path is being followed and that it is also being shared. You may then invoke appropriate deities, totems and ancestors to witness the rite, and then each swear the oath of kinship over Draupnir. Perhaps share a drinking horn of mead or ale to seal the oath, and affirm your commitment by shaking hands, laughing together, or some such thing.

We maintain that you should not forget that such an oath is sworn before the gods. To break it is to be untrue to one's self, to the gods, and to one's kindred. Never swear an oath which will be impossible to keep. And when you do swear an oath, be prepared to keep it, however small. Oathbreaking is against the Heathen code (see the section entitled 'Preface').

# – Chapter 7 –
# Magic - Working It / Making It Work

M agic cannot be written off as simply fantastical or
superstitious. The magic of childhood, as marked
at the outset of Galdrbok, is very powerful. Remember
when you played in the world of monsters and dragons?
That really was the world of monsters and dragons, at least
for as long as you were 'there'. More specifically, the magic
we are concerned with in this chapter is practical, working,
or useful magic. This is certainly related to, or draws upon
the power of the magic of childhood, but magic is – or can
be – put towards much more than that besides. Indigenous
shamans may not use the term 'magic' (they have their own
terms for magical practices), but interacting with spirits to
bring about healing or some other 'supernatural' feat is
certainly 'magical', and is much documented in the Norse
myths and sagas, as well as other literature of the Old
North such as the Anglo-Saxon 'Lacnunga' (a book of herb
lore and spells).

Magic is a way of interacting with the spirit world which
makes things 'happen' in the 'real' world – according to
Crowley's famous axiom, 'Magick' is 'the Science and Art
of causing Change to occur in conformity with Will'
(Crowley 1973: 131). Crowley used Magick with a 'k' to
distinguish it as a spiritual practice from more common
conjuring tricks (such as producing a rabbit from an empty
hat). We have used the more general 'magic' in Galdrbok
simply because our understanding of the term, and that of

our Heathen ancestors, was/is broader than Crowley's definition. In this chapter, the sort of magic we refer to is, however, broadly in agreement with Crowley's method – making change happen, by esoteric means.

There are many books on magic, some excellent, others not. Arguably some of the best expositions are by Aleister Crowley and Austin Osman Spare, but their discussions are often intractable. Indeed, Spare suggested people should not 'follow' his system, but should create their own. We agree in part, but would add that coming up with your own system is not only difficult and rather individualistic, but may also disregard important ancestral kennings – wisdom which was 'hard-won' or 'hard-learned'. None the less, the magical techniques of Crowley and Spare are 'classic' and retold in a highly accessible way by Jan Fries in his excellent work 'Visual Magick' (1992). Rather than repeat what has already been said by Fries and by other writers, we only discuss magic here in the context of the runes. Relevant books specific to Runic magic are listed at the end of this book.

## Working Magic

How is magic worked? Well, it is important to note that the essence of magic is in the 'in between' or liminal space(s) – in Ginnungagap, and Ginnungagap is the medium through which magic works. Human will (Hugr) is a real force which can act on the world and Magicians use ritual paraphernalia to steer/support the will and imagination towards the desired result (principles discussed by Humphries & Vayne 2004).

Essentially, simply willing (wishing) something to happen is unlikely to make that something happen. How often have your 'wishes' failed? One reason for this is that the Hugr (ego/mind) can latch on to the conscious thought, ridicule it, and stop it from happening. The key is to bypass the Hugr (conscious mind) using 'symbols' which are not recognisable, in this case symbols from Northern lore, and most obviously, various runes. The correct combination of symbols for the purpose at hand will manipulate the Hugr (mind), using the Hamr (non-conscious), into making the magic happen.

How magic happens is a debate best explored outside the remit of Galdrbok – besides, in terms of practice rather than theory, it is of no consequence. The point – and ask anyone who has tried magic a few times – is that it works. The 'symbols' used can be almost anything, but in this system of course we use runes. The runes are effective in isolation as symbols to make effective magic – what is required in more complex magic, however, is the manipulation of the runic symbols into something which is not recognisable, called a bind rune, 'sigil', or in Old Norse 'Galdrastafr'.

## Sigil Magic and Galdrastafr

In Galdrastafr, the Runic Magician chooses the runes to be used for the spell. These runes are combined into a composite image which, in its own right, is idiosyncratic to the spell – a Galdrastafr (examples of bindrunes composed of the authors' names can be found at the end of this book). The Runic Magician then internalises the image by meditating on it, chanting Galdr, even ingesting it – you could bake a cake with a rune image on it, for example, and then eat your spell! (See also Bennett 2003, on 'Eucharist Magick').

A major issue to address when preparing your spell is its potential consequences. Books on magic are replete with discussions over when and why to do magic, and when not to do it, for even the most innocent and well-meant spell may inadvertently have unexpected effects (the butterfly effect in chaos theory). Thus spell-working can have negative effects, or in other words can result in negative Orlog, for the Mage. An appropriate format for spell-working, we have tried and tested, which avoids negative Orlog, is as follows.

The Northern Magician chooses the runes suitable for the working. The Vitki then does a rune cast to elucidate whether Wyrd – the pattern of Orlog of the Mage – accords with the will of the Mage. If the answer is positive, the Vitki continues with the spell, if not, then it ends here. Essentially, the operative Hugr (conscious/ego) part of the spell is removed from the process and put into the hands of Wyrd.

If the spell is to continue, you then create a sigil from the aforementioned runes. Throughout this spell-making, the stanza from the Anglo-Saxon rune poem for each rune is recited, the rune sounds and seed sounds vibrated, and appropriate deities invoked. The ritual surrounding the making of the sigil can be as elaborate or as simple as required – some people require more to get their ego out of the way than others do, and hence make magic work.

Once the sigil is designed, the Heathen Magician then fixes it in a material form with pen on paper, or as a combination of sticks on the ground, with charcoal on birch bark, marked on a cake, biscuit, or in a fluid, or fixed in some other appropriate medium. Again, ritual should be an integral part of the fixing of the sigil. Next comes the most difficult part of the magic – making it happen. For this, the ego must be completely removed via entering trance. Trance is essential to working magic. You may employ the frenetic dancing of Disiric trance, or take on a deity form with appropriate Galdr. Thus a healing spell may best involve the invocation of Freyja, while a weather spell requires Thunor's presence and co-operation. Appropriate sacrifices, such as libations or other offerings to the deity, might encourage the co-operation required.

When trance is achieved, the Runester internalises the sigil by gazing at it. The well-seasoned Scryer should find this stage relatively easy. The longer the time spent internalising the sigil, the better the results are likely to be. If trance recedes but more internalisation is required, resume trance induction. Once internalisation is achieved, you should sign and send the sigil. Do this by marking it in the air (which is pregnant – is Ginnungagap – with fecund potential rather than 'nothing'!) with the Gandr, ritual blade or other suitable tool, while vibrating suitable Galdr, then sending or blasting (pointing) the Gandr into the air. In the spirit world this will be the signing and sending of the sigil into the Ginnungagap. Usually the Galdrastafr is signed in red, and is clearly visible to the Mage, in trance.

With the magic ritual done, the Heathen shaman must forget the experience as soon as possible since any Hugr memory (ego remembering) of why the spell was cast will negatively affect its taking effect. This is best achieved by flinging yourself back into the real world by thumping the ground, laughing heartily to thank the deities and other beings who helped, eating, drinking and/or conversing with friends if the rite was a communal one. When the spell does finally take effect, you might forget you had even produced it, but by that time it is of course 'bye-the-bye'!

Magic need not be as complicated as this, depending on the magnitude of the required effect, or on the time available. Simple spells can be conducted anywhere and at any time. Sign and send an Elksedge rune over your bicycle when you have forgotten the lock so that it will be safe, for instance. Or, when an ambulance, funeral procession or fire engine passes, cross your fingers into a need rune. This will facilitate, if only in a small way, a transferral of beneficial 'need' energies to assist those 'in need'. It also acts to remind you of your place in the world, of the transience of life, and the fact that there are always other beings (plant, animal, human or 'spirit') in greater need than ourselves.

The purpose is to establish, through participation, a powerful mnemonic (memory) device to act as a spur, an encouragement, like crowd support in a sport. Will such simple magic really work? Try it and see! Doing it is far more productive than thinking about it or attempting to rationalise it in terms of 'natural laws' such as 'cause and effect'. Don't let the veil of rationalisation and scepticism deprive you of the benefit of such a practical kind of magic. Given the chance, the rational ego will never let you up and out of your chair to try; it will either tell you that you do not know enough about the subject, or you will dismiss the whole procedure as superstitious auto-suggestion, or the like. It is the effort to create magic and the thrill that this alone can produce, which contributes immensely to its effects. Nothing kills this as surely as inappropriate intellectual speculation.

## Spellcraft - Shamanic Healing

Healing is a primary role of indigenous shamans. This healing may be of social tensions between community members, of psychological-type maladies, or of physical illnesses (and of course there may be a fine line between these three). The scope of healing in indigenous shamanic contexts is much wider than in the modern West. For we moderns, healing is something we tend to seek out only if we are 'ill'. We have difficulty understanding the notion of healing unless the 'healer' defines what is to be healed (and how). Your family doctor follows the protocol of identifying the symptoms and prescribing appropriate drugs. These drugs, more often than not, address the symptoms rather than the cause.

In other cultures and/or times, healing is/was considered to be an on-going and preventative process involving the whole being – 'physical', 'mental', and 'spiritual' (or 'mind, body, spirit'). Fortunately, 'alternative medicine' is no longer shunned entirely by Western medicine, and the latter is increasingly taking a more 'holistic' approach to health and well-being. 'Shamanic healing' is, we believe, as important as traditional Western medicine when treating sickness. Indeed it stands alongside and co-operates with other 'alternative' or 'complementary' therapies. Readers can use their own kennings to establish how to conduct appropriate healing rituals – we also provide some pertinent suggestions for components of a healing ritual below.

Consider your position very carefully before undertaking anything of this nature – it is up to you to decide whether or not you are prepared to undertake such a responsibility. Indeed this is true for all magic, from the simplest 'signing and sending' to a complex healing. If you are not sure of your ability, then you probably are not ready. If you really cannot decide for yourself, ask the advice of the runes.

Get to know your client as well as is possible in at least one consultation before moving on to any magical healing practice. The role of 'counselling', as we would put it in the West, is as much a part of the shamanic vocation as dealing with spirits. During the consultation your 'inner eye' (that is, Woden's eye) may already be establishing useful snippets of information, or the voices of spirits (your spirit-helpers) may enter your kenning. Listen to them. Take advice. Listen to your client and assess their situation. Before the consultation you may want to ritually prepare yourself by following rituals numbered one to three in the previous chapter, and by invoking appropriate spirits, gods and ancestors.

Let the healing then begin. Ask your client to lie down and close their eyes (or otherwise get comfortable). You, meanwhile, will induce trance and enter Yggdrasill at Midgard. Travel on the tree in the form you are used to, to the appropriate world for this type of healing. For a strengthening healing, it might be best to head to light elf world, and for expelling malignancy, to the dark elves. In that world, engage with the entities there. One may present itself to you as the appropriate spirit to assist you in the healing. But, always be sure this is the right spirit: question it. A common magical practice is to ask the spirit its name. If it will not comply with this simple request, do not trust

it. Tricksters come in many guises! Let this spirit take you
to the location of the malady, if there is one (a single organ,
for example). Here, another spirit may be present and it is
this 'illness' which must be extracted from the patient. It is
also possible to detect the illness by scanning your patient's
body with your crystal and 'seeing' through it. Such
malignant beings are often dull-coloured or you may
simply feel that they exude malignancy.

It is wise to familiarise yourself with this entity before
'touching' it in any way. For some shamanic healers, the
spirit may appear as a potentially dangerous creature, such
as a snake or spider. For others, a strange amorphous blob
will be seen. Remember that while it may be malignant, the
illness is likely to simply be doing what it does, following
its Wyrd. Better to communicate with it first than to
immediately assume it must be 'scared out'. Negotiation
with the spirit may work here, but it may well be reluctant
to leave, in which case it must be challenged. If so, use your
helpers to gain strength, intone appropriate runes, and ask
the help of deities.

Once you feel the time is right, attempt to 'pick up the
spirit' in the spirit world. Use special equipment where
necessary. If you feel uncomfortable using your hands on
'sickness', you could use your Gandr or some other ritual
tool. Either way, it may be necessary to 'see' the spirit in
both 'sides' of Midgard – the spirit and ordinary worlds –
for this kind of magic ritual often involves being present in
both worlds. So, at the same time as removing it in the
physical world, extract the spirit from the location of the
illness. Travel back then from the world you are in to
Midgard, and send the illness into the earth, and down to

Helheim, by thrusting it with your hands or pointing your Gandr. Send the illness from Midgard to Helheim, where it will be absorbed and recycled.

Let trance recede and your ordinary consciousness return. Thank those that helped you, and gently ease your patient into a comfortable space. They may want to remain laying down for a while. They may instead want a hot drink. Whatever else you do, endeavour to make them at ease. Spend some time with them after the healing to reassure them and make sure they are fully returned to this world too. Note any otherworldly experiences they may have had and, if necessary, have follow-up treatments or consultations to monitor their progress.

In this chapter we have detailed a number of magical techniques. Needless to say, the diverse possibilities for magical practice are virtually endless, dependent only on the required task at hand. It is important in all workings to be aware of and familiar with the 'how' and 'why'. Be aware of the implications of what you are doing, and be prepared to take on the responsibility of your actions. If in doubt, rune cast. Especially when conducting a healing, it is important to be familiar with the various aspects of your being, from your Lich ('body') to your Orlog ('fate'). It is these aspects of the Heathen shaman's being which we next briefly examine.

## The Heathen Shaman's Being

In previous chapters we have suggested that the map of Yggdrasill is reflected in the human body – 'man is a miniature macrocosm'. With dedicated practice, Runesters may build up an intimate relationship with the(ir) world tree, and just as the term Yggdrasill itself implies Woden is a part of the tree, so the Heathen shaman's being can be said to 'be' Yggdrasill. The aim of the Northern Mage is to harmonise these specific aspects of be-ing by altering consciousness, traversing the tree, and crafting positive Orlog. In common terminology, these aspects of personhood can loosely be termed 'body', 'mind' (ego), 'soul' and 'spirit' – but these are quite vague terms and the Northern traditions have a more complex and nuanced understanding of such concepts. The 'body' and the 'mind' (terms we have inherited from the Enlightenment tradition) are familiar concepts to most people since we are involved with body and mind all of the time in the everyday world, whether consciously or not. The 'soul' and 'spirit' are all of those aspects of being which are less obvious in 'physical' reality, though of course they are intimately related to the physical body. Indeed, the categories of mind, body, soul and spirit, and the divisions between them, are not entirely separate in the approach taken in Northern traditions – they are all a part of the single human be-ing.

All aspects of the Heathen shaman's being can be regarded intellectually as distinct entities, but in actuality there is much overlap. In essence, you are 'one being', and it is only intellectually that the various parts can be labelled. It is important to understand the workings of the various elements which go to make up your whole being, none the less, and the elements discussed here enable that process. Careful study of these aspects of yourself will bring various kennings into your practices. When diagnosing a patient for sickness, for instance, these terms and concepts act as useful reference points. Just as a medical doctor maps out illness on the 'plan' of the physical body, so the Runic healer maps out sickness – but in greater non-physical depth, on the seven parts of the material and spiritual human being. These seven component parts – seven of course in itself being a significant number in Northern lore – are named as follows:

1. Lich
2. Hugr
3. Hamr
4. Hamingja
5. Fylgja
6. Orlog
7. Ond

## 1. Lich

The human body itself is the Lich, the physical vehicle for life. It is also a manifestation of divinity, as laid out in the cosmogony. As such, the body and its intimate relationship to the physical world are to be celebrated. The strong and healthy Lich will promote strength in the other areas of being, while the lazy, lethargic Lich is prone to the stagnation of Ond. This, in turn, can lead to the diminishing of the Hamr (shape or 'shield skin' as Brian Bates [1983, 1996] names it), so that the Lich has a 'low immunity' (in medical terms), making it prone to invasion (including viral and bacterial infection) from outside. Sickness can be caused by medically recognised intrusions such as viruses, but also more subtle and medically unidentifiable spirit intrusions. The Anglo-Saxon term 'elf-shot' refers to such sicknesses.

The Lich can be manipulated through fasting, entheogen use, physical exertion, and other techniques, to promote various consciousness-altering effects. Such shamanic techniques can promote trance and shamanic journeying because the Hamr becomes permeable in order that the Fylgja can leave the Lich – on out of body travel in the otherworld. As a physical entity, the Lich is subject to the laws of space and time, and the body is a temple (shrine) within these laws. Approaching the body as a shrine does not require asceticism – at the simplest level, the body should be celebrated in many ways: sex, food, drink and a variety of entheogens mark examples of both recreational and esoteric celebrations. Inducing sensory deprivation in order to alter consciousness also involves approaching the body as a shrine, as a vehicle which engages with gnosis. Working with the body in this way, then, the Heathen shaman also celebrates and manipulates the other non-physical components of be-ing, as follows.

### 2. Hugr
Hugr is Old Norse for 'thought' or 'mind'. One of Woden's ravens is called Huginn ('thought', 'mind'), the other Muninn ('the thought', 'memory'), and Woden states in Grimnir's Sayings (Grimnismal 20) that he fears more for the loss of Muninn than Huginn – indeed what is the mind without the memories which hold thought together? The Hugr is, in particular, the conscious, intellectual, rational, and linear mode of thought, also known as the 'left' brain. It is the Hugr which is disrupted during trance / otherworld journeys. The Hugr is also harnessed and directed as 'will' (what Crowley termed 'True Will') in the process of magic.

### 3. Hamr

Hamr can be translated from Old Norse to English as the 'hide' or 'shape'. Brian Bates names it the 'Shield-Skin' (as noted above), meaning that while the 'soul' is non-physical, or hidden (from physical view), it does have shape – the shape of the human body. Hamr is comparable with the astral body of Western traditions (Gundarsson 1990: 15) which is allegedly encountered every night in our dreams. Hamr is also a shape which can be changed and re-formed by magic, that is, according to will – the Hugr (Thorsson 1984: 151). Working with and refining Ond can be described as 'crafting the Hamr' or soul.

With a strong Lich, the Runester can manipulate the Hamr into allowing the Fylgja to leave the Lich on out of body travel. A weak Lich also facilitates such a process, though often at such times the Fylgja leaves the body without permission – sometimes stolen by spirits – requiring a Heathen shaman to seek the lost Fylgja in what neo-shamans term 'soul retrieval'. The experienced Mage can also use such personal sickness to his/her advantage since the 'open' state brought on by fever and other conditions facilitates loosening of the Lich and hence out of body travel. On any such otherworldly travel, however, the Mage ensures the safety and protection of all other aspects of be-ing through precautionary ritual observances. These might include a simple Rune Row, Hammer Warding, or protective Galdrastafr and deity/spirit invocations.

### 4. Hamingja

Hamingja, at its simplest, is 'good fortune', personal luck or power (Gundarsson 1990: 14). There is some confusion between the Hamingja and the Fylgja in the lore, since both involve shape-shifting and both continue to exist after physical death. The main difference is that the Hamingja is personal luck or a 'guardian spirit' (a Bates term again), perhaps related to what Crowley called the 'Guardian Angel'. Indeed, Simek describes the Hamingja as a 'protective spirit' (Simek 1993: 129). The Hamingja can also be transmitted to someone else's being after death, beyond the constraints of familial links (Simek 1993: 129). In this way, the Hamingja is related to the Draugr, your 'ghost'.

### 5. Fylgja / Fetch

The Fylgja is Old Norse for 'follower' (Gundarsson 1990: 291), 'following spirit' or 'skin' (Simek 1993: 96-97). Like the Hamingja, it is an aspect of the 'soul' which can be separated from the Lich. The Fylgja can also be seen in dreams or visions, and leaves at death to become independent. It differs from the Hamingja, though, because after death the Fetch can transfer only to relations (Simek 1993: 96-97). This hints at a form of reincarnation in Nordic belief, though there appears to be no other evidence for such a belief. It may also refer to the phenomenon, particularly in Siberia, where someone is adopted – often by force – by the spirit of an ancestor shaman. This 'calling' to the shamanic vocation by the spirits is not uncommon in shamanisms worldwide. The Fylgja is therefore your own spirit-helper, be it in the form of an ancestor, animal or stone. When shape-shifting into spirit-helpers and undertaking out of body travel on the world tree, Heathen shamans are working with the Fylgja.

### 6. Orlog

Orlog is that part of being which is directly a part of Wyrd (Gundarsson 1990). Orlog is derived from the Old Norse 'or-', out of, and 'log', law – hence 'that which is of the law' (Stone 1989: 21). Each of us has Orlog and it has a pattern marked out on the Web of Wyrd. This pattern on the Web is attached to one's being by filaments of what Bates terms 'fibres'. The pattern can be determined through rune casting, so that the Wodenic Vitki is able to get 'in sync' with and negotiate Wyrd. Runic shamans who are aware of their pattern of Orlog can work with and re-manipulate this pattern – the process of overcoming negative Orlog. Orlog also means 'primal layers' (Thorsson 1984: 151), referring to the primal trinity of the Norns, and perhaps to how the past reflects on the present according to the Way of Wyrd.

### 7. Onð

Ond is the 'vital breath' (similar to the Hindu 'Prana') given to humans by Woden (see Cosmogony). It is the animating force which gives life to all things (including so-called inanimate objects) and leaves the body at death. At this point it returns to the earth where it gives life to another being, from the creatures such as worms and maggots which decompose the Lich, to the ravens, wolves, eagles and other scavengers at the top of the food chain. Thus any death is in a sense a reincarnation!

Ond is the vital spirit which resides at the base of the spine in the seething cauldron Hvergelmir. When wakened by the Seidrmadr, the Ond can be carefully trained by the Heathen Mage to shoot up through all the worlds, or up the Irminsul pillar, and into Asgard, resulting in shamanic ecstasy. How, when and why, to work with Ond, is determined by Orlog. The Lich is then 'seethed' according to various consciousness-altering practices (dancing,

Galdr, drumming, and so on) to waken and raise the Ond. The Lich itself cannot work or focus the Ond however because Ond is a 'spiritual' thing – Ond is instead manipulated and directed by the Hugr, shaped by the Hamr into a 'manageable' form, and is then directed with the Fylgja in the required direction. This direction is usually up the tree but Ond can also be directed towards someone else for healing (or indeed for harm), or the Heathen shaman may work with the Ond of the whole 'family' or even 'tribe' in Helheim.

# – Conclusion –
# Ragnarok

We intend this book to be both a manual and a source of inspiration: a manual for learning and practising initiatory, shamanic, animist Heathenry, and a source of inspiration for you to follow your own path. If you feel the system is completely for you that is fine, but you may choose not to follow the system presented in this book to the final letter. You might instead enjoy the Galdr, or the techniques of rune casting and scrying. Borrowing these elements of the practice may prompt you to produce different rituals, create your own Galdr, and develop different ways of following a Heathen path. If this is what you decide to do, then this book will have served its purpose.

All things must end, and our ancestors knew this well, as represented in Ragnarok, the 'final destiny' or 'twilight' of the gods. The Ragnarok of the Edda may well be a late addition to the myths, being reflective of the uncertain times encountered towards the end of the Viking period. But as an analogy for death, it also reminds us that death is ever present. This book has held this teaching – and other approaches to 'death' – at its core. And by practising the path herein detailed, it is possible to make journeys beyond death, beyond the barriers of space and time into the otherworld – the world tree of Northern mythology. What is more, this experience is by no means restricted to happening only at the time of physical death, for every rune cast, every scrying session, and every ecstatic ritual takes you beyond death. This is of course a preparation for the final death, Ragnarok itself.

But what is Ragnarok? The version of the afterlife among the Vikings which most of us encounter in the literature today seems to us to have been most prevalent amongst warriors. They saw death in battle and residing in the hall of the slain as the highest honour. These heroes may have been followers of the battle god Woden, but they were not the only ones dedicated to Woden for there were also Woden's shamans. Perhaps Ragnarok – the coming of death, the afterlife and its character – would have been rather different for Woden's shamans than for his warriors. No 'glory' or 'valour' for them, but a shamanic, ecstatic death. This is a death which can be induced throughout one's lifetime by utilising the practices of altering consciousness and engaging with otherworldly beings, as outlined in Galdrbok. But this is also a death in which the final journey out of the body is accomplished – sloughing off the Lich.

This multi-faceted 'death' is one meaning of Ragnarok for Heathen shamans today, and it is the theme with which we end this book. Ragnarok is by no means simply an 'end'. Just as a new world was promised after the Ragnarok of the Viking era, so a new beginning follows the Ragnarok of contemporary Heathenry, in a number of ways. For example, just as every otherworldly ritual involves the re-memberment of Ymir in the form of rune-casting or a cosmogony mimesis, so each ritual is also a death, a mini-Ragnarok. And each rebirth from the ritual is a birth into a new, more spiritually accomplished way of being which celebrates life and the world(s). The well-practised, many times transcended Northern Mage then, will at the final death encounter a familiar place, an otherworld which has been visited on many occasions. Death will be a well rehearsed and oft-experienced event, and the territory of Yggdrasill will be well known. Ragnarok, then, may be approached as the 'death of death'.

*Waes thu hael!*

# – Appendix A –
## The Anglo-Saxon Rune Poem

The translation of the Anglo-Saxon rune poem in this appendix was created expressly for this book. Each rune, its stanza of the rune poem and interpretation, fills one page. The Anglo-Saxon rune glyph is given first, followed by the Anglo-Saxon name, the Common Germanic name (in brackets) and a Modern English translation. After the Modern English translation of each stanza of the rune poem follows an interpretation and key words and phrases encapsulating the meaning of the rune, including those linked to the Cosmogony (see Chapter 2: Cosmogony). These interpretations are of our own kenning, or based on Thorsson (1984), Linsell (1992), Fries (1993) and Aswynn (1994). There are also adaptations of Thorsson's (1984) 'seed sounds' at the end of each section, which can be used to further connect with each rune.

Aspects of the translation require some explanation. For example, in the case of the Peorth rune it is typically alleged that due to a failure in 'meter', a word or idea is missing after 'spirited' in the Peorth stanza of the rune poem. Given the nature of Anglo-Saxon 'leisure' and the somewhat obscure nature of 'Peorth' as a lot box (chance box) and its association with 'chance', it is pertinent to note that one favourite pastime or 'leisure activity' in the 'beer hall' of our ancestors was 'riddling', as evinced by the 95 Anglo-Saxon riddles in the Exeter Book (e.g. Hamer 1970). Riddling is epitomised more recently by Tolkien (a

professor of Anglo-Saxon) in 'The Hobbit', as illustrated in
the original Gollum-Bilbo encounter where riddles are
exchanged. We strongly suspect that the missing
word/idea in the Peorth verse is 'riddling' – in a sense, we
have solved the riddle! The non-modern grammatical
placement of the word does not prejudice this view.

The term 'drihten', used in more than one instance in the
rune poem, translates as 'lord', referring to a deity (one of
many) as one's 'lord', as well as to a local nobleman. We
retain the original here, to embrace this ambiguity and
avoid the singular 'Lord' in the Christian sense. 'Metod' is
the Norn (Wyrd Sister) of the 'present', or 'life becoming'.
'Man' is not gender specific in Old English, so we retain its
use in this translation (rather than, for example, 'woman'
and 'yeoman', or pluralisation) both for consistency and in
adherence to the Old English language. Similarly, the term
'warrior' should not be seen as referring exclusively to
'soldiers' but also to ordinary folk, both men and women,
who 'battle' through life. Finally, note that 'folk' refers to all
people and is not racially aligned.

The translations of the Anglo Saxon words found in the
Rune Poem have been arrived at with reference to
Bosworth (1989), Mitchell and Robinson (1992) and
Pollington (1996[1993]).

# Feoh (Fehu): Fee/Wealth

WEALTH IS A COMFORT TO ALL MEN
THOUGH EACH MUST SHARE IT WELL
IF HE WILL CAST HIS 'LOT' BEFORE HIS DRIHTEN

Moveable wealth, cattle, fertility, energy, Vanir deities.

Mobile force/power. Creative and fertile potential and energy. The birth of Ymir. Wealth brings wolves from the woods. Wealth is not down to money alone. The 'sending' rune'. The horns of bovine livestock, two branches on a tree, two leaves on a stem.

fehu fehu fehu
fffffffffffff
fu fa fi fe fo
of ef if af of
fffffffffffff

## Ur (Uruz): Aurochs/Cattle

THE AUROCHS IS RESOLUTE AND HORNED OVERHEAD
FIERCE AND UNTAMED, IT FIGHTS WITH HORNS
THAT HUGE, PROUD, MOOR-STRUTTING BEAST

The sacred cow: the 'birth' of Audhumla.

The horns of the aurochs and the stance of the aurochs.

Courage, bravery, boldness, daring, defiance, firmness, vigorous, powerful, strong, determined. Health, healing and the maintenance of healing. Vital strength, causality. Induction of magnetic earth streams.

uruz uruz uruz
uuuuuuu
uuurrrrrr
uuuuuuu

## Thorn (Thurisaz): Thorn

THORN IS VERY SHARP FOR ALL WARRIORS
EXTREMELY GRIM AND EVIL TO GRASP
FOR ALL MEN WHO SETTLE IN ITS MIDST

Thurs, Giant, Thunor, Mjollnir. Destruction and regeneration. Active defence, awakening the will to action, knowledge of the division of all things.

Blasting force, forces of destruction and defence. A forward thrusting force – 'fucking'. Thunder and lightning. The thorn protects the flower, breaks down barriers and fecundates. The thorn on the branch, perhaps blackthorn or hawthorn. The sleep thorn of folklore. The shape of the hammer. Birth of Buri.

thurisaz thurisaz thurisaz
th th th th th th th th
thur thar thir ther thor
thu tha thi the tho
th th th th th th th th

# Os (As): Mouth

MOUTH IS THE SHAPER OF SPEECH

WISDOM'S PROP AND WISE MEN'S COMFORT

AND EVERY PEER'S EASE AND HOPE

The rune of the 'word', poetry, song, and Galdr. Convincing and magnetic speech. Acquisition of creative wisdom.

Woden, ecstasy, transformation, shaman, inspiration. Death mysteries, numinous knowledge, prophesy, communication. Challenging of death through the knowledge of Woden. The wind blown cloak of Woden. Ymir produces the first in the race of giants.

ansuz ansuz ansuz

aaaaaaaaaa

aaaaaaasssssss

aaaaa

aaaaaaaaaa

# Rað (Raidho): Riding

RIDING IN THE 'HALL' IS SOFT FOR WARRIORS
YET HARD WHEN SEATED HIGH UPON A MIGHTY HORSE
COVERING THE MILE-PATHS

Make the journey or delay the journey. Plan, prepare, strategy. Thinking is not doing! The act of riding. Rhythm, rhythmic movement, cosmic order. The solar wagon/chariot. Ymir produces the second in the race of giants. Sexual reproduction is possible.

raidho raidho raidho
rrrrrrrrrr
ru ra ri re ro
rudh radh ridh redh rodh
or er ir ar ur
rrrrrrrrrr

## Cen (Kenaz): Torch

TORCH IS FAMILIAR BY ITS QUICKENING FLAME
PALE AND BRIGHT IT BURNS MOST OFTEN
WHERE PRINCES REST, INSIDE

The fire rune, controlled energy. Smithing and crafting towards a willed result. The flame of the torch, the firebrand, a torch fixed at an angle to a wall. The responsibility of leadership. Voice opinions, share your strength of conviction with others and spur them into action. Lead, join, partnership, organise, unite, direct. Ideas, understanding, kenning. Control, creativity, regeneration. A six-headed son is born from Ymir.

kenaz kenaz kenaz
ku ka ki ke ko
kun kan kin ken kon
ok ek ik ak uk
keeeeennnnnnn

## Gyfu (Gebo): Gift/Giving

GIVING IS FOR MEN, NOBLE AND WORTHY

AND FOR OUTCASTS AND OTHERS WITHOUT MEANS

A SUSTENANCE, SUPPORT AND AN HONOUR

Sacrifice, shamanic sacrifice.

Open-handedness, hospitality. When others share with you what they have, however little it may be, show them respect. It is often easier to give than to receive. No person is so rich that he will not welcome thanks for a gift given gladly.

A gift well meant should be well received. The generous and the bold seldom have cares but the mean see evil everywhere and pine for gifts. Loyalty and obligation. Harmony between kin. Sex magic. Woden hanging on the tree. Buri and Bestla give birth to Woden, shaman-god.

gebo gebo gebo
gu ga gi ge go
gub gab gib geb gob
og eg ig ag ug
geeeeebooooo

## Wynn (Wunjo): Joy

JOY TOLERATES LITTLE OF WOE, SORROW OR ANXIETY
FOR HE THAT HAS FOR HIMSELF
HAPPINESS AND BLISS
AMIDST A TOWN OF 'PLENTY'

Joyful are those who recognise good fortune when it is with them. To know joy, you must also know sorrow, but do not seek it out as Wyrd has enough for all of us. The sorrow of others is not hard to find for those who have eyes to see. Be thankful for what you have and enjoy it.

Learn from the past and contemplate the future, but enjoy the present. Do not let the possibility of misfortune tomorrow spoil today's joy. Sorrow and despondency comes but joy returns. Harmony, well-being, joy, pleasure. Vili is born. The shape of the clan banner. On its back, the rune is also a couple making love with one partner on top.

wunjo wunjo wunjo
wu wa wi we wo
wun wan win wen won
wo we wi wa wu
wwwyyyyyynnnn

# Hagl/Hagel (Hagalaz): Hail/Snowflake

HAIL IS THE WHITEST 'CORN'
IT SWIRLS ALOFT
TUMBLES IN GUSTY WINDS
THEN TURNS INTO WATER

Dramatic change. Complete harmony.

Cosmic pattern, framework, completeness.

Overcome setbacks as best as you can and make provision in times of plenty for times of hardship and suffering. After the storm, security returns. Ve is born. The potential for Ymir's dismemberment and the creation of the tree. The 'primal' snowflake. The first of three 'Winter runes'.

hagalaz hagalaz hagalaz
h h h h h h h h h
hu ha hi he ho
hug hag hig heg hog
(hul hal hil hel hol)
oh eh ih ah uh
h h h h h h h h h

# Nyð (Nauð): Need

NEED, LIKE A STRICTURE ABOUT THE BREAST
THOUGH OFT' A MORTAL SIGN, CAN AUGUR WELL
HELP AND HEAL, IF ATTENDED-TO QUICKLY

Resistance, distress, need.

Hardship, like guilt, causes us discomfort but it can also bring contentment if we confront it. Confront hardship when it first appears. The Gods help those who help themselves. Endure hardship and when it goes, which it surely will if you act wisely, you will be stronger and better able to make your way in the world.

Overcome negative Orlog. Use the force of resistance under will for magic. Recognise personal need. Use your Wyrd, do not strive against it. The bore and bow which turns it to kindle the need-fire. Wildfire, two fingers crossed in need. The second 'Winter rune'. Adversity as a test of fortitude. Love magic – to attract a lover.

naudhiz naudhiz naudhiz
nnnnnnnnnnnnnn
nu na ni ne no
nudh nadh nidh nedh nodh
un an in en on
nnnnnnnnnnnnnn

# Isa (Is): Ice

ICE IS EXCEEDING COLD, VERY SLIPPERY
GLISTENS LIKE GLASS, MUCH LIKE A JEWEL
FLOOR-FROST, FAIR-WROUGHT, A FINE SIGHT

Much of what we desire is difficult or dangerous to gain, painful to hold, and easily slips from our grasp. What looks resplendent from afar is often dull to the touch.

Disappointment, illusion, selfishness, individuality, ego, polarity, balance. World Ice, development of firm will and control, freezing of negative forces (such as giants). Stillness, concentration. The Gods create the first human, Ask. The icicle, the 'primal' ice of Nifelheim, from which everything else was created. The third 'Winter rune'.

isa isa isa
iiiiiiiii
iiiissssss
(ssssss iiiii)
iiiiiiiiii

# Gera (Jera): Year

YEAR BRINGS HOPE FOR MEN

WHEN GODS IN HAVEN

PERMIT THE EARTH TO GIVE FORTH BRIGHT CROPS FOR RICH AND POOR

Frigg is Earth and of Earth. She is her own daughter and is known by many names. Frigg is the Goddess of Fertility and Love; she brings us the fruits of the earth and the fruits of our loins. She is the Goddess of the Harvest and Mother of People. Use her gifts wisely and care for her, so that she is able to care for those who come after us. Love and love-making, fertility and bountiful harvest. A loving and fertile relationship.

Attainment of a goal, Peace. Reaping the rewards of earlier work. Cycles, annual solar cycle. Fruition, peace, plenty. Realisation of cyclical nature, bringing of concepts into material manifestation, the fruits of magical work. The second human, Embla, is born marking the potential for sexual reproduction. Midway in the Futhark, Jera is the rune of cycles and sexual reproduction. A rune of the spring and Summer months, and the time from springtime to harvest.

jera jera jera
jjjeeeeerrrraaaa
jjjjjjjjjjjj
ju ja ji je jo
(jur jar jir jer jor)
jjjeeeerrrraaaa

# Eoh (Ehwaz): Yew

YEW IS OUTWARDLY AN UNSMOOTH TREE
HARD, FAST IN THE GROUND, A KEEPER OF FIRES
ROOTS 'WRITHING-BENEATH', A JOY ON HOMELAND

The yew is very strong and long of life. Its roots and branches, like the Web of Wyrd, reach out into the seven worlds. The yew is ever green. It is the tree of life and death, the world tree Yggdrasill. Spiritual Journey. An opportunity for self discovery and inner peace. A search for meaning and values.

Spiritual discovery and fulfilment. A reassessment of values and the way you wish to live your life. A new outlook on life. A change of direction. A new path. The vision of the worlds on the tree. Shamanic travel on the world tree. The Yggdrasill world tree and its creation.

Shamanic initiation. The tree sacred to Woden.

eihwaz eihwaz eihwaz
eeeeeeeeeeeeee
iwu iwa iwi iwe iwo
iwo iwe iwi iwa iwu
eeeeeeeeeeee

# Peorth (Perthro): The Lot Box/Dice Cup

PEORTH IS UNFAILING RECREATION AND LAUGHTER
WHEN SPIRITED WARRIORS SIT BLITHELY TOGETHER
RIDDLING IN THE BEER-HALL

Ease and openness are joys to be had when kin or companions sit together playing, riddling and story-telling around the hearth in relaxed friendship. Fellowship and friendship, trust and ease. Companionship, loyalty.

Wyrd and according/discording with Wyrd, harmony, the runic oracle, divination, Orlog, the rune of time, escaping time, cause and effect.

perthro perthro perthro
pu pa pi pe po
purdh pardh pirdh perdh pordh
po pe pi pa pu
peeeerrrrththththththrrrroo

# Eolh (Elhaz/Algiz): Elksedge

ELKSEDGE OFT' INHABITS FENLAND
GROWING IN WATER, IT GRIMLY WOUNDS
AND BURNS WITH BLOOD ANY MAN WHO GRASPS IT

Be wary even in times of need. Grabbing quickly for support at that which comes easily to hand can bring pain and sorrow.

Protection, guard, resilience and hardiness. Endurance and the ability to withstand adverse conditions. Strengthening of the Lich, Hamr, Hugr and Hamingja. Caution. A splayed hand, Antlers of the elk, Branches of a tree, a Swan in flight. A (protective) sanctuary for the gods. The Stadrgaldr of connection with the gods. Be careful whom you trust and what you clutch at. Connections between gods and people. Discretion, prudence, circumspection, foresight, vigilance.

elhaz elhaz elhaz
zzzzzzzzzzzzzz
uz az iz ez oz
oz ez iz az uz
zzzzzzzzzzzzzz

## Sigel (Sowilio): Sun

SUN FOR SEAFARERS ALWAYS GIVES HOPE
TO THOSE WHO FERRY OVER THE 'FISHES BATH'
'TIL THEIR 'SEA - STALLION' BRINGS THEM TO LAND

Sun brings a fair journey and good fortune. Its bright light chases away fear, and warms the sea and soil. Success, achievement, well-being, safety, happiness.

The feminine Solar wheel, its turning, and its energies. The thunderbolt. Spiritual Will as expressed through the Hvels of the Lich.

sowilo sowilo sowilo
sssssssssssssss
sssoooooooooolll
su sa si se so
(sul sal sil sel sol)
us as is es os
ssssssssssss

# Tiw (Tir/Tiwaz): The God Tiw

TIW IS A CLEAR DEPENDABLE SIGN
KEEPS STEADY WITH PRINCES, IS EVER ON COURSE
AND NEVER WANDERS OVER THE NIGHT MIST

Tiw is the warriors friend, a god of courage. Like the guiding star which bears his name, he shines out of the darkness and is always there for those who need him. Tiw the Sky Father, watches over us as provider; the god of order and justice. Tiw is unflinching in battle and in all he does. Warriors and travellers look to his brightly burning light.

Courage and glory. Protection in conflict, and help in overcoming fear and doubt. Giver of confidence and destroyer of doubt. Development of conscience and right direction in life. Building spiritual will. Divine order, passive regulation. The Sword or Spear point, the Arrow, the shape of the Irminusl pillar, Mjollnir inverted – the scales of justice.

A victory rune – often found on ancient weapons and funerary urns.

tiwaz tiwaz tiwaz
tiiiiwwwwww
tu ta ti te to
tur tar tir ter tor
ot et it at ut
tiiiiwwww

## Beorc (Berkano): Birch

BIRCH HAS NO FRUIT

BEARS SHOOTS WITH NO SEED

A LEAF-LADEN CROWN AMIDST HIGH SHINING BRANCHES

DELIGHTFUL GARLAND ALOFT IN THE SKY

The Birch is a tree of fertility, healing and magic. Its branches seem bare of flower and seed, yet it is very fertile and sprouts many shoots. Woden marked runes on nine birch twigs then struck an adder with them, so that it flew into nine parts. The Birch is the tree of the wise ones who can heal us. Birch is the wood of rune wands and magic.

Inspiration. Fertility of the mind. Inspiration swirls in the head and sprouts many shoots. Vision, dream, idea, brain-wave, understanding. Magic and the onset of magical abilities. The power to influence, and affect people and things. A wish or desire fulfilled. Influence, foresee, foretell, knowledge, understanding, wisdom. Containment and works of concealment. The Birch Goddess, her breasts. A rune of spring rites.

berkano berkano berkano
bu ba bi be bo
beeeeeerrrrr
(burk bark birk berc bork)
ob eb ib ab ub
beeeeeerrrr

# Eh (Ehwaz/Ehwo): Horse

HORSE IS FOR NOBLES, A PRINCELY JOY
HORSES 'HOOFING' PROUDLY WHERE
WEALTHY RIDERS BANDY WORDS
A STEED TO THE RESTLESS, IS EVER A COMFORT

It is a pleasure to own something which gives pride in its possession and joy in its use. A horse gives the freedom to meet people, seek adventure and visit far-away places. The Heathen shaman is now capable of shamanic travel on Yggdrasill (Sleipnir). Travel and adventure. New people, partnerships, new places, new experiences, venturesome, pioneering, progressive, opportunist, explorer, trek, voyager. Boredom, loneliness, tedium, frustration, weariness, jaded.

The sign of two horses facing one another, two humans facing one another and holding hands, and the horse (with bent back, drooping belly). A beast sacred to our Heathen ancestors.

ehwo ehwo ehwo
eeeeeehwwwooooo
ehwu ehwa ehwi ehwe ehwo
ehwo ehwe ehwi ehwa ehwu
eeeeeehwwwoooo

## Mann (Mannaz): Humankind

MAN IN HIS GLEE IS DEAR TO HIS KIN

THOUGH EACH MUST BETRAY HIS FELLOWS

WHEN THE DRIHTEN DECREES

THE PITIFUL FLESH CONDEMNED TO THE EARTH

Friendship brings great joy and comfort. Value it highly and tend it carefully. Wyrd has a grave for us all. Go often to the homes of your friends: weeds and brambles grow quickly on a neglected path. Enjoy the company of your fellows while you may; friendships do not endure forever. Friends are difficult to find but easy to lose.

Companionship, relations, trust, appreciation, support, loyalty, fellowship, genetics. Change; the old makes way for the new. Rarely such a thing as the lone sage. Community of humans and spirits. The divine human ancestor. Must 'die ' to enter the tree. Posture of death; two people, clasping.

mannaz mannaz mannaz
mmmmmmaaaaaaannnnnnn
mu ma mi me mo
mun man min men mon
um am im em om
mon men min man mun
mmmmmmaaaaaaannnnnnn

# Lagu (Laguz): Water

WATER TO FOLKS SEEMS NEVER-ENDING
TO HIM WHO MUST VENTURE ON AN UNSTEADY SHIP
WHILE HIGH WAVES TERRIFY
AND THE 'SEA-STALLION' HEEDS NOT THE 'BRIDLE'

On earth no-one can venture over the whale's domain without fear of what Wyrd will bring. Still, seafarers return to the salt waves and undertake journeys to the land of strangers.

Opportunity and new horizons. Be bold and seize an opportunity but do not be over-confident. Opening, turning point, new ideas, uncertainty, need for courage, determination and clear thinking to survive the rough passage. Endure hardship and uncertainty, and reap the reward which awaits you. Guidance through difficult initiatory tests. The entering of the tree through 'submergence', but trepidation over the unknown. Any body of water (lake, river, stream, sea, raindrop, etc).

laguz laguz laguz
IIIIIIIIIIIIII
lu la li le lo
(lug lag lig leg log)
ul al il el ol
lo le li la lu
llllllaaaaaaaguuuuuuu

# Ing (Ingwaz): The God Ing

ING WAS FIRST SEEN AMONGST THE EAST DANES
'TIL HE DEPARTED OVER THE WAVES
HIS WAGON FOLLOWING BEHIND HIM
THUS THE 'HARDY MEN' NAMED THAT HERO

When the English lived in Angel they gave praise to Mother Earth and called her Nerthus. Ing is the son of Nerthus, and he and his sister Eostre are called Lord and Lady. Each Winter Ing leaves us and travels over the sea but bonfires, merriment and the burning of holly rouse him from his Winter sleep and he returns with a sheaf of corn as his pillow. He alone shall unbind the frost's fetters and drive away Winter, so that spring shall return to give the fields lush grass and the trees a crown of green.

The divine hero and consort of the mother goddess. Rebirth, regrowth, fertility, renewal. Excellent prospects for growth. Recognition of (the beauty of) life cycles and the possibility of shamanic ecstasy and wisdom.

ingwaz ingwaz ingwaz
iiiiiinnnnnnnggggg
ung ang ing eng ong
ong eng ing ang ung
iiiiinnnnnngggggg

# Daeg (Dagaz): Day

DAY IS THE DRIHTEN'S HERALD, DEAR TO MEN
GREAT METOD'S LIGHT, A JOY AND A HOPE
TO RICH AND POOR – FOR ALL TO USE

Day is reason and understanding; it brightens the life of all men and brings many rewards.

Reason, safety and justice. Good health, light, brightness, understanding. The balance between day and night. The day and daylight. The shape of Mjollnir. Wodenic paradox, the cycle of 'cosmic' life and potential for achieving shamanic wisdom.

dagaz dagaz dagaz
dhdhdhdhdhdhdhdhdh
daaaaaaaaaagaaaaazzzz
du da di de do
dh dh dh dh dh
odh edh idh adh udh
daaaaaaaaaagaaaaazzzz

# Aethel (Odal): Home/Land

HOME IS EXCEEDINGLY LOVED BY EACH MAN
IF HE MAY OFTEN ENJOY ITS DUE RIGHTS
HAPPY AT HOME, IN PROSPERITY

Home, in our sacred landscape, is security and stability, peace and prosperity – an inheritance to be treasured. A sense of belonging and being at ease with the land and its people. Peace, freedom and security. Inherited property.

Unity, community, cohesion, comradeship, empathy, trust, loyalty, peace, prosperity, well-being, confidence, stability, strength, freedom, security, continuity, survival. The shape of an enclosure, the vulva. Coming (closer to) home, closer to the wisdom of the heart, and the potential for dissolving individuality. Moving from ego-centricity to clano-centricity.

othala othala othala
oooooooooooooo
ooooooo
othul othal othil othel othol
othol othel othil othal othul
ooooooo

# Ac: Oak

OAK ON LAND, TO THE OFFSPRING OF MEN, IS
FODDER FOR FLESH, FARES OFTEN
OVER THE GANNET'S BATH WHERE THE SEA TESTS
WHETHER OAK BE 'NOBLE' AND 'TRUE'

As the 'Donar-' or 'Thunor-Oak', the tree is sacred to Thunor. It is the tree of the lightning bolt of creation and Oak trees seem particularly prone to lightning strike. Oaks were often meeting places, locations for the 'Thing'. One of these in Hampshire is recorded in the Domesday Book. The Oak is the tree of long life and endurance, famed for its prowess in shipbuilding. The Acorn is the classic symbol of fertility, shaped like the glans penis.

Honour, trust, strength, resilience (developed beyond Elksedge). Strength and the ability to face death.

## Asc: Ash

ASH OVERHEAD IS BELOVED OF MEN
WELL-POSITIONED AND STANDING FIRM
IT ENDURES LIVING MEN AS FOES

Woden's ash spear Gungnir, the spiritual weapon, is made from Ash. The shape of the rune is related to the Os rune, thus note the connection between Ash and Woden.

The Rowan or Mountain Ash was used to make small crosses (Gift runes – note the Woden connection again), which were bound with red cord. They were carried on the person or placed in a suitable place (such as the threshold of the home) to ensure protection.

Determination, direction, resolution (emphasised further than in the rune of Tiw).

# Yr: Weapon/Bow

BOW IS FOR EACH PRINCE AND NOBLE, A

JOY, A SYMBOL OF WORTH, LOOKS FAIR ON A STEED

SECURES SWIFTLY ITS MARK – AN OUTSTANDING BATTLE-WEAPON

The spiritual weapon, more pronounced than in the Thorn rune (also linking back to the Yew rune and the Yew longbow), which represents compassion. It is the weapon for 'killing' death and overcoming darkness. Fries suggests the shape resembles that of a horse's saddle, a tent, or a blanket.

## Iar: Beaver

BEAVER IS A RIVER-FISH, IT EXPLOITS
FOOD ON THE GROUND AND HAS A FAIR DWELLING
BOUNDED BY WATER, WHERE IT LIVES JOYFULLY

Happiness, contentment (further than in Wynn), spiritual bliss and shamanic ecstasy. Glimpses of Bilrost.

Fries mentions that at the time of the Rune Poem, Beavers (and the Otter – also a 'river-fish') were considered to be 'fish'.

# Ear: Grave

GRAVE IS WEARISOME TO ALL WHO ARE NOBLE

WHEN DEAR-HELD FLESH BEGINS TO COOL

CHOOSES BLEAK EARTH FOR SPOUSE, LIFE-BREATH FALLEN

JOYS DEPARTED, PLEDGES CEASING

Give thanks for life, the greatest of gifts, and dwell not on the grave which awaits you. We wrestle with old age in an unequal struggle from the day we are born, but even the strong are humbled by death. Let the certainty of an end to this life be a spur to acts of courage and glory.

The experience of Death, both momentarily in life through regular induction of the trance states, and the final death itself when the Lich is sloughed off.

The rune appears to resemble the shape of the Irminsul Pillar which, at the world's axis, supports the sky.

## – Appendix B –
## Synopsis of Galdrbok's Path
## of Shamanic Initiation

We understand that many readers will read Galdrbok purely out of general interest. Yet for some readers the path of Heathen shamanic initiation may appeal as a lifeway. For those prepared to apply the system, we briefly explain here how to use this book as a path of Heathen shamanic initiation, comprising a 'synopsis'. This is presented in a sequence of nine (that sacred number of the North, again!) numbered stages which correspond with the practices outlined in chapters one to seven. We recommend that you read each chapter in turn and follow the recommended procedures in them before moving on to later chapters.

The practical basis of the system is to be found in the use of the runes and a crystal ball, and the practices of rune casting and scrying associated with them (Chapter 1), in sacred landscapes. All other practices stem from here.

The theoretical basis of the system is the Norse (or more loosely 'Northern') cosmogony and cosmology which chart the Heathen otherworld (Chapters 2 and 3). The path of initiation itself and its rituals, follow stages contained within the cosmogony. The theoretical and methodological considerations on trance (altering consciousness), Galdr (sung or chanted spells), ritual (e.g. offerings to gods), magic (casting spells) and the

Heathen shaman's being (Chapters 4 to 7) all tie into the practices of rune casting and scrying (with a crystal ball), and they also refer back to the cosmogony and cosmology.

Galdrbok is thus self-contained, consistent and offers a complete, practical system of initiation for today, following in the traditions of shamanic Heathenry.

As said, we recommend that you resist skipping any step, as much as you may want to. It is important to become adept at 'the basics' before moving on to more advanced work.

## The Synopsis

This synopsis introduces terms which may not be familiar to the reader at this stage. But do not be put off! Each of these terms is introduced in detail at the relevant point in the relevant chapters. Use this synopsis to get an overall 'feel' of the Heathen initiation system initially, and then refer back to it at will. Note that there are 29 Anglo-Saxon runes and that a stanza of the Anglo-Saxon rune poem supports each of them. In Galdrbok, these 29 runes are understood to represent (among other things) the creation of the universe. They also provide insights into its workings, and the workings of all things.

1. Read up to and including Chapter 1.

2. Acquire a rune set and crystal ball (any size will do). Familiarise yourself with rune casting and scrying, and try to learn by heart the rune poem.

3. Read Chapters 2 and 3.

4. Apply the rituals associated with the use of the runes and the use of the crystal ball to 'internalise' the cosmogony (the mythology/ancient memory of how the universe was made) and cosmology (plan of the universe, from an animistic/shamanistic perspective). Study these until they become a part of you (and your community) in a personal (and communal) vision. This vision sets the territory for exploring Yggdrasill and its worlds.

5. Read chapters 4-6, in turn.

6. Begin practising the trance states and Galdr, and familiarise yourself with rituals 1-4 in Chapter 6: Ritual.

All practices to this point relate to the Runic cosmogony (see Chapter 2) up to and including rune 18, Berkano. But, the initiatory practices surrounding rune 13, Yew, are only undertaken at stage 7 (see below). Nonetheless, the worlds of Yggdrasill can still be seen or descried, if not entered, before then. The runes 14 to 18 furthermore, will 'open the way' to shamanic wisdom and magical abilities. However, the experience of these runes will be enhanced further after stage 7 has been completed. This underlines the importance of practising Vaniric trance before progressing on to Aesiric and Disiric trances.

7. When you are sufficiently accomplished, undertake the shamanic self-initiation described in ritual 5 (Hung on the Tree, Chapter 6). Having practised with the runes, you can now experience how Woden won them. In the cosmogony, this stage corresponds mainly with rune 13 Yew – the

Yggdrasill tree itself on which Woden hung. It logically follows that runes 14 Perthro to 18 Berkano which 'open the way' (unlock the magical door), are also important here, since as Woden's experiences in the Havamal indicate, it is after shamanic initiation proper that magical and other abilities progress. This is the level of shamanic journeying proper, moving the adept beyond passive scrying, so runes 19 Horse (the means to travel) to 24 Odal, native or home land (the return home from the shamanic journey), are particularly involved. Stages 8 and 9 next deal with the runes 17 Tiw to 29 Grave.

8. As you see fit, practice ritual 6 (Deity/Ancestor Communication and Shape-Shifting, Chapter 6) and thereby familiarise yourself more fully with the three trance states and deity/ancestor invocation (Galdr). On the cosmogony, these are broadly the rune stages 14 Perthro to 28 Beaver.

With the completion of stage 8, you should explore the remaining ritual procedures, such as the first four chapters of the Edda, the Wheel of the Year, and Oath Swearing. Once accomplished in these practices, read chapter 7 and undertake the procedures of magic and shamanic healing if and when required. Again, these are the cosmogony stages relating to runes 14 Perthro to 28 Beaver.

9. Overall in these practices you are persistently 'opening the way' to descrying and entering the otherworld (runes 14 Perthro to 18 Berkano). You are also undertaking shamanic initiation and the benefits that brings (runes 13 to 18), as well as shamanic travel on the tree symbolised by rune 13 but expressed in runes 19 Horse (the means

to travel) to 24 Odal (the return home to 'ordinary' consciousness).

With stage 9 completed, you should undertake any or all of these practices and rituals as often as possible. At the simplest level, this will comprise rune casting and scrying, and at the most complex level, the shamanic self-initiation (ritual 5). In this way you will become more familiar with the otherworlds which are outside the circles of space and time, and beyond death, embodied in the cosmogony by rune 29 Grave. We know from the ancient sources that Woden was preoccupied by his own death and acquiring the knowledge of it. While one aim of the system in Galdrbok might be construed as engaging with the reality of death, every ritual in itself involves a kind of death and therefore an experience of transcendence (importantly, this transcendence is the 'ecstasy' of shamanisms rather than 'escape' from reincarnation – which is unnecessary in a Heathen animistic worldview). Every ritual, even in a small way, is a form of shamanic experience, initiation, and transcendence.

The stages of the cosmogony and the traditional order of the runes provide a practical framework for sequencing the system. Just as the runes are not fixed or dogmatic, the stages of the cosmogony are not mutually exclusive and there is much cross-referencing. For example, the grave rune is referenced in the 'mini-death' which is experienced during Vaniric trance (rune 14 Perthro).

Galdrbok's path of shamanic initiation demands dedication and time. Do not expect to be sufficiently accomplished to be able to move from one stage to the next in a matter of days or weeks. The time frame of months and years should be seriously entertained. An adept Heathen Runester will understand the undertaking of Galdrbok's entire path of shamanic initiation as a life's work – resonating with what the occultist Aleister Crowley termed the 'great work'. Such a practitioner will also return to the basic elements of the system on a regular basis: 'going back to basics' facilitates new insights through altered eyes.

The Ulfhednr group, who follow the path outlined in Galdrbok, have no strict hierarchies, priests or dogma. Direct contact with the otherworld removes the need for such intermediaries and protocols. Individual practitioners may choose to express their allegiance based on the number of seasons and years they have dedicated to their Heathen path. Thus, after one year's practice, started at the beginning of Winter, an adept may use the title 'Ulfhednr One Winter Old', and after two years 'Ulfhednr Two Winter's Old', and so on. Practitioners attaining nine years dedicated practice may in addition use the title 'Ulfhednr Elder'. These titles offer an indication of dedication and experience only, and do not denote privilege or authority.

# References Cited and Further Reading

There are many books and numerous articles on runes, Heathenry, and related subjects. Some of these, including those cited in the text, are listed below. We suggest you approach all of them, as we expect you have approached the current volume itself, with an open but critical mind.

## The Runes and Heathenry

Aswynn, F. 1994. Leaves of Yggdrasill. Minnesota: Llewellyn.

Elliott, R.W.V. 1989 [1959]. Runes: An Introduction. Manchester: Manchester University Press.

Fries, J. 2002 [1993]. Helrunar: A Manual of Rune Magick. Oxford: Mandrake Press.

Gundarsson, K. 1990. Teutonic Magic: The Magical and Spiritual Practices of the Germanic Peoples. Minnesota: Llewellyn.

Howard, M. 1985. The Wisdom of the Runes. London: Rider.

Linsell, T. 1992. Anglo-Saxon Runes. Middlesex: Anglo-Saxon Books.

Linsell, T. 1994. Anglo-Saxon Mythology, Migration and Magic. Middlesex: Anglo-Saxon Books (reprinted and revised edition of Linsell 1992).

Loewe, M. and C. Blacker (eds) 1981. Divination and Oracles. London: Allen and Unwin.

Osborn, M. and S. Longland. 1987. Rune Games. London: Routledge and Kegan Paul.

Page, R.I. 1964. Anglo-Saxon Runes and Magic. Journal of the Archaeological Association 27: 14-31.

Page, R.I. 1987. Runes. London: British Museum Publications.

Page, R.I. 1995. Runes and Runic Inscriptions: Collected Essays on Anglo-Saxon and Viking Runes. Woodbridge, Suffolk: The Boydell Press.

Pennick, N. 1992. Rune Magic: The History and Practice of Ancient Runic Traditions. London: Thorsons.

Pennick, N. 1999. The Complete Illustrated Guide to Runes. Shaftesbury, Dorset: Element Books.

Pollington, S. 1995. Rudiments of Runelore. Hockwold-cum-Wilton, Norfolk:Anglo-Saxon Books.

Taylor, P. 1992. The Message of the Runes: Divination in the Ancient Germanic World. In: Matthews, J. (ed.) The World Atlas of Divination: 33-44. London: Tiger Books.

Thorsson, E. 1984. Futhark: A Handbook of Rune Magic. York Beach, Maine: Samuel Weiser.

Thorsson, E. 1987. Runelore: A Handbook of Esoteric Runology. York Beach, Maine: Samuel Weiser.

Thorsson, E. 1988. At the Well of Wyrd: A Handbook of Runic Divination. York Beach, Maine: Samuel Weiser.

Thorsson, E. 1993. Green Runa: The Runemaster's Notebook – The Shorter Works of Edred Thorsson, Volume 1 (1978-1985). Austin, Texas: Runa-Raven Press.

## General Heathenry / Peoples of the North

Adalsteinsson, J.H. 1978. Under the Cloak: The Acceptance of Christianity in Iceland with Particular Reference to the Religious Attitudes Prevailing at the Time. Uppsala: Acta Universitatis Upsaliensis.

Alexander, M. (Translator). 1970 [1966]. The Earliest English Poems. London: Penguin.

Alexander, M. (Translator). 1973. Beowulf. London: Penguin.

Arnold, C.J. 1997. An Archaeology of the Anglo-Saxon Kingdoms. London: Routledge.

Banard, H.E. 1945. Some English Sites of Ancient Heathen Worship. The Hibbert Journal: A Quartely Review of Religion, Theology and Philosophy XLIV: 76-79.

Barley, N. 1972. Anglo-Saxon Magico-Medicine. Journal of the Royal Anthropological Society of Oxford 3: 67-76.

Bates, B. 1996. The Wisdom of the Wyrd: Teachings for Today from Our Ancient Past. London: Rider.

Blain, J. 2000. Understanding Wyrd: The Norns and the Tree. An Introduction to the Cosmology of Northern European Spiritual Practice. Devizes, Wiltshire: Wyrd's Well – contact: jenny@wyrdswell.plus.com

Blain, J. Wights and Ancestors: Heathenism in a Living Landscape. Hathersage, Derbyshire: Wyrds Well – contact: jenny@wyrdswell.plus.com

Bonser, W. 1926. Magical Practices Against Elves. Folk-Lore 37: 350-363.

Bonser, W. 1932. Survivals of Paganism in Anglo-Saxon England. Transactions of the Birmingham Archaeological Society 56: 37-70.

Bonser, W. 1962. Animal Skins in Magic and Medicine. Folk-Lore 73: 128-129.

Bonser, W. 1963. The Medical Background of Anglo-Saxon England. London: Wellcome Historical Medical Library.

Borovsky, Z. 1999. Never in Public: Women and Performance in Old Norse Literature. Journal of American Folklore 112: 6-39.

Bosworth J. 1989. Anglo-Saxon Dictionary. London: Oxford University Press.

Branston, B. 1957. The Lost Gods of England. London: Thames and Hudson.

Branston, B. 1955. Gods of the North. London: Thames and Hudson.

Budd, P. and T. Taylor. 1995. The faerie smith meets the bronze industry: magic versus science in the interpretation of prehistoric metal-making. World Archaeology 27(1): 133-143.

Chadwick, H.M. 1899. The Cult of Othin. Cambridge: Cambridge University Press.

Clemoes, P. (ed.) 1959. The Anglo-Saxons: Studies in Some Aspects of Their History and Culture Presented to Bruce Dickens. London: Bowes and Bowes.

Cockayne, T.O. 1864-1866. Leechdoms, Wortcunning and Starcraft of Early England. Reissued 1961, London: Holland Press.

Crawford, J. 1963. Evidences for Witchcraft in Anglo-Saxon England. Medium Aevum 32 (2): 99-116.

Crossley-Holland, K. 1980. The Penguin Book of Norse Myths: Gods of the Vikings. London: Penguin.

Davidson, H.E. 1943. The Road to Hel. Cambridge: Cambridge University Press.

Davidson, H.E. 1950. The Hill of the Dragon: Anglo-Saxon Burial Mounds in Literature and Archaeology. Folk-Lore 61 (4): 169-184.

Davidson, H.E. 1964. Gods and Myths of Northern Europe. London: Pelican.

Davidson, H.E. 1967. Pagan Scandinavia. London: Thames and Hudson.

Davidson, H.E. 1993. The Lost Beliefs of Northern Europe. London: Routledge.

Dickens, B. 1915. Runic and Heroic Poems of the Old Teutonic Peoples. Cambridge: Cambridge University Press.

Dickinson, T.M. 1993. An Anglo-Saxon 'cunning woman' from Bidford-on-Avon. In: M. Carver (ed.) In Search of Cult: Archaeological Investigations in Honour of Philip Ratz: 45-54. Woodbridge, Suffolk: The Boydell Press.

Dubois, T. 1999. Nordic Religions in the Viking Age. Philadelphia: University of Pennsylvania Press.

Dumézil, G. 1977. Gods of the Ancient Northmen. California: University of California Press.

Ellis, H.R. 1943. The Road to Hel: A Study of the Conception of the Dead in Old Norse Literature. Cambridge: Cambridge University Press.

Elton, O. 1999 [1905]. (translator) Saxo Grammaticus' Gesta Danorum, Book 6. Electronic Document: http://www.inform.umd.edu:8080/EdRes/ReadingRoom/Nonfiction/Saxo/Danes/book06 (accessed 13.9.99).

Faulkes, 1998[1987]. Edda by Snorri Sturluson. London: Everyman.

Flowers, S. 1989. The Galdrabók: An Icelandic Grimoire. York Beach, Maine: Samuel Weiser, Inc.

Frazer, W.O. and A. Tyrell (eds) 2000. Social Identity in Early Medieval Britain. London: Leicester University Press.

Glover, J.; Mackie, S. and M. Magnusson. 1995[1987]. Beowulf. Stroud, Gloucestershire: Alan Sutton Publishing Limited.

Gordon, E.V. 1962. An Introduction to Old Norse (Third Edition). Oxford: Oxford University Press.

Grattan, J. 1952. Three Anglo-Saxon Charms from the Lacnunga. Modern Language Review XXII: 1-6.

Grattan, J.H.G. and C. Singer. 1952. Anglo-Saxon Magic and Medicine. Wellcome Historical Medical Museum: Oxford University Press.

Griffiths, B. 1996. Aspects of Anglo-Saxon Magic. Frithgarth, Norfolk: Anglo-Saxon Books.

Grundy, S. 1995. The Cult of Odhinn: God of Death. PhD Thesis, University of Cambridge.

Grundy, S. 1996. Freyja and Frigg. In: S. Billington and M. Green (eds) The Concept of the Goddess: 56-67. London: Routledge.

Gundarsson, K. 2001. Spae-Craft, Seidr, and Shamanism. Available online: www.thetroth.org/resources/kveldulf/spaecraft.html

Hamer, R. (translator). 1970. A Choice of Anglo-Saxon Verse. London: Faber and Faber.

Harvey, G. 1995. Heathenism: A North European Pagan Tradition. In: Harvey, G. and C. Hardman (eds) Paganism Today: Wiccans, Druids, the Goddess and Ancient Earth Traditions for the Twenty-First Century: 49-64. London: Thorsons.

Haugen, E. 1983. 'The Edda as ritual: Odin and his masks'. In: R. J. Glendinning and H. Bessason (eds) Edda: A Collection of Essays. Manitoba: University of Manitoba Press.

Heaney, S. 1999. Beowulf: A New Translation. London: Faber and Faber.

Herbert, K. 1994. Looking for the Lost Gods of England. Frithgarth, Norfolk: Anglo-Saxon Books.

Herbert, K. 1996 [1993]. Spellcraft: Old English Heroic Legends. Frithgarth, Norfolk: Anglo-Saxon Books.

Hinton, D. 1993. Archaeology, Economy and Society: England from the Fifth to the Fifteenth Century. London: Routledge.

Hollander, L.M. (translator) 1999. Heimskringla: History of the Kings of Norway by Snorri Sturluson. Austin: University of Texas Press.

Howard, M. 1985. The Wisdom of the Runes. London: Rider.

Hübener, G. 1935. Beowulf and Germanic Exorcism. Review of English Studies 42: 163-181.

Johnston, G. (translator) and P. Foote (notes and essay) 1963. The Saga of Gisli. London: Aldine Press / J.M. Dent and Sons Ltd.

Kelchner, G.D. 1935. Dreams in Old Norse Literature and Their Affinities in Folklore. London: Cambridge University Press.

Kunz, K. (translator) 2001. The Saga of the People of Laxardal. In: The Sagas of Icelanders: 270-421. London: Penguin.

Larrington, C. 1993. A Store of Common Sense: Gnomic Theme and Style in Old Icelandic and Old English Wisdom Poetry. Oxford: Clarendon Press.

Larrington, C. (Translator) 1996. The Poetic Edda. Oxford: Oxford University Press.

Lethbridge, T.C. 1951. A Cemetery at Lackford, Suffolk: Report on the Excavation of a Cemetery of the Pagan Anglo-Saxon Period in 1947. Cambridge: Cambridge Antiquarian Society, Quarto Publications, New Series 6.

Long, C. 1985. Spirituality: Ancient People. New Jersey: Crossroads Press.

Lucy, S.J. 1997. Housewives, Warriors and Slaves? Sex and Gender in Anglo-Saxon Burials. In: J. Moore and E. Scott (eds) Invisible People and Processes: Writing Gender and Childhood into European Archaeology: 150-158. Leicester: Leicester University Press.

McGregor, R. 1995. Skirnismal as Ritual Drama: A Summary of Scholarship this Century. Deep South 1(3): Available online: http://www.islandia.is/~sighar/edda1/skirnissum.html

Magnusson, M. and Palsson, H. (translators) 1965. The Vinland Sagas: The Norse Discovery of America. London: Penguin.

Mattingly, H. (Translator) 1948. Tacitus on Britain and Germany. London: Penguin.

Meaney, A.L. 1981. Anglo-Saxon Amulets and Curing Stones. British Archaeological Reports 96. Oxford: B.A.R.

Meaney, A.L. 1989. Women, Witchcraft and Magic in Anglo-Saxon England. In: D.G. Scragg (ed.) Superstition and Popular Medicine in Anglo-Saxon England: 9-40. Manchester: Manchester Centre for Anglo-Saxon Studies.

Metzner, R. 1994. The Well of Remembrance: Rediscovering the Earth Wisdom Myths of Northern Europe. Boston: Shambhala.

Mitchell, B. and F.C. Robinson. 1992. A Guide to Old English: Fifth Edition. Oxford: Blackwell.

Mitteilungen, K. 1935. Runic Rings and Old English Charms. Archiv für das Studium Der Neueren Sprachen 67: 252-256.

Morris, K. 1991. Sorceress or Witch?: The Image of Gender in Medieval Iceland and Northern Europe. New York: University Press of America, Inc.

Nässtrom, B-M. 2003[1996]. Freyja: Great Goddess of the North. Harwich Port, Cape Cod: Clock & Rose Press.

Nässtrom, B-M. 1996a. Freyja and Frigg: Two Aspects of the Great Goddess. In: J. Pentikäinen (ed.) Shamanism and Northern Ecology: 81-96. Berlin and New York: Mouton de Gruyter.

Nässtrom, B-M. 1996b. Freyja: A Goddess with Many Names. In: S. Billington and M. Green (eds) The Concept of the Goddess: 69-75. London: Routledge.

North, R. 1997. Heathen Gods in Old English Literature. Cambridge: Cambridge University Press.

Orchard, A. 1997. Cassell Dictionary of Norse Myth and Legend. London: Cassell.

Owen, G.R. 1981. Rites and Religions of the Anglo-Saxons. New York: Barnes and Noble Books.

The Pagan Federation. 1997. Northern Tradition Information Pack. London: The Pagan Federation.

Page, R.I. 1970. Life in Anglo-Saxon England. London: B.T. Batsford.

Palsson, H. (Translator). 1971. Hrafnkel's Saga and Other Stories. London: Penguin.

Pennick, N. 1989. Practical Magic in the Northern Tradition. Wellingborough, Northants: The Aquarian Press.

Pollington, S. 1996 [1993]. Wordcraft, Wordhoard and Wordlists: Concise New English to Old English Dictionary and Thesaurus. Frithgarth, Norfolk: Anglo-Saxon Books.

Pollington, S. 2000. Leechcraft: Early English Charms, Plantlore and Healing. Hockwold-cum-Wilton, Norfolk: Anglo-Saxon Books.

Ring of Troth (Europe). 1997. Elder Troth: An Introduction to the Northern Tradition. London: Ring of Troth.

Ring of Troth (USA). Our Troth. (Currently out of print). Available online: http://asatru.knotwork.com/troth/ourtroth/index.htm

Richards, J.D. 1991. Viking Age England. London: B.T. Batsford/English Heritage.

Robertson, D. 1976. Magical Medicine in Viking Scandinavia. Medical History 20: 317-322.

Rodrigues, L.J. 1993. Anglo-Saxon Verse Charms, Maxims & Heroic Legends. Middlesex, Pinner: Anglo-Saxon Books.

Rooth, A.B. 1961. Loki in Scandinavian Mythology. Lund, Sweden: C.W.K. Gleerups.

Rosedale, E. et.al. 1981. The Vikings in England. London: The Anglo-Danish Project.

Ryan, J.S. 1963. Othin in England: Evidence from the Poetry for a Cult of Woden in Anglo-Saxon England. Folk-Lore 74: 460-480.

Salmon, V. 1960. 'The Wanderer' and 'The Seafarer', and the Old English Conception of the Soul. Modern Language Review LV(1): 1-10.

Scudder, B. (translator) 2001. Egil's Saga. In: The Sagas of Icelanders: 3-184. London: Penguin.

Semple, S. 1998. A Fear of the Past: the Place of the Prehistoric Burial Mound in the Ideology of Middle and Later Anglo-Saxon England. World Archaeology 30 (1): 109-126.

Shepherd, C. 1998. A Study of The Relationship Between Style I Art and Socio-Political Change in Early Medieval Europe. B.A.R. International Series 745. Oxford: British Archaeological Reports.

Simek, R. 1993. A Dictionary of Northern Mythology. Bury St. Edmunds: St. Edmundsbury Press.

Sørensen, P.M. 1983. The Unmanly Man: Concepts of Sexual Defamation in Early Northern Society. Odense, Denmark: Odense University Press.

Speake, G. 1980. Anglo-Saxon Animal Art and its Germanic Background. Oxford: Clarendon Press.

Stanley, E.G. 1964. The Search for Anglo-Saxon Paganism. Cambridge: Brewer.

Stenton, F. 1971. Anglo-Saxon England. The Oxford History of England Volume II Third Edition. Oxford: Oxford University Press.

Stone, Alby. 1989. Wyrd: Fate and Destiny in North European Paganism. London: Privately Published.

Stone, Alby. 1997. Ymir's Flesh: North European Creation Mythologies. Loughborough, Leicestershire: Heart of Albion Press.

Stoodley, N. 1999. The Spindle and the Spear: A Critical Enquiry into the Construction and Meaning of Gender in the Early Anglo-Saxon Burial Rite. B.A.R. British Series 288. Oxford: British Archaeological Reports.

Storms, G. 1948. Anglo-Saxon Magic. The Hague: Martinus Nijhoff.

Ström, F. 1974. Nid, Ergi and Old Norse Moral Attitudes. London: Viking Society for Northern Research.

Strömbäck, D. 1935. Sejd: textstudier i nordisk religionshistoria. Nordiska texter och undersökningar 5. Stockholm: Hugo Gebers Förlag.

Stuart, H. 1976. The Anglo-Saxon Elf. Studia Neophilogica 48: 313-320.

Strutynski, U. 1975. Germanic Divinities in Weekday Names. Journal of Indo-European Studies 3: 363-384.

Stuart, H. 1976. The Anglo-Saxon Elf. Studia Neophilogica 48: 313-320.

Thorpe, L. (translator) 1974. Gregory of Tours, The History of the Franks. London: Penguin.

Thun, S. 1969. The Malignant Elves. Studia Neophilologica 41: 378-396.

Turville-Petre, E.O.G. 1964. Myth and Religion of the North: The Religion of Ancient Scandinavia. London: Weidenfeld and Nicolson.

Van Hamel, A. 1932. Odin Hanging on the Tree. Acta Philologica Scandinavia 7: 260.

Wawn, A. (translator) 2001. The Saga of the People of Vatnsdal. In: The Sagas of Icelanders: 185-269. London: Penguin.

Welch, M. 1992. Anglo-Saxon England. London: B.T. Batsford/ English Heritage.

Williams, H. 1998. Monuments and the Past in Early Anglo-Saxon England. World Archaeology 30 (1): 90-108.

Wilson, D. 1992. Anglo-Saxon Paganism. London: Routledge.

Wilson, D.M. 1959. A Group of Anglo-Saxon Amulet Rings. In: P. Clemoes (ed.) The Anglo-Saxons: Studies in some Aspects of their History and Culture presented to Bruce Dickens: 159-170. London: Bowes and Bowes.

# Other Paganisms, Indigenous Religions and Related Subjects

Anthony, D.W. 1995. Nazi and Eco-feminist Prehistories: Ideology and Empiricism in Indo-European Archaeology. In: Kohl, P.L. and C. Fawcett (eds) Nationalism, Politics, and the Practice of Archaeology: 82-96. Cambridge: Cambridge University Press.

Bender, B. 1998. Stonehenge: Making Space. Oxford: Berg.

Blain, J., D. Ezzy and G. Harvey (eds) 2004. Researching Paganisms: Religious Experiences and Academic Methodologies. Walnut Creek, California: AltaMira.

Blain, J. and R.J. Wallis 2002. A living landscape? Pagans and Archaeological Discourse. 3rd Stone: Archaeology, Folklore and Myth – The Magazine for the New Antiquarian 43 (Summer): 20-27.

Clifton, C. and G. Harvey (eds) 2004. The Paganism Reader. London:Routledge.

Cope, J. 1998. The Modern Antiquarian: A Pre-Millennial Odyssey Through Megalithic Britain. London: Thorsons.

Deren, M. 1975. The Voodoo Gods. St. Albans, Hertfordshire: Paladin.

Eisler, R. 1987. The Chalice and the Blade. San Francisco: HarperSanFrancisco.

Fatunmbi, A.F. 1991. Ìwa-pèlé: Ifá Quest; The Search for the Source of Santería and Lucumí. Bronx, New York: Original Publications.

Gallagher, A-M. 1999. Weaving a Tangled Web: History, 'Race' and Ethnicity in Pagan Identity. The Pomegranate: A Journal of Neo-Pagan Thought 10: 19-29.

Gimbutas, M. 1974. The Gods and Goddesses of Old Europe: 7000-3500 B.C. London: Thames and Hudson; Berkeley, Los Angeles and London: University of California Press.

Gimbutas, M. with M. R. Dexter (as ed.) 1999. The Living Goddesses. Berkeley, Los Angeles and London: University of California Press.

Harvey, G. 1997. Listening People, Speaking Earth: Contemporary Paganism. London: Hurst & Co.

Harvey, G. 2000a. Boggarts and Books: Towards an Appreciation of Pagan Spirituality. In: Sutcliffe, S. and M. Bowman (eds) Beyond New Age: Exploring Alternative Spirituality: 155-168. Edinburgh: Edinburgh University Press.

Harvey, G. (ed.) 2000b. Indigenous Religions: A Companion. London: Cassell.

Harvey, G. (ed.) 2002. Readings in Indigenous Religion. London: Continuum.

Harvey, G. 2004a. Animals, Animists and Academics. Paper presented at Exploring Consciousness – With What Intent? Bath Spa University College Sophia Centre Conference in association with the Academy for Cultural and Educational Studies and Psychonaut UK, 24-26 June.

Harvey, G. 2004b. Animism. London: Hurst & Co / Columbia: Columbia University Press.

Harvey, G. and C. Hardman 1995. (eds) Paganism Today: Wiccans, Druids, the Goddess and Ancient Earth Traditions for the Twenty-First Century. London: Thorsons (Re-published as 'Pagan Pathways').

Hutton, R. 1991. The Pagan Religions of the Ancient British Isles: Their Nature and Legacy. Oxford: Blackwell.

Hutton, R. 1996. The Stations of the Sun: A History of the Ritual Year in Britain. Oxford: Oxford University Press.

Hutton, R. 1999. Triumph of the Moon: A History of Modern Pagan Witchcraft. Oxford: Oxford University Press.

Jones, P. and N. Pennick 1995. A History of Pagan Europe. London: Routledge.

MacLellan, G. 1994. Small Acts of Magic. Manchester: Creeping Toad.

MacLellan, G. 1997. Sacred Animals. Berkshire: Capall Bann.

MacLellan, G. 1998. A Sense of Wonder. Performance Research 3(3) ('On Ritual'): 60-63.

Neihardt, J. G. 1993[1932]. Black Elk Speaks: Being the Life Story of a Holy Man of the Ogala Sioux. Lincoln: University of Nebraska Press.

Roscoe, W. 1998. Changing Ones: Third and Fourth Genders In North America. London: Macmillan.

Sutcliffe, S. and M. Bowman (eds) 2000. Beyond New Age: Exploring Alternative Spirituality. Edinburgh: Edinburgh University Press.

Wallis, R.J. and J. Blain. 2003. Sites, sacredness, and stories: interactions ofarchaeology and contemporary Paganism. Folklore 114(3): 307-321.

Wallis, R.J. and J. Blain. In preparation. Sacred Sites, Contested Rites/Rights: Contemporary Pagan Engagements with the Past. Brighton: Sussex Academic Press.

# Shamans, Past and Present

Aldhouse Green, M. 2001. Gender Bending Images: permeating boundaries in ancient European iconography. In: R.J. Wallis and K.J. Lymer (eds) A permeability of boundaries: new approaches to the archaeology of art,religion and folklore: 19-29. B.A.R. International Series 936. Oxford: British Archaeological Reports.

Atkinson, J.M. 1989. The Art and Politics of Wana Shamanship. California: University of California Press.

Balzer, M. 1997. Introduction. In: M. Balzer (ed.) Shamanic Worlds: Rituals and Lore of Siberia and Central Asia: xiii-xxxii. New York: North Castle Books.

Blacker, C. 1975. The Catalpa Bow: A Study of Shamanistic Practices in Japan. London: George Allen and Unwin.

Bourguignon, E. 1976. Possession. San Francisco: Chandler and Sharp.

De Rios, M.D. 1984. Hallucinogens: Cross-Cultural Perspectives. Bridport,Dorset: Prism Press.

Devereux, P. 1992. Shamanism and the Mystery Lines: Ley Lines, Spirit Paths, Shape-Shifting and Out-of-Body-Travel. London: Quantum.

Devereux, P. 1997. The Long Trip: A Prehistory of Psychedelia. New York: Arkana.

Dowson, T.A. In preparation. Rock Art and the Shaman. London: Routledge.

Eliade, M. 1964. Shamanism: Archaic Techniques of Ecstasy. London: Penguin Arkana.

Flaherty, G. 1992. Shamanism and the Eighteenth Century. New Jersey: Princeton University Press.

Halifax, J. 1979. Shamanic Voices: A Survey of Visionary Narratives. London: Arkana.

Halifax, J. 1982. Shaman: The Wounded Healer. London: Thames and Hudson.

Harner, M. 1972. The Jivaro: People of the Sacred Waterfalls. Berkeley: University of California Press.

Harner, M. (ed.) 1973. Hallucinogens and Shamanism. Oxford: Oxford University Press.

Harner, M. 1980. The Way of the Shaman. London: Harper Collins.

Harvey, G. 1998. Shamanism in Britain Today. Performance Research 3(3) ('On Ritual'): 16-24.

Harvey, G. 2002. Shamanism: A Reader. London Routledge.

Harvey, G. and R.J Wallis. Forthcoming 2006. Shamanism: An Encyclopedia. Lanham, Maryland: Scarecrow Press.

Hoppál, M. 1996. Shamanism in a Postmodern Age. Folklore: An electronic Journal of Folklore. Available online: http://haldjas.folklore.ee/folklore/vol2/hoppla.htm

Humphrey, C. 1996. Shamans and Elders: Experience, Knowledge, and Power among the Daur Mongols. Oxford: Clarendon Press.

Hutton, R. 1993. The Shamans of Siberia. Glastonbury, Somerset: The Isle of Avalon Press.

Hutton, R. 2002. Shamans: Siberian Spirituality and the Western Imagination. London: Hambledon.

Jakobsen, M.D. 1999. Shamanism: Traditional and Contemporary Approaches to the Mastery of Spirits and Healing. Oxford: Berghahn Books.

Katz, R. 1982. Boiling Energy: Community Healing Among the Kalahari !Kung. Cambridge, Massachusetts: Harvard University Press.

Leto, S. 2000. Magical Potions: Entheogenic Themes in Scandinavian Mythology. Shamans Drum 54: 55-65.

Lewis, I. M. 1989 [1971]. Ecstatic Religion: A Study of Shamanism and Spirit Possession. London: Routledge.

Lewis-Williams, J.D. and T.A. Dowson. 1989. Images of Power: Understanding Bushman Rock Art. Johannesburg: Southern Book Publishers.

MacLellan, G. 1995. Dancing on the Edge: Shamanism in Modern Britain. In: Harvey, G. and C. Hardman (eds) Paganism Today: Wiccans, Druids, the Goddess and Ancient Earth Traditions for the Twenty-First Century: 138-148. London: Thorsons.

MacLellan, G. 1999. Shamanism. London: Piatkus.

Myerhoff, B. 1974. Peyote Hunt: The Sacred Journey of the Huichol Indians. Ithaca, New York: Cornell University Press.

Noel, D.C. 1997. The Soul of Shamanism: Western Fantasies, Imaginal Realities. New York: Continuum.

Pinchbeck, D. 2002. Breaking Open the Head: A Visionary Journey from Cynicism to Shamanism. London: Flamingo.

Rätsch, C. 1992. A Dictionary of Sacred and Magical Plants. Bridport, Dorset: The Prism Press.

Rudgley, R. 1993. The Alchemy of Culture: Intoxicants in Society. London: British Museum Press.

Shirokogoroff, S. 1935. Psychomental Complex of the Tungus. London: Kegan and Paul.

Taussig, M. 1987. Shamanism, Colonialism and the Wild Man: A Study in Terror and Healing. Chicago: The University of Chicago Press.

Vitebsky, P. 1993. Dialogues With the Dead: The Discussion of Mortality among the Sora of Eastern India. Cambridge: Cambridge University Press.

Vitebsky, P. 1995. The Shaman. London: Macmillan.

Wallis, R.J. 1998. Journeying the Politics of Ecstasy: Anthropological Perspectives on Neo-shamanism. The Pomegranate: A Journal of Neo-Pagan Thought 6:20-28.

Wallis, R.J. 1999. Altered States, Conflicting Cultures: Shamans, Neo-shamans and Academics. Anthropology of Consciousness 10 (2-3): 41-49.

Wallis, R.J. 2000. Queer Shamans: Autoarchaeology and Neo-shamanism. World Archaeology 32(2): 251-261.

Wallis, R.J. 2002a. The Bwili or 'Flying Tricksters' of Malakula: a critical discussion of recent debates on rock art, ethnography and shamanisms. Journal of The Royal Anthropological Institute 8(4): 735-760.

Wallis, R.J. 2002b. Waking the Ancestors: Neo-shamanism and Archaeology. In: G. Harvey (ed.) Shamanism: A Reader: 402-423. London: Routledge.

Wallis, R.J. 2003. Shamans / neo-Shamans: Ecstasy, Alternative Archaeologies and Contemporary Pagans. London: Routledge.

Wallis, R.J. 2004. Between the Worlds: Autoarchaeology and neo-Shamans. In: J. Blain, D. Ezzy and G. Harvey (eds) Researching Paganisms: Religious Experiences and Academic Methodologies: 191-215. Walnut Creek, California: AltaMira.

Wallis, R.J. In preparation. Shamans and Art.

# Heathen Shamans, Past and Present

Bates, B. 1983. The Way of Wyrd. London: Arrow.

Bates, B. 1996/7. Wyrd: Life Force of the Cosmos. Sacred Hoop 15 (Winter): 8-13.

Buchholz, P. 1971. Shamanism: the Testimony of Old Icelandic Literary Tradition. Mediaeval Scandinavia 4: 7-20

Blain, J. 2000. Speaking Shamanistically: Seidr, academia, and rationality, DISKUS. Available HTTP: http://www.unimarburg.de/religionswissenschaft/journal/diskus/blain.html

Blain, J. 2001. Shamans, stones, authenticity and appropriation: contestations of invention and meaning. In: R.J. Wallis and K.J. Lymer (eds) A Permeability of Boundaries: New Approaches to the Archaeology of Art, Religion and Folklore: 47-55. B.A.R. International Series 936. Oxford: British Archaeological Reports.

Blain, J. 2002. Nine Worlds of Seidr-Magic: Ecstasy and Neo-shamanism in North European Paganism. London: Routledge.

Blain, J. and R.J. Wallis. 1999. Men and 'Women's Magic': Gender, Seidr, and 'Ergi'. The Pomegranate: A New Journal of Neo-Pagan Thought 9: 4-16.

Blain, J. and R.J. Wallis. 2000. The 'ergi' seidman: contestations of gender, shamanism and sexuality in Northern religion past and present. Journal of Contemporary Religion 15(3): 395-411.

Campbell, M. 1999. Ergi: A Personal Perspective on Men and Seidr. SpiritTalk: A Core Shamanic Newsletter 9 (Early Summer): 22-24.

Fries, J. 1996. Seidways: Shaking, Swaying and Serpent Mysteries. Oxford: Mandrake.

Glosecki, S.O. 1986. Wolf Dancers and Whispering Beasts: Shamanic Motifs from Sutton Hoo? Mankind Quarterly 26: 305-319.

Glosecki, S.O. 1988. Wolf of the Bees: Germanic Shamanism and the Bear Hero. Journal of Ritual Studies 2/1: 31-53.

Glosecki, S.O. 1989. Shamanism and Old English Poetry. New York: Garland Publishing.

Høst, A. 1999. Exploring Seidhr: A Practical Study of the Seidhr Ritual. Paper presented at 'Religious Practices and Beliefs in the North Atlantic Area' seminar, Århus University.

Kelly, K. 1999. Close to Nature: an interview with Annette Høst.
    Spirit talk: A Core Shamanic Newsletter 9 (Early Summer): 5-9.
Lindquist, G. 1997. Shamanic Performance on the Urban Scene:
    Neo-Shamanism in Contemporary Sweden. Stockholm Studies
    in Social Anthropology 39. Stockholm, Sweden: University
    of Stockholm.
Linzie, B. 1999. Seething: Where Does a Seidrman Go? Spirit talk: A
    Core Shamanic Newsletter 9 (Early Summer): 27-29.
Paxson, D.L. 1992. The Seid Project: A Report on Experiences and
    Findings. Unpublished manuscript: Hrafnar Monograph #1.
Paxson, D.L. 1993. Heide: Witch-Goddess of the North. Available
    online: www.hrafnar.org/godesses/heide.html Originally
    published in Sagewoman, Fall 1993.
Paxson, D.L. 1997. The Return of the Volva: Recovering the Practice of
    Seidh. Available online: http://www.vinland.org/Heathen/
    hrafnar.seidh.html, accessed 18.11.97
Paxson, D. 1998. "This Thou Dost Know… ": Oracles in the
    Northern Tradition. Idunna: A Journal of Northern Tradition:
    no page numbers.
Paxson, D. 1999. Seeing for the People: Working Oracular Seidr in the
    Pagan Community. Spirit talk: A Core Shamanic Newsletter 9
    (Early Summer): 10-13.
Price, N. 2000. Shamanism and the Vikings? In: W.W. Fitzhugh and E.I
    Ward (eds) Vikings: The North Atlantic Saga: 70-71. Washington
    D.C.: Smithsonian Institution.
Price, N. 2002. The Viking Way: Religion and War in late Iron Age
    Scandinavia. Uppsala: Department of Archaeology and
    Ancient History.
Solli, B. 1999. Odin the queer? On ergi and shamanism in Norse
    mythology. In: A. Gustafsson and H. Karlsson (eds) Glyfer och
    arkeologiska rum – en vänbok till Jarl Nordbladh: 341-349.
    Gotarc Series A volume 3. Göteborg, Sweden: University
    of Göteborg.
Wallis, R.J. 2003. Taliesin's Trip / Wyrd Woden: Druid and Heathen
    neo-Shamans, and 'Celtic' and 'Northern' Shamanisms: Contesting
    the Past: Chapters 3 & 4 in: Shamans / neo-Shamans: Ecstasy,
    Alternative Archaeologies and Contemporary Pagans.
    London: Routledge.

Williams, H. 2001. An ideology of transformation: cremation rites and animal sacrifice in early Anglo-Saxon England. In: N. Price (ed.) The Archaeology of Shamanism: 193-212. London: Routledge.

## Occult, Magic and Esoteric Subjects

Bennett, A. 2003. Eucharist Magick or How to Have Your Cake and Eat It. Available online: www.dowhatthouwilt.com/resources/members/eucharist.asp (accessed 15.09.03).

Carroll, P.J. 1987. Liber Null and Psychonaut. York Beach, Maine: Samuel Weiser, Inc.

Chumbley, A.D. 2002. AZOËTIA: A Grimoire of the Sabbatic Craft. Sethos-Behena Edition. Xoanon Publishing.

Crowley, A. 1973. Magick. London: Routledge and Kegan Paul.

Crowley, A. 1990 [1976]. The Book of the Law (Liber Al vel Legis). York Beach, Maine: Samuel Weiser, Inc.

Crowley, A. 1991 [1973]. 777 and Other Qabalistic Writings of Aleister Crowley. York Beach, Maine: Samuel Weiser, Inc.

Farrar, J and S. Farrar. 1990. Spells and How They Work. Bury St. Edmunds: St. Edmundsbury Press.

Fortune, D. 1987 [1935]. The Mystical Qabalah. London: Aquarian.

Fries, J. 1992. Visual Magick: A Manual of Freestyle Shamanism. Oxford: Mandrake Press.

Grant, K. 1973. Aleister Crowley and the Hidden God. London: Frederick Muller Ltd.

Grant, K. 1975. Cults of the Shadow. London: Frederick Muller Ltd.

Grant, K. 1980. Outside the Circles of Time. London: Frederick Muller Ltd.

Grant, K. 1991 [1972]. The Magical Revival. London: Skoob Books.

Grant, K. 2002. The Ninth Arch. London: Starfire.

Grant, K. and S. Grant 1998. Zos Speaks: Encounters with Austin Osman Spare. London: Fulgur Limited.

Grant, K. 2003. Images and Oracles of Austin Osman Spare. London: Fulgur Limited.

Green, M. The Elements of Natural Magic. Bridport, Dorset: Elements Books Limited.

Hay, G. 1992. The Necronomicon: The Book of Dead Names. London: Skoob Books Publishing.

Humphries, G. and J. Vayne 2004. Now That's What I Call Chaos Magick. Oxford: Mandrake.

Johari, H. 1986. Tools for Tantra. Vermont: Destiny Books.

Johnson, N.J. 2000. Barefoot Zen: The Shaolin Roots of Kung Fu and Karate. York Beach, Maine: Samuel Weiser, Inc.

Parfitt, W.1988. The Living Qabalah: A Practical Guide to Understanding the Tree of Life. Bridport, Dorset: Element Books Limited.

Ra Un Nefer Amen I. 1990. Metu Neter Volume 1: The Great Oracle of Tehuti and the Egyptian System of Spiritual Cultivation. Brooklyn, New York: Khamit Corporation.

Schwaller De Lubicz, I. 1981 [1979]. The Opening of the Way: A Practical Guide to the Wisdom Teachings of Ancient Egypt. Rochester, Vermont: Inner Traditions International.

Spare, A.O. 1993. From the Inferno to Zos: The Writings and Images of Austin Osman Spare (Volume 1). Seattle: First Impressions.

## Other Resources, Journals and Magazines

3rd Stone: The Magazine for the New Antiquarian, PO Box 961, Devizes, Wiltshire SN10 2TS (due to be re-launched in the near future... ).

Idunna: A Journal of Northern Tradition, The Troth, Box 472, Berkeley, CA 94701, USA.

Pagan Dawn: The Journal of the Pagan Federation, BM Box 5896, London WC1N 3XX.

Runa: Exploring Northern European Myth, Mystery and Magic, Rune-Gild, BM Sorcery, London WC1N 3XX.

Sacred Hoop Magazine: A Practical Guide to shamanic Living, PO Box 16, Narberth, Pembrokeshire SA67 8YG.

Shaman's Drum: A Journal of Experiential Shamanism, PO Box 311, Ashland, OR 97520, USA.

Spirit Talk: A Core-Shamanic Newsletter, 120 Argyll Street, Cambridge CB1 3LS.

The Pomegranate: The International Journal of Pagan Studies, Equinox Publishing www.equinoxpub.com

Widowinde, The English Companions, BM Box 3346, London WC1N 3XX.

19.99

Printed in the United States
126776LV00005B/66/A